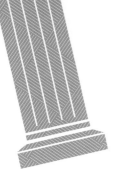

WITHDRAWN

CULTURE TRAILS

52 PERFECT WEEKENDS FOR CULTURE LOVERS

Copenhagen's waterways:
see page 92; Havana's music
scene (right): see page 86

SA.98

© Sarah Coghill / Lonely Planet

INTRODUCTION

How can the term 'culture' be defined? For some people it's manifestations of human achievement — paintings that capture a moment in history, emotive operas or classic literature. For others, it's the social rituals and customs of a particular place or group of people. More often than not, the two are intertwined. When we travel, the cultures of the countries we visit are usually what we notice first, and it is often what inspires us to visit in the first place. The memories we take home with us may be of artisans hammering on the streets, historic architecture looming around a plaza, or music wafting from a backalley doorway: culture exists everywhere, and it means everything to the curious traveller.

If that's you, you'll love this tour of the world in 52 short trips — one for every week of the year. We've scoured the globe to find the richest cultural enclaves, where the arts have had a profound, lasting impact and local culture is being protected and nurtured; where old customs hold true, new ones are being forged, or the past is melding with the future in fascinating ways. The cultural spectrum is broad: literature, art, architecture, music, theatre, dance, festivals, TV, film, comics — you name it, it's in here. All you need to do is bring your curious minds, and explore.

A classic
lighthouse at
Provincetown in
Cape Cod: see
page 308

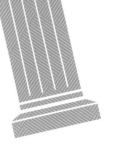

CONTENTS

INDONESIA
↓
Bali 170

JAMAICA
↓
Kingston 200

MEXICO
↓
Mexico City 224

PORTUGAL
↓
Lisbon 248

SPAIN
↓
Catalonia 266

Madrid 272

Seville 278

USA
↓
Los Angeles 290

Deep South 296

New York 302

Cape Cod 308

Washington, DC
& around ~~214~~ 314

IRELAND
↓
Dublin 176

West Ireland 182

JAPAN
↓
Tokyo 206

Naoshima Islands
212

MOROCCO
↓
Marrakesh 230

ROMANIA
↓
Transylvania 254

TAIWAN
↓
Taipei & around
284

ITALY
↓
Venice 188

Florence 194

LEBANON
↓
Beirut 218

NEW ZEALAND
↓
North Island 236

South Island 242

SCOTLAND
↓
Glasgow 260

Australia

ABORIGINAL ART IN THE NORTHERN TERRITORY

The cracked landscapes and creation stories of the Top End are writ large across its rock walls and galleries: welcome to the heartland of Indigenous Australia's artistic communities.

The Northern Territory's Top End is a land rich in Aboriginal culture and art, both ancient and painted before your very eyes. The story begins back in the centuries before white settlement, when expert artists adorned their rock shelters with vivid interpretations of their world — animals no longer imaginable in such places remain where they were painted on remote rock walls. You'll find them across Kakadu National Park and out on the private concession that surrounds Hawk Dreaming Lodge.

Fast forward centuries and Aboriginal art is undergoing a remarkable and long-overdue renaissance — local art centres have become places of refuge and fair remuneration for the Aboriginal community's modern artists, both well-known and those yet to make their name. They are also places where white and Aboriginal worlds most easily intersect — here you can sit down with the

NEED TO KNOW
Four days is comfortable for this trail; the easiest way to get around is by car, preferably a 4WD (hire one in Darwin).

artists, watch them paint and pass time together in a way that is rarely so easy elsewhere.

As is so often the case in indigenous Australia, art and life are utterly inseparable from the land from which they arise. A little exploration of this terrain — the crocodile-rich rivers, the blood-red escarpments, the ghost gum trees — provides the essential context to the art that adorns both rock and art gallery walls. In fact, it is impossible to understand what you see without travelling through Aboriginal country in the company of its local people, listening to stories of the land and its inhabitants.

And then there's Darwin, a gateway to the Aboriginal worlds that lie beyond and where so much of what is good in Aboriginal art resides. The galleries of the Northern Territory's state capital are a critical part of the whole experience, and the perfect primer for the journey that lies ahead.

01 © Sam Earp/Tourism NT

Timor Sea
Gardangarl (Field Island)
AUSTRALIA
03
OENPELLI
South Alligator River
KAKADU NATIONAL PARK
05
02
04
JABIRU
07
06
GALURRUYU

Van Diemen Gulf
01
GUNBALANYA (OENPELLI)
DARWIN
JABIRU
BATCHELOR
KAKADU NATIONAL PARK

01 MUSEUM & ART GALLERY OF THE NORTHERN TERRITORY

Welcome to what could be the finest repository of Aboriginal art anywhere in Australia. Carvings from the Tiwi Islands, bark paintings from Arnhem Land, and the dot paintings that are a hallmark of the Western Desert – the walls here are like a journey through the remote communities of the Northern Territory, as seen through the eyes of their artists.

While this modern exhibition space is no substitute for feeling the hot desert wind on your face as you sit down in the red sand to watch an artist paint, Darwin is an essential part of the story – if your work is exhibited in the capital, you've made it to the big time. Getting a feel for the works here is like taking the pulse of the Northern Territory's world of indigenous art. *www.magnt.net.au; 19 Conacher St, Darwin; tel +61 8 8999 8264; 9am-5pm Mon-Fri, 10am-5pm Sat & Sun*

02 UBIRR ROCK ART SITE

It's only a three-hour drive from Darwin to the east of Kakadu National Park, but it's a journey from one world into an altogether different one. Ubirr is one of the finest open-air galleries of rock art anywhere on earth and the many rock walls here tell stories ancient and steeped in mystery.

On one wall is the story of the rainbow serpent, the creation myth for Aboriginal people across the Top End; on another a gallery that is considered a thousands-of-years-old visual menu of animals portrayed in that distinctive x-ray style typical of Aboriginal rock art. Just around the corner from the main panel, improbably high on a rock wall, is a representation of the thylacine, or Tasmanian tiger.

For the rock art, come in the morning when things are cooler and quieter. But plan to return in the late afternoon, to join the crowds climbing the escarpment for Kakadu's best sunset views.

'Injalak is a place to sit under the shade of the eucalypts while locals dye pandanus fronds ready for weaving'

01 Twin Falls in Kakadu National Park

02 The rock art at Nourlangie has World Heritage status

03 Viewing rock art at Nourlangie site

04 Spot crocs on the Guluyambi Cultural Cruise

03 INJALAK ARTS & CRAFTS CENTRE, GUNBALANYA

Much of Arnhem Land remains off-limits to outsiders, but a brief foray to Gunbalanya (also known as Oenpelli) is well worth the effort. You'll need a permit (issued on the spot by the Central Lands Council in Jabiru) and to check in at the Border Store in Ubirr for an update on water levels at the crossing over the East Alligator River; crocs lie in wait for those who ignore this warning. Once across the river, the road runs alongside stunning Arnhem Land escarpments and on into Gunbalanya and its wonderful Injalak Arts & Crafts Centre.

One of the great producers of Arnhem Land artworks, Injalak is also a place to sit under the shade of the acacias and eucalypts while local women dye their pandanus fronds ready for weaving. Or pull up a chair and watch as the master painters of Injalak paint their intricate works on the back verandah.

It's one of the Territory's best community art centres; a fine place to shop, and a priceless opportunity to not just buy a piece of art but watch it being made and talk to the artist as he or she brings each creation into being.
www.injalak.com; Gunbalanya; +61 8 8979 0190; 8.30am-5pm Mon-Fri, 9am-2pm Sat

04 GULUYAMBI CULTURAL CRUISE

Back on the East Alligator River, from the upstream boat ramp on the Kakadu side of the river, the Aboriginal-led Guluyambi Cultural Cruises get you up close and personal with semi-submerged crocs, talk you through the stories passed down through generations of local Aboriginal communities and take you ashore at one of the loveliest corners of Western Arnhem Land. There's even a demonstration of spear-throwing.

These cruises represent a great leap forward for the local community — finally it is the Aboriginal people

who are telling their own stories. Initiating outsiders into the land defines who they are, and gives them a voice after decades of marginalisation. www.kakaduculturaltours.com.au/ guluyambi-cultural-cruise; tel 1800 525 238

05 HAWK DREAMING LODGE

If you stood at Ubirr to watch the sunset and wondered what lay beyond, the answer is Hawk Dreaming – park your car in the Border Store compound and the good people from Hawk Dreaming Lodge will take you there.

At this upmarket tented lodge, where wallabies lounge on the grass and bird song is the only soundtrack, you find yourself immersed in the silence of a Kakadu that few visitors see. The light eucalyptus woodland is a precursor to a towering escarpment considered sacred to the local Aboriginal people, associated as it is with the Hawk Dreaming, an Aboriginal Dreamtime creation story.

The rock art here, finely rendered and little known, is like stumbling upon hidden treasure (look for the expertly drawn crayfish), while the sunset-viewing locations are glorious. www.kakaduculturaltours.com.au/ hawk-dreaming-wilderness-lodge; tel 1800 525 238

06 NOURLANGIE ROCK ART

A short drive down the road from Jabiru in the direction of Yellow Water, and 12km down a sealed side road, Nourlangie is classic Kakadu escarpment country with its red sandstone bluffs and sacred cliffs. Here the ancient artists created some of the most striking images anywhere in the Top End.

The Angbangbang Gallery in particular showcases thought-provoking Dreaming characters, some of which date back 20,000 years but which were repainted in the 1960s. Most memorable of all is Nabulwinjbulwinj, a dangerous fellow from the spirit world who likes to eat females after banging them on the head with a yam...

07 WARRADJAN ABORIGINAL CULTURAL CENTRE

For your last stop on this journey, return to the Kakadu Highway, turn left, and barely 30km later take the

07

turn-off to Yellow Water. Just before the resort, this Aboriginal Cultural Centre is an informative place to bring your trip to a close.

The creation stories and panels explaining the rock-art context answer so many of the questions that arise when viewing remote rock walls. They help to demystify the soulful, if at times confusing, link between the land through which you've travelled and the artwork that you've encountered along the way.

Up here in the Top End, as you'll have no doubt discovered, art is the domain of Aboriginal storytellers and dreamers — and a very beautiful world indeed.
Tel +61 8 8979 0051; off Kakadu Hwy; 9am-5pm
BY ANTHONY HAM

07 © Parks Australia

05 Jim Jim Falls in Kakadu National Park

06 A local guide on the Guluyambi river cruise

07 A brolga (Australian crane) stalks the wetlands

WHERE TO STAY
HAWK DREAMING LODGE
Out in a corner of Kakadu National Park that few visitors get to see, this fine place is like an African safari tented camp. It inhabits a lovely area of escarpments, waterholes and woodlands.
www.kakaduculturaltours. com.au/hawk-dreaming-wilderness-lodge; tel 1800 525 238

ANBINIK KAKADU RESORT
Award-winning, design-led rooms are the highlight at this resort, a three-hour drive from Darwin, but there's something for everyone – from camping to supremely comfortable rooms with balconies. You can organise tours here.
www.kakadu.net.au; 27 Lakeside Drive, Jabiru; tel +61 8 8979 3144

WHERE TO EAT & DRINK
BORDER STORE
It may not be anything fancy, but there's a really friendly frontier feel to this place in Ubirr, close to where Kakadu National Park meets Arnhem Land. The Thai food is excellent, and you can buy books and local artwork here as well as book tours.
Tel +61 8 8979 2474; 8am-8pm Jun-Oct

CRUSTACEANS
Darwin has an excellent waterfront food scene, but it's here that you'll find the city's best seafood. Locally caught barramundi is the highlight, along with a first-class wine list and first-class harbour views.
www.crustaceans.net.au, tel +61 8 8981 8658; Stokes Hill Wharf, Darwin; 5.30pm-11.30pm

CELEBRATIONS
DARWIN ABORIGINAL ART FAIR
Held over three days in August, this is an art-lover's highlight of the year with works from Aboriginal communities all across the Northern Territory.
(www.darwinaboriginal artfair.com.au)

MAHBILIL FESTIVAL
This one-day celebration of local indigenous culture takes over Jabiru in early September. Expect art demonstrations, spear throwing, didgeridoo blowing, magpie-goose cooking, music and dance.
(www.mahbililfestival.com)

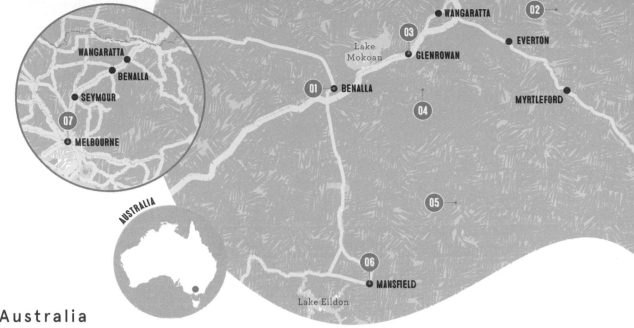

The map shows locations numbered 01 through 07, including: WANGARATTA, GLENROWAN (03), BENALLA (01), EVERTON, MYRTLEFORD, 02, 04, 05, MANSFIELD (06), SEYMOUR, MELBOURNE (07), Lake Mokoan, Lake Eildon, AUSTRALIA.

Australia

NED KELLY'S BUSHRANGER TRAIL

Starting out from Melbourne, tour the gold-mining towns, hills and valleys of Victoria's High Country in pursuit of Ned Kelly, the 19th-century outlaw and Australian icon.

Ned Kelly: hero or villain? Or a bit of both? One thing that is certain is that the story of Australia's legendary outlaw (1855-1880), a bushranger about whom we still talk today, is interwoven with one of the most beautiful and fascinating corners of Australia, the high country of northeast Victoria.

Numerous books and films have been produced about Ned's exploits. Forget the films. Neither Mick Jagger's nor Heath Ledger's efforts give a true flavour of this man and his landscape. Instead, bring two paper companions on this trail: local author Ian Jones's *Ned Kelly: A Short Life*, for the facts, and Peter Carey's *The True History of the Kelly Gang* for the most evocative (and fictionalised) account of the Kelly family. It's a rare treat to read a true story in a pub that the protagonist would have frequented.

The trail touches on the country towns about a

NEED TO KNOW
This circular trail takes a minimum of three days by car, starting from Melbourne.

three-hour drive northeast of Melbourne that sprang up during the 19th-century gold rush. Beechworth remains a handsome destination for weekend visits. Of the town, Peter Carey writes: 'There were much higher country to the south and east but no one could see that from Beechworth for there the law did sit in pomp and majesty and there were no higher place than its own elevated opinion.'

Using the Hume Freeway out of Melbourne as the spine of the story, it's possible to get an evocative snapshot of the legend and the man while travelling through the country he called home.

The ending of this bushranger's tale should come as no surprise: 'America has Jesse James, England has Robin Hood,' says Ian, Beechworth's walking tour guide. 'We have a man who wore a bucket on his head.' Ned Kelly, hero or villain? Make up your own mind on this trail through Victoria's High Country.

01 BENALLA

The Hume Freeway first passes Ned's birthplace (he was one of 14 Kelly kids) at Avenel, which is where, at the age of 10, he earned a prized green sash for saving the life of a boy drowning in Hughes Creek. But the first stop on this trail is Benalla, where the sash is displayed (bloodstains and all) in the town's Costume and Kelly Museum.

Also stop by the Benalla Art Gallery, where Australian artist Sidney Nolan's tapestry *Glenrowan* (c1974) depicts the siege in the town that was the beginning of Ned's end. Benalla was also where the police who hunted Ned were based. *www.benallaartgallery.com.au; tel +61 3 5760 2619; Bridge St, Benalla;*

'Since 2013 Ned has been buried in an unmarked grave in Greta's dusty country cemetery, next to his mother, Ellen Kelly'

10am-5pm Wed-Mon; Benalla Costume and Kelly Museum, www.home.vicnet.au/~benmus/; tel +61 3 5762 6093; 14 Mair St, Benalla; 9am-5pm

02 BEECHWORTH

Australia's best-preserved town from the gold-mining era is the nexus of Ned's story. He passes through numerous times and it's the site of his darkest moments and times of triumph. Beechworth had several notable features: a courthouse, a gaol and lots of pubs. In fact, with a population of 60,000 in its heyday (today it's 3000) there were more than 50 pubs here alone.

A few remain, but your focus should be on the cluster of granite buildings around the present-day tourist information office in the Historic Precinct: the gaol, the cells and the courthouse where Kelly, his mother,

01 Beechworth's old
buildings preserve a
Kelly atmopshere

02 The open road in
Victoria's High Country

03 Historic Precinct,
Beechworth

04 Hills and valleys
characterise the land in
which Ned roamed

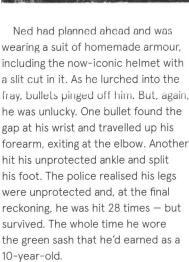

and his mentor Harry Powers were tried and incarcerated at varying times.

The guided walking tour that starts from the tourist office is recommended and visits the key sites. *www.explorebeechworth.com.au*

03 GLENROWAN

'I'm sorry but I must detain you.' With those words Ned Kelly and his gang held hostage the occupants of Glenrowan's Ann Jones Inn in 1880. Many of the hostages were friends or sympathisers of his cause to create a Republic of North East Victoria. Outside Ann Jones Inn, on the north side of the bridge in this town, were 60 police waiting. In the final shoot-out three of his gang, including his brother Dan, were shot dead.

Ned had planned ahead and was wearing a suit of homemade armour, including the now-iconic helmet with a slit cut in it. As he lurched into the fray, bullets pinged off him. But, again, he was unlucky. One bullet found the gap at his wrist and travelled up his forearm, exiting at the elbow. Another hit his unprotected ankle and split his foot. The police realised his legs were unprotected and, at the final reckoning, he was hit 28 times — but survived. The whole time he wore the green sash that he'd earned as a 10-year-old.

By the end of the siege, the inn had been destroyed by fire and today a simple sign marks the site at 1 Siege St. A giant statue of Ned stands at the corner of Gladstone and Kate Sts.

04 GRETA

Detour off the Hume Fwy, along eucalypt-lined country roads, to reach Greta (there's no shortage of Scottish or Irish echoes in this part of Australia). Greta is Kelly country: Ned lived on Fifteen Mile Creek from the age of 12 and his descendants still live in the same house.

Its place in this bushranger's tale is assured thanks to two facts: it was from Greta that a drunk police constable, Alexander Fitzpatrick, rode out to arrest Ned's brother Dan or seduce his sister Kate one evening. His mission didn't go to plan and, after a fracas in which he received a self-inflicted bullet wound, events were set in motion for Ned and the Kellys.

(05)

Since 2013 Ned has been buried in an unmarked grave in Greta's dusty country cemetery, next to his mother, Ellen Kelly; you can sign the visitor book in the rotunda.

05 POWERS' LOOKOUT RESERVE

It's time to turn south and head back to Melbourne, taking a rural route (the C521) rather than the freeway. From Greta, follow signs eastward for the King Valley, now famed for its food and drink: there are lots of stops for sampling wine, cheese, and olives.

Between Whitfield and Tolmie lies Harry Powers' Lookout. Harry was known as the Gentleman Bushranger, because he never used violence to achieve his aims. Instead,

being an imposing fellow, he merely cocked his rifle and suggested his victims donate their valuables to him. He had an especial fondness for quality footwear.

At the age of 14, Ned was already an accomplished cattle rustler and horse thief. Harry heard of his talents and went to the Kelly home in Greta to propose an apprenticeship for Ned. He received a fusillade of crockery from Mrs Kelly, but eventually took Ned on and the pair lived in a series of hideouts in the bush.

Harry's lookout has an incredible view of King Valley, with steps leading up to an airy viewing platform from which to survey the land.
www.parkweb.vic.gov.au

06 MANSFIELD

From the Powers' Lookout, continue south to the small town of Mansfield, passing Stringybark Creek (signposted), where the Kelly Gang shot three policemen in a shootout in October 1878. On 15 November 1878 the Kelly Gang were declared outlaws from the steps of Mansfield's courthouse, which is still in use today.

The three policemen are buried in Mansfield cemetery and there's a marble memorial to them on the town's main street roundabout. Mansfield is also a local hub for activities on Lake Eildon and Mt Buller. From here, make your way back to Melbourne by either the freeway or meander via country roads to Healesville, depending on the time you have.

07 OLD MELBOURNE GAOL

Your final stop (and Ned's) is the Old Melbourne Gaol in the centre of Victoria's state capital city — today one of Australia's best culture hubs, framed by Kelly-era Victorian buildings and skyscrapers.

Kelly's mother was already in the gaol, working in the laundry. When the day of Ned's execution arrived — 11 November 1880 — she was offered the day off but refused it. On the other side of the laundry's wall was the gallows. At 11.14am, so the story goes, Ellen Kelly fainted as a thud was heard the other side of the wall. *www.oldmelbournegaol.com.au; tel +61 3 8663 7228; 377 Russell St, Melbourne; 9.30am-5pm*

BY ROBIN BARTON

05 Old Melbourne Gaol in the state capital

06 Ned Kelly statue in Glenrowan

06 © Robin Barton

WHERE TO STAY

THE ARMOUR MOTOR INN
Beechworth's best motel is in a prime location close to the creek, the town's pubs and an ice-cream parlour. It's a cosy building with a garden, pool, balconies and owners happy to tell guests about Ned Kelly. *www.armourmotorinn.com.au; tel +61 3 5728 14666; 1 Camp St, Beechworth*

MANSFIELD MOTEL
This convenient overnight stop on the way back to Melbourne is a clean, functional motel on the edge of town, with a cafe and pub within easy walking distance. *www.mansfieldmotel.com.au; tel +61 3 5775 2377; 3 Highett St, Mansfield*

WHERE TO EAT & DRINK

BRIDGE ROAD BREWERS
Kelly iconography abounds at this craft brewery in central Beechworth. Pair a sensational pizza with one of Ben Kraus's beers. Toppings on the thin, handmade bases often use local, seasonal produce. If you don't fancy pizza, come just for a drink and then hop over to nearby Tanswell's Commercial Hotel, a historic place with above-average pub food. *www.bridgeroadbrewers.com.au; +61 3 5728 2703; The Old Coach House, Browers Ln, 50 Ford St, Beechworth; food daily 12-3pm, plus 5.30-8.30pm Thu-Fri & 6-8.30pm Sat-Sun*

DAL ZOTTO
From Friday to Sunday, stop at this Italian themed winery in Whitfield for lunches of pizza or pasta, often made with local ingredients. From the restaurant window view sanglovese, nebbiolo and other Italian varieties of vines. Alternatively, grab an award-winning pie from Whitty's cafe to eat at Harry Powers' Lookout. *www.dalzotto.com.au; tel +61 1300 725 484; 4861 Main Rd, Whitfield*

CELEBRATIONS

NED KELLY WEEKEND
For one weekend every August, Beechworth turns back the clock to the 1880s with reenactments of key events in the Kelly story, as well as walking tours, live music and lots of activities for children. *(www.beechworth.com/events_calendar)*

Australia

GOTHIC TASMANIA

Tasmania's legacy as an ends-of-the-earth island penitentiary casts a macabre shadow over one of Australia's prettiest isles — come in winter to fully experience its gothic spirit.

Tasmania — Australia's island state, adrift in the Southern Ocean some 200km south of the Australian mainland — is a uniquely fated place, crossed with a gothic, otherworldly spirit that seems to hang in the cobweb corners of the latitude.

The island's capital city is Hobart: here, in the depths of winter, sheets of ice wind whip down the face of kunanyi/Mt Wellington behind the city, tearing at the cuffs of your jeans. Thin feathers of cirrus speed above on faster, more elevated planes. Foothills cut deep silhouettes against the evening sky, humping reluctantly down to the slate-grey Derwent River. Quite unexpectedly, a profound sense of loss and oblivion can bear-down here, making you feel utterly insignificant, transporting you back to the difficult and at times bleak days of 19th-century colonisation.

Indeed, before the British showed up in 1803, Tasmania's indigenous population lived here harmoniously for tens of

NEED TO KNOW
A three-day weekend in and around Hobart will infuse you with Tasmania's gothic spirit. Hire a car to get around.

thousands of years, maintaining a seasonal culture of hunting, fishing and gathering. It's logical to conclude that, across the span of millennia, this beautiful island has only relatively recently lost its sense of ease; and it's easy to imagine that the first bloom of British sail cloth on the Derwent — and with it the guns, disease and alcohol that decimated Tasmania's Aboriginal population — may have somehow cursed this place.

British convicts suffered here too: 70,000 of them were sent to Tasmania until the 1850s, locked in prisons so inhumane that today, among their ruins, the sense of sadness is palpable.

History can't be rewound and the mistakes of the past can't be dismissed. But a visit to Hobart today will shed some light on how Tasmanians have begun to embrace the gothic solitude of their island, and — through the lens of art, festivals and culture — are making headway towards better defining, if not forgiving, themselves.

01 © Marcus Mok / Alamy

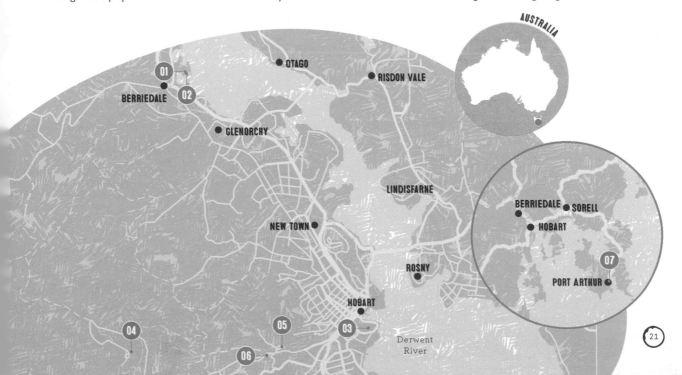

'To the Mouhineener people,
Mt Wellington is *kunanyi* —
a place of shelter, of beauty
and of refuge'

02 © Mona–Rémi Chauvin, Image Courtesy Mona Museum of Old and New Art. Hobart, Tasmania, Australia. 03 © Auscape / Getty Images

01 DARK MOFO

When the winter solstice creaks around in June, Dark Mofo stirs in the half-light. This fabulous annual festival — featuring live music, installations, readings, film noir and midnight feasts, all tapping into Tasmania's edgy gothic undercurrents — has grown in popularity to rival Hobart's long-running New Year's festival scene.

Locals rug-up, drink red wine around bonfires, talk and eat, ruminating over the macabre, the unexpected and the surprisingly good. *www.darkmofo.net.au*

02 MONA

Even if you're not in Hobart for Dark Mofo (accommodation gets tight!), a visit to the festival's home turf is mandatory. Since it opened in 2011, Mona — the Museum of Old & New Art — has put Hobart on the world art map. Occupying a saucepan-shaped peninsula jutting into the Derwent River 12km north of central Hobart (get here by car, shuttle bus, or aboard the museum's own sleek catamaran), Mona is arrayed across three underground levels abutting a sheer rock face. Described by philanthropist owner David Walsh

as 'a subversive adult Disneyland', the museum showcases ancient antiquities next to challenging contemporary works.

Sexy, provocative, disturbing and deeply engaging: expect to experience at least three of these adjectives, and to walk away reeling. *www.mona.net.au; tel +61 3 6277 9900; 655 Main Rd, Berridale; 10am–6pm Wed-Mon*

03 BATTERY POINT

An empty rum bottle's throw from the Hobart waterfront, the old maritime village of Battery Point is a tight nest

01 The gothic facade of Cascade Brewery

02 Revelry on the dark side during Dark Mofo

03 Snow-capped peak of Mt Wellington

04 Port Arthur, Tasmania's infamous former penal colony

05 The Museum of Old & New Art

of lanes and 19th-century cottages, packed together like shanghaied landlubbers in a ship's belly.

After a day at Mona, backtrack to Hobart and spend the early evening exploring: stumble up the sandstone Kelly's Steps and dogleg into South St, where the red lights once burned night and day.

Spin around picturesque Arthur Circus, a ring of Georgian cottages encircling a village green, then ogle the lonesome spire of St George's Anglican Church. The veneer of history here can sometimes seem a tool for contemporary commerce —

but it doesn't take much imagination to conjure up visions of mariners, merchants and the hardships of life here by the cold harbour, 150 years ago.

www.batterypoint.net

04 KUNANYI/MT WELLINGTON

Kunanyi/Mt Wellington (1270m) towers over Hobart like a benevolent overlord. To the Mouhineener people, the mountain is *kunanyi* — a place of shelter, of beauty and of refuge. In the early 1800s they watched from the foothills as the intruders cleared the forest and built their city below.

Hacked out of the mountainside during the Great Depression, the sealed road to the summit — a 30-minute morning drive from central Hobart — winds up through thick temperate forest, opening out to winter snowdrifts, stunted heathers and lunar rockscapes at the top. Don't be deterred if the sky is overcast: often the peak rises above cloud level and looks out over a magic carpet of cloud-tops.

This dichotomy of views — the new city beneath and the timeless cloudscape above — reflects the experience of the Mouhineener, who

06 © Andrew Watson / Alamy

lost their lands but will forever be imbued in the spirit of this place. *www.wellingtonpark.org.au; tel +61 03 6238 2176; Pinnacle Rd, Fern Tree*

05 CASCADES FEMALE FACTORY HISTORIC SITE

Finally being recognised as an important historic site, this barren backblock was where Hobart's female convicts were incarcerated. In fact, one in four convicts transported to Van Diemen's Land (Tasmania's first European name) was a woman.

As you wander among the ruins of high-walled work yards, next to the cold-running Hobart Rivulet and below towering kunanyi/Mt Wellington, the ghosts of the past seem all too real. It's a 20-minute drive down from the mountain summit: explore the site on

your own, book a guided tour or watch 'Her Story' – a vivid dramatisation of the suffering these women (and their children) experienced. *www.femalefactory.org.au; tel +61 3 6233 6656; 16 Degraves St, South Hobart; 9.30am-4pm*

06 CASCADE BREWERY

Standing in bleak, startling isolation next to the Hobart Rivulet (the city's original water source) Cascade is Australia's oldest brewery (1832) and is still bottling brilliant beers. The brewery is a short walk (or shorter drive) from the Cascades Female Factory Historic Site in South Hobart: you may be in need of a little light relief after your experiences there, but the brewery's imposing, gothic-looking façade is downright spooky.

Fear not: entertaining tours involve plenty of history, with tastings at the end to soothe your ragged nerves. *www.cascadebreweryco.com.au; tel +61 3 6224 1117; 140 Cascade Rd, South Hobart; 10am-5pm*

07 PORT ARTHUR HISTORIC SITE

On your last day in Hobart, take a drive to the Tasman Peninsula, 96km southeast of Hobart. Waiting portentously at the end of Arthur Hwy is the Unesco World Heritage–listed Port Arthur Historic Site, the infamous and allegedly escape-proof penal colony dating from the early 19th century. Here today, kids kick footballs and dads poke sausages on barbecues, but it's impossible to totally blank out the tragedy of this place, both

historically and more recently (in 1996 a lone gunman killed 35 people here, and in the surrounding area).

Dozens of structures and ruins remain, including an asylum, penitentiary, church, boys' prison, island graveyard and 'Separate Prison' built to punish inmates through isolation and sensory deprivation. To make sense of things, take a guided tour or come back at night for a ghost tour. Still not quite disturbing enough? Read *Gould's Book of Fish* by Man Booker Prize-winning Tasmanian author Richard Flanagan — an unhinged portrait of Tasmanian convict life. www.portarthur.org.au; tel +61 3 6521 2310; 6973 Arthur Hwy, Port Arthur; 9am-late
BY CHARLES RAWLINGS-WAY

06 Hobart's historic Salamanca Place

07 Penguin sculptures, by Stephen Walker, look out across Hobart's now-idyllic harbourfront

07 © John White Photos / Alamy

WHERE TO STAY
HENRY JONES ART HOTEL
In Hobart's restored waterfront Henry Jones IXL jam factory, with remnant bits of jam-making machinery and huge timber beams, super-swish HJs oozes class. Modern art enlivens the walls, while its bar and restaurant are world class. www.thehenryjones.com; tel +61 3 6210 7700; 25 Hunter St

ASTOR PRIVATE HOTEL
There are new hotels and apartments popping up all over Hobart these days, but how about something with a bit more soul? This lovely, rambling 1920s charmer is all stained-glass windows, antique furniture and lofty ceilings. www.astorprivatehotel.com.au; tel +61 3 6234 6611; 157 Macquarie St

WHERE TO EAT & DRINK
REPUBLIC BAR & CAFE
The Republic is a raucous art-deco pub hosting live music every night. It's the number-one rock room around town, with an always-interesting line-up, loads of goods beers and excellent food.

www.republicbar.com; tel +61 3 6234 6954; 299 Elizabeth St, North Hobart; 11am-late

JACKMAN & MCROSS
Early-morning cake and coffee at this conversational bakery-cafe may evolve into a quiche, tart or baguette for lunch, or perhaps a blackberry-and-wallaby pie. Tel +61 8 6223 3106; 57-59 Hampden Rd, Battery Point; 7am-6pm Mon-Fri, to 5pm Sat & Sun

CELEBRATIONS
FESTIVAL OF VOICES
Sing to keep the winter chills at bay during this quirky July festival, featuring performances, workshops, cabaret and choirs at venues around Hobart and beyond. (www.festivalofvoices.com)

TEN DAYS ON THE ISLAND
Tasmania's premier cultural festival is a biennial event (odd-numbered years, usually late March to early April) celebrating Tasmanian arts, music and culture at statewide venues. Expect concerts, exhibitions, dance, film, theatre and workshops. (www.tendays.org.au)

01

Australia

ADELAIDE: AUSTRALIA'S LIVE MUSIC CITY

Adelaide's wild world-music extravaganza WOMADelaide is just the tip of the iceberg in South Australia's capital, where locals roll with rhythm and rock all year round.

In 2015, Adelaide — the most modest and middle of the road of Australia's state capitals — was anointed a Unesco 'City of Music', an honour awarded to cities where cultural, political and creative forces combine to create a perfect musical storm.

Adelaide? Really? Well, this big country town may seem shy and retiring, but 'Radelaide' has a lengthy rock 'n' roll lineage. It has been the founding ground for classic Oz rock acts such as AC/DC, Cold Chisel and The Angels, who tore it up in legendary outer-suburbs rock pubs such as the Largs Pier, Elizabeth and Pooraka hotels. More recently, there's been The Superjesus, hip-hoppers The Hilltop Hoods and the astonishingly talented Sia.

These days it's not just radio hits that come out of Adelaide: this is a town overflowing with buskers, jazz ensembles, metal bands and alt-country ramblers, all of whom find plenty of venues and plenty of listeners

NEED TO KNOW
Try to hit this three-day trail Friday to Monday. Walk between venues in the CBD; hop in a cab for the suburbs.

to dig their creative crafts. The small-bar scene here has exploded in the past few years — the product of a savvy council initiative to relax liquor licensing laws and allow small-capacity venues, many of which have regular live tunes. A crop of stalwart pubs dotted around the city also host nightly live bands, defying 'Turn it down!' next-door-neighbour complaints. The talent has always been here, and now so are the venues. Adelaide is no longer a city that musicians must leave in order to make it big.

Music festivals, too, are a big deal in Adelaide. The city's annual world-music showpiece is WOMADelaide, during which 20,000 people descend on the city each day. Then there's the Adelaide Fringe festival, second only to the Edinburgh Fringe in its appeal to street artists of all creeds and calibres. City street corners are on high rotation during the summer festival season, with busker after busker peddling their wares.

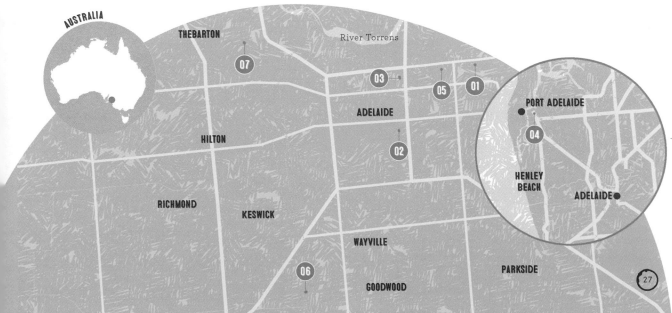

01 EXETER HOTEL

Rolling into town on a Friday night, adhere to the 'when in Rome' dictum and head straight to the Exeter Hotel on Rundle St in downtown Adelaide's East End. Surrounded by high-rent boutiques and restaurants, the Exeter remains defiantly down-at-heel — a charismatic, weathered old boozer attracting an eclectic brew of post-work, punk and uni drinkers, shaking the day off their backs.

Pull up a table in the grungy beer garden and settle in for the evening. Original nightly music treads a line between indie rock, electronica and acoustic — something of a lottery, but never dull. Keep an eye out for

'Local musos head here to hang, drink and converse — Wheatsheaf is the place to come to check the pulse of Adelaide's music scene'

the Bastard Sons of Ruination, a local rock outfit who conjure up a hellish alt-country ruckus (staying still is not an option).
www.theexter.com.au; tel +61 8 8223 2623; 246 Rundle St; 11am-late

02 CENTRAL MARKET

If you're feeling sub-par on Saturday morning, reconstitute over a big breakfast at Adelaide's fabulous

Central Market, an undercover food haven in the West End of Adelaide's CBD with 250-odd stalls and myriad cafes and coffee opportunities. It's all very loud, aromatic, hyperactive and stimulating in here: salami vendors, yoghurt stalls, nut shops, pasta outlets... as much an insight into Adelaide's multicultural soul as anything else. But on this musical pilgrimage, the

01 Music-lovers
spread out for an
Adelaide Symphony
Orchestra concert

02 Rundle Mall: busker
heaven

03 Drinkers roll into
the Exeter Hotel on a
Friday night

04 A performance by
Compagnie Luc Amoros
at WOMADelaide

the selfportrait
is not a
portrait that
paints itself.

main attraction is the market buskers, who must be talented and inoffensive enough to perform here: expect sincere interpretations of Coldplay/ Eric Clapton fare and impeccable classical renditions. *www.adelaidecentralmarket.com. au; tel +61 8 8203 7494; Gouger St; 7am-5.30pm Tue, 9am-5.30pm Wed & Thu, 7am-9pm Fri, 7am-3pm Sat*

03 CASABLABLA

As Saturday night thins towards the wee smalls, Adelaide's cool new crop of laneway bars continues to thrum. On Leigh St (not technically a laneway but slender nonetheless), this good-time late-nighter operates under a broad live-music remit, rolling from swing to funk, latin, reggae and '60s R&B. Inside (and outside in the courtyard), the fit-out would best be described as Marrakesh meets Mumbai: flickering lanterns, big Buddhas, fish tanks, burnt-ochre walls...

Local band Gorilla Jones plays here regularly: funky soul with lots of brass and va-va-va-voom. You can walk here from the Central Market if you're still hanging around the West End — an easy 10-minute amble to collect your musical consciousness. *www.casablabla.com; tel +61 8 8231 3939; 12 Leigh St; 3.30pm-late Tue-Thu, noon-3.30am Fri, 5pm-3.30am Sat*

04 NEWMARKET HOTEL

Jazz more your thing? On Sunday afternoon, hop in a cab and roll 14km northwest of the city to Port Adelaide, an old shipping enclave that's riddled with heritage pubs, decaying warehouses and sea-salty maritime soul. The Newmarket Hotel has live trad jazz every Sunday: sit at the bar, bend an elbow with Adelaide's bohemian set and dig the finger-snappin' zah-bah-dee-bop. *www.newmarkethotelptadel.com.au; tel +61 8 8447 2400; 132 Commercial Rd; 8am-10pm Mon, to midnight Tue-Thu, open till late Fri, 9.30am-late Sat, 11am-10pm Sun*

05 RUNDLE MALL

Back in the city centre on Monday, head for Adelaide's commercial epicentre Rundle Mall. Weary aesthetics and mainstream chain stores aside, the mall is a honey-pot lure for local and peripatetic buskers. On any day of the week — but especially on weekday lunch breaks when the city suits are out and about — grab a bench seat or stand around in a circle and see who's playing.

Regulars include offbeat entertainers such as a biker guy who plays delicate flute ballads, but also plenty of vocal soloists, guitar balladeers, harmonica guys and keyboard hymnists. Throw a few coins their way, depending on your satisfaction reaction.
www.rundlemall.com

06 DERRINGERS MUSIC

Swim a little way out of the mainstream and there are some quirky, quality music shops in Adelaide's inner suburbs. If you're into guitars, point your compass towards Derringers Music, a 5km taxi ride south of the city centre in funky Forestville. This compact cave-of-wonders corner shop is hung with gorgeous vintage, new and rare guitars (and mandolins, ukuleles, banjos...). If you're visiting Adelaide on a long weekend you're probably not about to carry a 1964 US Gibson Hummingbird out the door with you, but here's your chance to play one. (And if you really like it, they'll ship it back home for you.)
www.derringers.com.au; tel +61 8 8371 1884; 66-72 Leader St; 9.30am-5.30pm Mon-Fri, to 4pm Sat, noon-4pm Sun

07 WHEATSHEAF HOTEL

On Monday night, jump in a taxi and head 3km west of the city centre to semi-industrial Thebarton where the everlovin' Wheatsheaf Hotel plies its beery musical trade. This hidden gem draws an offbeat, arty crowd of students, lesbians, gays, punks and rockers. Even if they're not performing, local musos head here to hang, drink and converse – this is the place to come to check the pulse of the local music scene.

The ramshackle music room out the back is where you want to be. Grab a craft beer and tune in to eclectic musical offerings from acoustic and blues to country and jazz. If you can, time your visit with Creative Original Music Adelaide (aka COMA; www.coma.net.au), which

convenes here every first and third Monday of the month. This non-profit enterprise was set up by local musos in 2005, committed to increasing opportunities for Adelaide original musical performance.

Expect jazz, improv, electronic and new classical acts; COMA creative director Jamie Capatch is usually on hand and keen for a chat. Don't let the flightpath sonics put you off: this is Adelaide music at its most informal, sociable and accessible — an amiable way to round out your musical long weekend in this city of many sounds.
39 George St, Thebarton; www.wheatsheafhotel.com.au ; +61 8 8443 4546; 1pm-midnight Mon-Fri, noon-midnight Sat, noon-9pm Sun
BY CHARLES RAWLINGS-WAY

05 Sunset at the Adelaide Festival Centre

06 Solar-powered lighting doubles as street sculpture in central Adelaide

WHERE TO STAY

ADABCO BOUTIQUE HOTEL
This central Adelaide hotel has at various times been an Aboriginal education facility, a roller-skating rink and an abseiling venue. These days you can expect lovely rooms, interesting art and quality linen. *www.adabcohotel.com. au; tel +61 8 8100 7500; 223 Wakefield St*

MAYFAIR HOTEL
Central Adelaide's old gargoyle-studded Colonial Mutual Life insurance company building (1934) has been reborn as this very luxe hotel. It's been fabulously done, incorporating bars, eateries and smiling staff. *www.mayfairhotel.com. au; tel +61 8 8210 8888; 45 King William St*

WHERE TO EAT & DRINK

MAYBE MAE
Peel St in Adelaide's West End is the city's after-dark epicentre. Down a stairwell off an alleyway here, Maybe Mae doesn't loudly proclaim its virtues to the world (can you even find the secret door?). But once you're inside, let the good times roll

with classic rock, booth seats and brilliant beers. *www.maybemae.com; +61 421 405 039; 15 Peel St; 5pm-late Mon-Fri, 6pm-late Sat & Sun*

GIN LONG CANTEEN
Expect chipper staff, communal tables and pan-Asian cuisine at this energetic North Adelaide food room. Meals are bolstered by jumbo bottles of Vietnamese beer. *www.ginlongcanteen.com. au; tel +61 8 7120 2897; 42 O'Connell St; noon-2.30pm Tue-Fri, 5.30-late Tue-Sat*

CELEBRATIONS

WOMADELAIDE
Family-friendly and slightly new-age, WOMADelaide is one of the world's best live-music events, with more than 300 musicians and performers from around the globe. *(www.womadelaide.com.au)*

ADELAIDE FRINGE
This annual independent arts festival held in February/March entices wandering musos from around the planet to venues across the city. Weird, funky, unpredictable and downright hilarious. *(www.adelaidefringe.com.au)*

INNERE STADT 1

AUSTRIA

05

04

06

02

VIENNA

01

BURGGARTEN

STADTPARK

07

03

Wien

08

RESSELPARK

Austria

ON A CLASSICAL HIGH IN VIENNA

During the Viennese Classical period, the world's greatest composers sought fame and fortune in Vienna's coffee houses and opera halls. Today, the city's love of music lives on.

In the Musikverein's Golden Hall, the crowds are dressed in their concert-going finery. The hum of excited chatter fades as the Vienna Philharmonic takes to the stage. Expectant silence falls. The orchestra strikes up and a trembling violin chord in A major drifts across the audience. It is that most famous of waltzes: Strauss's The Blue Danube. The conductor's baton seems to move of its own accord to this joyous, swaying number; an ode to the river that runs with gentle grace through the heart of the Austrian capital. For others, the waltz conjures images of bashful debutantes and their beaux twirling across a chandelier-lit ballroom. Either way, there can be no doubting where you are. This is Vienna in a nutshell.

No city has shaped classical music more than Vienna. In the heyday of the late 18th and early 19th centuries — the Viennese Classical period — the world's greatest composers sought their fortunes in its alleyways. The

NEED TO KNOW
The trail is doable in a day, though two days would allow more time to attend live performances.

highly cultured Hapsburgs, Vienna's ruling royal family, were generous patrons and passionate music lovers. It was here that child prodigy Mozart made his sparkling debut; and here that Schubert, Haydn and Beethoven lived, toiled and penned some of their greatest works. Concert halls of unsurpassed lavishness were built to do justice to such talent: each one an architectonic and acoustic masterpiece

Classical music still runs in Vienna's blood today. You'll hear it on the streets, in parks and coffee houses, or perhaps wafting from open windows. On any given night of the week, orchestras perform for some 10,000 music fans. Joining them is your golden ticket to the city's soul. And however formidable the concert halls seem, they are by no means the preserve of the elite. Classical music here is open to one and all, with last-minute, standing-room tickets sometimes costing as little as a cup of coffee. Sold? Waltz this way.

01 © B.O'Kane / Alamy

01 STADTPARK

Step off Vienna's monumental Ringstrasse boulevard to reach this quiet pocket of greenery, which straddles both banks of the Wien River. You might want to twirl over to the statue of Johann Strauss II (1825-1899) first — the golden, violin-playing wonder set high on a marble pedestal makes for some terrific photo ops. Wander further and you'll come across other classical legends peeking out of the foliage: Schindler, Bruckner and Schubert included.

02 CAFÉ FRAUENHUBER

A short five-minute amble west along Himmelpfortgasse in Vienna's historic centre brings you to Café Frauenhuber, the city's oldest coffee

'Little has changed in the vaulted interior of Café Frauenhuber since the days when Mozart and Beethoven gave performances here'

house. Retaining plenty of old-school swagger, little has changed in the vaulted interior since the days when Mozart (1756-1791) and Beethoven (1770-1827) gave public performances here, and you half expect to see bewigged composers at its tables.

The *kaffeehaus* has always been an extension of society: a place to play cards, listen to music, browse the daily papers, eat cake and set the world to rights — and Frauenhuber

is no exception. Over properly flaky strudel and a *kleiner brauner* (espresso with a dash of milk), watch a little slice of Viennese life unfold. *www.cafefrauenhuber.at; tel +43 1 5125353; Himmelpfortgasse 6; 8am-midnight Mon-Sat, 10am-10pm Sun*

03 HAUS DER MUSIK

Two blocks south of Café Frauenhuber, the Haus der Musik propels you into a playful, interactive world of music

01 Statue of Johann
Strauss II in Stadtpark

03 Double bass leans
against a chair

02 Vienna city view
from Stephansdom

04 Vienna's elegant
Staatsoper (opera house)

behind its elegant façade. Don't be fooled into thinking this museum's just for kids — you're never too old to want to compose your own waltz by throwing dice, and attempting to virtually conduct the Viennese Philharmonic Orchestra is bound to have you in fits of giggles. The museum is spread across four floors and its concert hall occasionally hosts live classical music events, including some geared towards kids — 'Mozart and Vivaldi for Children', for instance. www.hausdermusik.com; tel +43 1 513 48 50; Seilerstätte 30; 10am-10pm

04 MOZARTHAUS

Mozart may have been born in Salzburg but, let's face it, he was much fonder of Vienna. His enduring love affair with the Austrian capital was ignited at the tender age of six when he first performed for an enraptured Empress Maria Theresa in the Mirror Room at Schloss Schönbrunn. Later, he spent 2½ prolific years at this address, where he penned *The Marriage of Figaro*.

During his 11-year stint in the city he inhabited several residences, but this is the only one that still exists. The rooms whisk you through scores, paintings and hologram scenes from *The Magic Flute*, providing some insight into Mozart's work, life and vices — when not composing, Mozart enjoyed heavy drinking sessions, swearing, bawdy humour, billiards, womanising and teaching his pet starling to sing. The Mozarthaus is a 10-minute stroll north of Haus der Musik. www.mozarthausvienna.at; tel +43 1 512 17 91; Domgasse 5; 10am-7pm

05 STEPHANSDOM

Just across the way rises Vienna's Gothic crowning glory: Stephansdom. Affectionately nicknamed Steffl (Little Stephan) by locals — not without a hint of irony — the 12th-century cathedral is an elaborate confection, its steeply pitched, mosaic-tiled roof glimmering with rows of chevrons.

The cathedral is where Franz Joseph Haydn (1732-1809) began his career as a choirboy at the age of eight. It also formed the backdrop to

Vivaldi's funeral in 1741 and Mozart's marriage to Constanze Weber in 1782. Beethoven, too, has a connection with the cathedral — he supposedly discovered the totality of his deafness when he saw pigeons fluttering out of the bell tower yet could not hear the bells toll.

The cathedral stages summer concerts on Fridays and Saturdays from July to October, and festive advent concerts in the run-up to Christmas. Year round, the 10.15am Mass on Sundays is something else, as it's conducted with full choral accompaniment. *www.stephanskirche.at; tel +43 1 515 323 054; Stephansplatz; public visits 9-11.30am & 1-4.30pm Mon-Sat, 1-4.30pm Sun*

06 HOFBURGKAPELLE

Follow the rhythmic clip-clop of *fiaker* (horse-drawn carriages) south along the Graben and Kohlmarkt to Vienna's resplendent Hofburg — a palace fit for Hapsburg emperors from 1279 until 1918. Its Gothic Hofburgkapelle (Royal Chapel) is a sublime backdrop to hear the celestial tones of the Wiener Sängerknaben (Vienna Boys' Choir).

The world's most celebrated choir performs a repertoire of Schubert, Mozart and other classical greats during Sunday Mass; it also stages a diverse line-up of classical and contemporary music across town in MuTh, its own performing space. *www.hofmusikkapelle.gv.at; tel +43 1 533 99 27; Schweizerhof; Sunday Mass 9.15am Sep-Jun*

07 STAATSOPER

A few minutes' walk south brings you to the Ringstrasse, where trams trundle past the opulent, neo-Renaissance State Opera. Opened in 1869, this showstopper of a concert hall has housed some of the most iconic directors in history, including Gustav Mahler, Richard Strauss and Herbert von Karajan.

For a taste of its architectural brilliance and musical genius, hook onto one of the guided tours, which zoom in on highlights such as the foyer adorned with busts of Beethoven, Schubert and Haydn, the Tea Salon glittering in 22-carat gold leaf, and the Gustav Mahler Hall festooned with tapestries inspired by Mozart's *The Magic Flute*. The

website lists tour dates and times.

Staging some 300 lavish productions a year, this is Vienna's premiere opera and classical music venue. Dress up and book in advance — if performances are sold out, try for standing-room tickets (€3 to €4), sold 80 minutes before curtain time at the box office. www.wiener-staatsoper.at; tel +43 1 514 44 7880; Opernring 2

08 MUSIKVEREIN

The only serious contender to the Staatsoper's classical music crown is the Musikverein, which sits on Karlsplatz on the opposite side of the Ringstrasse, 10 minutes' walk away. Its acoustics are legendary – the best in Austria, apparently – and it's a fittingly grand home for the resident Vienna Philharmonic Orchestra.

The palatial interior can be visited on a guided tour, but to really see it come to life you should try to snag tickets for a performance – cheap-as-chips standing-room tickets (€4 to €6) are often available last minute. Tickets for the famous New Year's Even concert, however, are more expensive and like gold dust. Register interest months ahead. www.musikverein.at; tel + 43 1 505 81 90; Musikvereinsplatz 1; guided tours 10am, 11am & noon Mon-Sat
BY KERRY CHRISTIANI

05 Preparing for an intimate performance at Mozarthaus

06 Conducting a virtual orchestra at the Haus der Musik

WHERE TO STAY
OPERA SUITES
The Staatsoper is right on your doorstep at this sweet, family-run guesthouse, lodged in a turn-of-the-century house in Vienna's historic centre. Comfy rooms have plush perks. www.operasuites.at; tel +43 1 512 93 10; Kärntner Strasse 47

HOTEL LAMÉE
Lamée is dark, decadent and as sexy as its namesake movie starlet Hedy Lamarr. The gold-kissed rooms and suites are pure 1930s glamour, and the roof terrace with Stephansdom views is the perfect pre-concert cocktail spot. www.hotellamee.com; tel +43 1 532 22 40; Rotenturmstrasse 15

WHERE TO EAT & DRINK
BITZINGER WÜRSTELSTAND
Behind the Staatsoper, Vienna's best sausage stand attracts ladies and gents dressed up to the nines, with its contrasting offer of fried-onion-topped sausages and Joseph Perrier Champagne. It's open until 4am so ideal for midnight, post-concert munchies. www.bitzinger-wien.at; tel +43 660 815 24 13; Albertinaplatz; 8am-4am

GRIECHENBEISL
Vienna's oldest restaurant opened its doors in 1447 and has welcomed the likes of Beethoven, Brahms, Schubert and Strauss. Classics such as tafelspitz (boiled beef) are served in vaulted rooms. www.griechenbeisl.at; tel +43 1 533 19 77; Fleischmarkt 11; 11.30am-11.30pm

CELEBRATIONS
OPERNBALL
Of the 300 or so balls in January and February, none is more lavish than the Opernball. Held in the Staatsoper on the Thursday preceding Ash Wednesday, it's an exuberant affair with formal dress. (www.wiener-staatsoper.at)

OSTERKLANG FESTIVAL
Orchestral and chamber music recitals fill some of Vienna's best music halls during the OsterKlang Festival, held around Easter each year. The highlight is the opening concert with the Vienna Philharmonic. (www.wien.info)

Belgium
BRUSSELS & THE 9TH ART

The quirky underbelly of Belgium's capital is the epicentre of a European comic-strip movement that began with Tintin and lives on in museums, galleries and on the streets.

It may be the headquarters of the European Union, but there's much more to Belgium's capital than stuffy institutions and bureaucrats. Fun, friendly and cosmopolitan, it is also the irreverent European Capital of the Comic Strip.

While most people around the world associate comics and cartoons with Mickey Mouse and Donald Duck, Snoopy and Charlie Brown, or superheroes such as Batman and Superman, in Belgium and the rest of Europe there is a whole different appreciation of comic strips. Known as *'La Bande Dessinee'*, shortened to BD and pronounced 'bay day', the humble comic strip here is a far more surreal, absurd and often political medium that lampoons politicians and addresses sensitive issues such as global warming, racism and terrorism.

So it is hardly surprising that the city that gave the world the iconic surrealist paintings of Rene Magritte has grandly christened the work of modest comic-

strip creators 'The Ninth Art', and has its own museum dedicated to cartoons.

Hergé's intrepid reporter Tintin made his first appearance in 1929, immediately capturing the nation's imagination, and Belgians have since grown up with a love of eccentric comic-strip heroes, who keep their fans faithful from childhood through to old age. And while Tintin may be Belgium's most famous creation, there is a whole universe of weird and wonderful characters waiting to be discovered by those who make a pilgrimage to Brussels — the laconic cowboy Lucky Luke and his dastardly enemies, the Dalton brothers, the bouncy spotted Marsupilami, cheerful Smurfs, and Asterix and Obelix, to name a few.

Brussels is already one of Europe's best-kept secret destinations, with great restaurants and bars, a wild nightlife scene and brilliant shopping. Its comic-strip heritage adds another dimension to this surprising city.

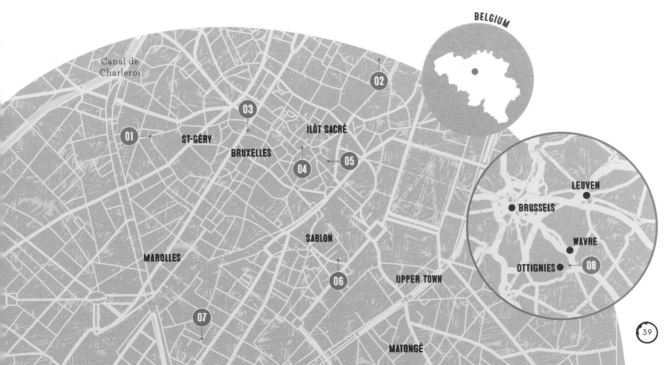

'While Tintin travelled the world, Hergé was a reserved person who spent most of his life quietly in Brussels'

01 COMIC STRIP TRAIL

Launched in 1991, the Brussels Comic Strip Trail has grown into more than 40 eye-catching cartoon murals across the city centre. Tracking them down is fun for kids and adults, and an ideal way to explore the backstreets of Brussels, armed with the trail map that explains who each character is. Most are within walking distance of each other in the city centre.

Kick off at Rue de la Buanderie, five minutes from the Grand Place, with an action scene of a bank hold-up by cowboy Lucky Luke, and don't miss the murals close to the Jeu de Balle flea market. Tintin, Snowy and Captain Haddock decorate a wall just by the famous Manneken Pis statue. *www.brussels.be/artdet.cfm/5316*

02 BELGIAN COMIC STRIP CENTER

Just behind La Monnaie, Brussels' grand opera house, this unique museum is housed in a magnificent old department store, designed by Victor Horta, Belgium's master of art nouveau. The palatial entrance is filled with fun statues of comic heroes and even a physical sculpture of Tintin's distinctive red-and-white rocket from *Destination Moon*.

One gallery illustrates the comic strip's history, from humble beginnings in late 19th-century American newspapers to the magic of Disney and cult Belgian magazines. An educational gallery explains the A to Z of creating a comic strip, starting with black-and-white sketches and ending with sophisticated storyboards coloured by painters.

A whole section is dedicated to Tintin, illustrating the changes over the years in Hergé's drawings and the increasing sophistication of subject

01 & 04
Comic-strip murals
around Brussels
city centre

02 The Hergé
Museum, outside
the city

03 Grand Place, the
heart of Brussels

05 Display at the
Belgian Comic
Strip Center

matter, such as *Tintin in Tibet*. This adventure, in which the cartoonist subtly addressed geo-political issues concerning the Chinese occupation of Tibet, is thought to have been Herge's favourite. It was serialised weekly for a year in 1958, eight years after the Chinese entered Tibet. *www.comicscenter.net, tel +32 2 2191980; 20 Rue des Sables; 10am-6pm*

03 BRÜSEL BOOKSHOP

Situated just off the Grand Place, Brüsel is more than a bookshop; it is a temple consecrated to the Ninth Art. Comic books are piled high all over the three-floor emporium: not just with Belgian favourites such as *Le Chat* — a wonderfully sardonic cat — but Japanese manga and cult books by global Bande Dessinee authors, from Mexico to Canada.

The first floor and basement double as galleries, exhibiting framed cartoon posters and original comic drawings. Nearby are top second-hand stores Little Nemo (25 Boulevard Lemonnier), named after the first-ever animated cartoon, and Le Depot (108 Rue du Midi), which has been drawing collectors for more than 50 years. *www.brusel.com; tel +32 2 5110809; 100 Boulevard Ansbach; 10.30am-6.30pm Mon-Sat, noon-6.30pm Sun*

04 LA BOUTIQUE DE TINTIN

On the other side of the Grand Place is an Aladdin's cave for Tintin fans. This official boutique dedicated to Hergé's young reporter stocks every gadget imaginable: think Tintin figurines and Captain Haddock keyrings, Snowy fridge magnets and even Madame Castafiore mugs. *www.boutique.tintin.com; tel +32 2 5145152; 13 Rue de la Colline; 10am-6pm*

05 MOOF MUSEUM

Up the hill from the Tintin boutique sits Brussels's imperious train station, La Gare Centrale, and hidden inside is Galerie Horta, where the MOOF opened its doors in 2010. Although officially called the Museum of Original Figurines, it is better known as La BD en 3D for its 1000 spot-lit figurines of dozens of comic strip heroes.

The entrance is marked by a striking statue of a Smurf — another inimitable Belgian cartoon creation, known here as Schtroumpfs. The first cartoon Smurfs appeared in French in 1958, but they did not become a worldwide pop-culture phenomenon until the 1980s, when the characters were turned into a hit TV animation series by an American-Belgian company. More than 300 million figurines have been made since then and millions of copies of their inimitable songs sold. Finally, the Smurfs found their way to Hollywood and the movies in 2011. *www.moof-museum.be; tel +32 2 2653325; 116 Rue du Marche-aux-Herbes; 10am-6pm Thu-Sun*

06 HUBERTY & BREYNE GALLERY

A 10-minute walk from Gare Centrale through Brussels' museum district brings you to the stately Place du Grand Sablon. Les Sablon is home to gourmet chocolate shops, chic antique stores and an art gallery that is internationally recognised for exhibiting original comic strip art.

For 25 years, Alain Huberty and Marc Breyne have organised shows where collectors can find signed storyboards, illustrations, prints and drawings, paintings and watercolours by many of the world's most famous comic-book creators, Hergé to Walt Disney's studio among them, as well as more contemporary voices. *www.hubertybreyne.com; tel +32 2 8939030; 8a Rue Bodenbroeck, Place du Grand Sablon; 11am-6pm Wed-Sat, to 5pm Sun*

07 JEU DE BALLE FLEA MARKET

There are always crowds walking up Rue Blaes, a street lined with tempting art deco stores stretching from Sablon to Place du Jeu de Balle. Nothing prepares, though, for the sight of the hundreds of traders occupying the immense square each day.

This is Europe's most authentic flea market, established a century ago, and amid the piles of bric-a-brac, comic-book fans search for vintage copies of *Le Journal de Tintin* or its great competitor, *Spirou* magazine, founded in 1939 with a host of light-hearted characters in a bid to appeal to a younger audience than aficionados of Hergé's more complex stories.

Amid the lively bars and cafes that line the square is the fun Jeu de Bulles gallery (www.jeudebulles.be), specialising in BD collectors' items. *www.marcheauxpuces.be; Place du Jeu de Balle; 6am 2pm*

08 HERGÉ MUSEUM

The figure of Hergé still towers over Belgium's world of comics, 30 years after Tintin's creator passed away. In 2009 a museum dedicated to him opened its doors, an hour's train trip south of Brussels.

The 24 comic albums chronicling *The Adventures of Tintin* have been translated into more than 70 languages, selling some 200 million copies across the globe. In this museum nine galleries include sections devoted to Hergé's lesser-known characters and his work in the cinema.

While Tintin travelled the world, Hergé — whose real name was Georges Prosper Remi — was a reserved person who shunned attention and spent most of his life quietly in Brussels. Despite his immense success, though, Hergé often attracted controversy. There have been claims of collaboration during the Nazi occupation of Belgium, and more recent criticisms of racism and misogyny in his comic strips. *www.museeherge.com; tel +32 10 488421; 26 Rue du Labrador, Louvain-la-Neuve; 10.30am-5.30pm Tue-Fri, 10am-6pm Sat & Sun*
BY JOHN BRUNTON

06 L'Art de la Fugue breakfast room

07 Treasures at the Jeu de Balle flea market

08 Comic-strip mural hangs above a cafe

WHERE TO STAY
L'ART DE LA FUGUE
Housed in a rambling townhouse, this fabulous B&B has guestrooms named after movies, including Farinelli, a riot of baroque antiques; and Absolutely Fabulous, a treasure trove of 1970s decor. *www.lartdelafugue.com; tel +32 478 695944; 38 Rue de Suede*

VINTAGE HOTEL
Every room in this hip design hotel is furnished with the owners' extraordinary collection of kitsch 1970s decor. Parked in the forecourt there is a unique glamping site: a retro 1958 Airstream caravan, luxuriously restored to its former glory. *www.vintagehotel.be; tel +32 2 5339980; 45 Rue Dejoncker*

WHERE TO EAT & DRINK
MER DU NORD
This fishmonger turned outdoor tapas bar attracts huge crowds to its pavement bar, serving grill-seared tuna, swordfish, scallops and squid, along with wine and champagne. Belgian specialities include creamy shrimp croquettes and fish soup. *www.vishandelnoordzee. be; tel +32 2 5131192; 45 Rue Sainte Catherine*

L'ARCHIDUC
The legendary Archiduc boasts a grand piano amid art deco interiors, and serves its bohemian-chic clientele gin martinis, bourbon sours and Belgian abbey ales such as Orval and Chimay. It hosts live jazz at the weekend. *www.archiduc.net; tel +32 2 5120652; 6 Rue Antoine Dansaert*

CELEBRATIONS
COMIC STRIP FESTIVAL
On the first weekend in September Brussels celebrates comic art with a parade of huge helium-inflated balloons of characters such as Tintin, plus exhibitions, shows and workshops. *(www.fetedelabd.brussels)*

SALON DU CHOCOLAT
It's a given that Brussels and chocolate go together, and this February event shows off the city's love for the sweet stuff; there is even a fashion show with models wearing chocolate dresses. *(brussels.salon-du-chocolat.com)*

Baía de Todos os Santos

BRAZIL

SANTO ANTÔNIO

CARMO

PELOURINHO

COMÉRCIO

06

01

02

04

05   NAZARÉ

CIDADE BAIXA (LOWER CITY)

03

Brazil

CAPOEIRA IN SALVADOR

Martial art, dance, art form... however you define it, Afro-Brazilian capoeira is a unique performance not to be missed, and the bay city of Salvador da Bahia is the place to catch it.

It's the capital of the state Brazilians call *a terra da felicidade* (the land of happiness). But Salvador da Bahia, strategically positioned at the confluence of the Atlantic Ocean and the Baía de Todos os Santos on the northeast coast of Brazil, isn't just a tropical paradise. It's the beating heart of Afro-Brazil — a destination rich in colour, joy and sunshine, but also a profound and lingering sadness.

Once a proud Portuguese colonial settlement, Salvador was a stronghold in the New World during the 16th century. But the slave trade quickly cast a shadow over the brand-new city's picturesque houses and wide beaches. It's estimated that four million African slaves were brought to Brazil in the three centuries that followed; most were sent to work on the massive sugar plantations that drove the young economy. It was there, in the *senzalas* — crowded, poorly maintained slave quarters — that the

NEED TO KNOW
Most stops on this two-day trail can be reached on foot, with a not-to-be-missed whizz up the Elevador Lacerda.

stage was set for the invention of a new art form. Slaves originally created capoeira, a form of martial arts that's likely based on a ritualistic African dance, as a form of self-defence against oppressive masters. To disguise their training, early capoeiristas made their sport look more like acrobatics or dance, using simple percussion instruments to create rhythm and music. Eventually the slave masters caught on, and capoeira was officially outlawed.

Through the 1920s, slaves continued to practise capoeira covertly. It was around this time, in the early 20th century, that two modern practitioners, Mestre Pastinha and Mestre Bimba, developed capoeira into two distinct schools, elevating the slaves' self-defence system to a nationally recognised (and legal) art form. Today, Salvador da Bahia is the best place in the world to see real capoeira — in all its elegance, athleticism, and melancholy — in action.

01 MERCADO MODELO

Sejam bem-vindos (welcome) to the Cidade Baixa, or Lower City. The Mercado Modelo is a popular artisan marketplace bustling with travellers: some are shopping, others are kicking back with a cold beer or waiting to catch a boat across the bay.

But this harbourfront landmark has a dark backstory. The building was originally constructed in the mid-19th century to serve as the city's third Customs House. Even though the slave trade into Brazil was technically outlawed in 1831, enslaved Africans were shipped into Salvador for decades afterwards — and local legend has it some of them were held here, in the oft-flooded basement, while awaiting placement.

'Capoeira was elevated into a nationally recognised art form when Mestre Bimba performed for the president of Brazil in 1928'

Today, the busy marketplace isn't the best place in town to see capoeira in action. The capoeiristas regularly performing on the lower terrace are catering to tourists. Throw some coins in the hat, anyway: the *mercado* is a fitting place to contemplate the experience of slaves and the circumstances that prompted them to develop capoeira in the first place. Cross the street and ride the historic Elevador Lacerda to the Cidade Alta

(Upper City) — home to the Pelourinho, Salvador's historic centre, and the city's numerous capoeira schools. *www.mercadomodelobahia.com. br; Praça Visconde de Cayru; 9-7pm Mon-Sat, 9am-2pm Sun & holidays*

02 ASSOCIAÇÃO DE CAPOEIRA MESTRE BIMBA

It's true that capoeira was born on Brazilian sugar plantations in the 16th century. But it wouldn't

01 Colonial buildings
echo 16th-century
Portuguese rule

02 Capoeira
performers throng the
streets of old Salvador

03 Brazilian beachlife
laps at the edges of
this bayside city

look the way it does today without its development in the city, or without the contributions of Mestre Bimba (1900-1974) — the modern practitioner whose son is still in charge of the Associação de Capoeira Mestre Bimba, the oldest and most famous capoeira school in the world.

Born Manuel dos Reis Machado, the Salvador native was the youngest of 25 children. From an early age he worked as a carpenter on the docks, building his personal strength and learning Capoeira Angola from an African sailor. Frustrated by how the original form had devolved into a tourist attraction, he developed 'regional' capoeira. Mestre Bimba's system was governed by a strict code: participants were required to wear clean white garments, for example, and coloured scarves that indicated rank.

Mestre Bimba took capoeira seriously and demanded the same of his students. In doing so, he pushed the form into the future, ultimately introducing choreography and flamboyant flips into the repertoire.

Capoeira was elevated to a nationally recognised art form after the Mestre performed for the governor of Bahia, in 1928. With the government's approval, the impassioned practitioner went on to found the world's first official capoeira academy in 1932. Mestre Bimba died suddenly in 1974, but his legacy is deeply felt in Bahia. Classes are available for adults and children at the organisation's HQ in the Pelourinho;

in the evening, you can also stop in to watch the masters practising. *www.capoeiramestrebimba.com.br; tel +55 71 3322 0639; Rua das Laranjeiras 1; Mon-Fri, class times vary*

03 FORTE DA CAPOEIRA

In the adjacent neighbourhood of Santo Antônio, you'll find the so-called Forte da Capoeira. The old fortress, recently refurbished and offering views over the bay, is a landmark (and a photo op) in its own right, especially at sunset. But it's nicknamed 'the Capoeira fort' because it's a hub of capoeira-related activities.

One non-profit organisation dedicated to the preservation of the 'original' form of capoeira — Angola, the more naturalist, less structured style that Mestre Bimba broke away from to develop Capoeira Regional — stages regular *rodas* (capoeira circles) here. Events often occur on Saturdays at 7pm, but for capoeira enthusiasts, it's worth a stop any time, as local organisations post their upcoming schedules around the fort. *www.cultura.ba.gov.br; +55 71 3117 1488; Praça Santo Antônio Além do Carmo; event times vary*

04 ATELIER MESTRE LUA RASTA

On the hunt for a unique souvenir? Look no further than the workshop of the multitalented Mestre Lua Rasta, a capoeira master, musician, craftsman and scholar of Afro-Brazilian percussion instruments. Born as Gilson Fernandes in 1950, Mestre Lua Rasta studied capoeira

under Mestre Bimba in 1968. His true passion, however, was the music that creates the rhythm for capoeira, such as the *berimbau* (a bow-shaped, single-string percussion instrument that sets the rhythm of capoeira), the *atabaque* (a tall wooden drum), and the *agogô* (a high-pitched bell that's also used in samba). He went on to become a respected maker of traditional percussion instruments.

Today, Mestre Lua Rasta lives across the bay from Salvador on the island of Itaparica, where he tans leather and harvests wood that he brings back to his urban atelier to craft beautiful, one-of-a-kind musical instruments. Stop in to see his process and perhaps even buy something; he can also arrange percussion or capoeira classes. *www.atelierlua.com.br; tel +55 71 3322 6750; Rua Inácio Accioli 3, Pelourinho; hours vary*

05 IGREJA E CONVENTO SÃO FRANCISCO

A few blocks away, in the Pelourinho plaza of Cruzeiro São Francisco, take a peek inside one of the most magnificent churches in Brazil. The baroque Igreja features over-the-top displays of wealth, including an 80kg silver chandelier.

But many tourists don't notice the disguised details added by the African slave artisans that played a key role in building the church. In a show of rebellion, early 19th-century slaves crafted cherubs with grotesquely distorted faces, huge sex organs, even pregnant bellies. Most of these darkly humorous details were later covered up or changed, but their very existence serves as an intriguing parallel with capoeira: in both cases, masters could force their slaves to work in the fields or the churches, but they couldn't stop them from subtler forms of individual expression, whether in martial arts or visual arts. *Cruzeiro de São Francisco; +55 71 3322-6430; 9am-5.30pm Mon & Wed-Sat, 9am-4pm Tue, 10am-3pm Sun*

06 BALÉ FOLCLÓRICO DA BAHIA

Finish your day at a nearby theatre — the Teatro Miguel Santana is our pick — catching a show by the world-

renowned Balé Folclórico da Bahia. The folkloric ballet of Bahia features dozens of musicians, dancers and singers in a repertory of traditional 'slave dances', capoeira, samba, and ceremonial dances associated with Candomblé, a cult-like religion that developed in Afro-Brazil.

It's not like any ballet you've seen before; it's an explosive spectacle of cultural pride and athleticism, of joy and melancholy, with fire-dancers twirling and capoeiristas high-kicking to the rhythm of traditional bells, drums and African percussion instruments.

The troupe earned international acclaim for its lively performance at the Biennale de la danse in Lyon, France, back in 1994. Afterward, the troupe started taking its show on the road more regularly, performing in places as far and wide as New York, Sydney and Stockholm.

When they're not travelling the globe, these talented performers put on frequent shows at Teatro Miguel Santana, a small theatre just off the Largo do Pelourinho. *www.balefolcloricodabahia.com.br; tel +55 71 3322 1962; Teatro Miguel Santana, Rua Gregório de Matos 49, Pelourinho; performances 8pm daily; confirm ahead*
BY BRIDGET GLEESON

04 Looking out over the Mercado Modelo and Elevador Lacerda (left)

05 Rainbow-striped berimbau instruments

WHERE TO STAY
CASA DO AMARELINDO
A lovely boutique hotel housed inside a colonial mansion, this cheerful *casa* has an adorable rooftop pool and bar where guests can swim and sip caipirinhas while overlooking the bay. *www.casadoamarelindo. com; +55 71 3266 8550; 6 Portas do Carmo*

HOSTEL GALERIA 13
Budget travellers love the breakfast buffet, Moroccan-style lounge and refreshing swimming pool at this popular hostel in the Pelourinho. Solar panels also make it an eco-friendly choice. *www.hostelgaleria13.com; +55 71 3266 5609; 23 Rua da Ordem Terceira*

WHERE TO EAT & DRINK
CAFÉLIER
It's hard to decide what's nicest about this quaint cafe: the frothy cappuccino and chocolate cake, the ice-cold caipirinhas, the charmingly antique interior, or the clifftop views over the water. *www.cafelier.com.br; tel +55 71 3241 5095; Rua do Carmo 50*

BAR ZULU
On a cobblestoned side street, this laid-back cafe-bar is a good place to try a healthier, modern take on Bahian *moqueca* (fish stew.) At night, try the potent house cocktail made with *cachaça* (a Brazilian rum-like spirit). *www.facebook.com/bar zulu; tel +55 71 98784-3208; Rua das Laranjeiras 15*

CELEBRATIONS
CARNAVAL
Second only to Rio's Carnaval, Salvador's festivities attract more than two million revellers for six days leading up to Ash Wednesday (usually in February). Look for *blocos afros* — powerful drum corps that use instruments you'll also see in capoeira performances.

LAVAGEM DO BONFIM
Outside of Carnaval, this festival is Salvador's largest and a not-to-be-missed party. It takes place on the second Thursday in January, featuring processions of costumed women carrying buckets of flowers to the church of Igreja Nosso Senhor do Bonfim. Associated festivities happen across the city.

Bulgaria

CONFRONTING SOVIET GHOSTS IN BULGARIA

The legacy of socialist rule and Soviet influence endures in remarkable architectural relics across Bulgaria. Touring these structures is a fascinating journey into a dark past.

Soviet architecture: instantly, the phrase conjures forests of tower blocks and steely grey statues. From the 1930s until the crumbling of the Soviet Union in 1991, super-sized monuments sprouted across Eastern Europe. Bulgaria was closely tied to the Soviet Union between 1946 and 1990, as the socialist People's Republic of Bulgaria, and the country harbours many remarkable relics of this period, from angular high-rise blocks to space-age monuments. Young Bulgarians can regard them without too much bitterness; but for those who lived through socialism, these structures are anchors to a past better forgotten.

For many visitors to this rugged Balkan country, Soviet buildings are mere curiosities. After all, Bulgaria has the Rodopi Mountains, a golden swathe of Black Sea Coast, and thousand-year-old Rila Monastery as its spiritual heart. But spectral Soviet buildings tap into

NEED TO KNOW
Four days and a car are ideal for completing this trip. With more time, it's possible to travel by bus and taxi.

Bulgaria's dark past, and span intriguing styles.

Most recognisable is Stalinist design: tiered high-rises of brick and concrete built in the 1930s and 1950s. Socialist realism developed around the same time, depicting communist values in grandiose sculptures (workers clutching wheat sheaves, grim-faced factory women), along with murals and mosaics of leaders. Overlapping with Soviet style is Brutalism — a raw, modernist art movement known for stark angles and unabashed use of concrete.

Soviet buildings are inescapably associated with the era's state control and repression. Consequently, they are in varying states of preservation. Some that symbolise enduring values such as power and freedom are beautifully maintained; others, inextricably linked to politics, have fallen into disrepair. Whether you're faced with bombastic statues or sinister ruins, their ambiguity is compelling.

01 © nikolay100 / Getty Image.

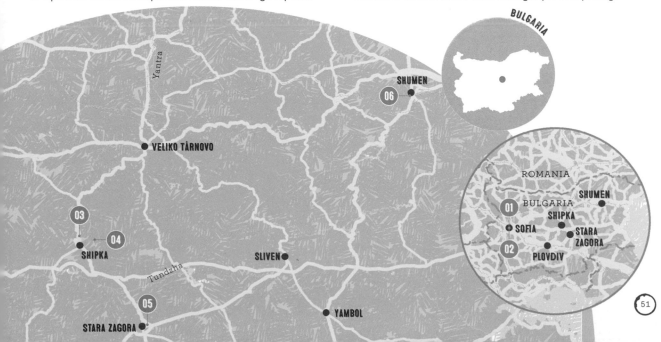

02 © Sean Gallup / Getty Images

01 FORMER COMMUNIST PARTY HEADQUARTERS

Built by a co-operative of architects in the mid-1950s, Sofia's former Communist Party HQ has all the features of early Soviet architecture: neoclassical columns reach up towards a tiered tower, crowned with a sharp spire.

The building narrowly escaped extinction at the end of Bulgaria's socialist regime when protesters tried to torch it. Today it sports a Bulgarian flag rather than a glittering red star, and houses government offices and a concert hall. It's 250m from central metro station Serdika.
Pl Alexander Battenberg 1, Sofia

02 NATIONAL PALACE OF CULTURE

Just 1.5km south of Sofia's Communist HQ you can grab a coffee, watch a movie, or go to the theatre within another socialist relic: sci-fi-style National Palace of Culture (NDK) is the friendly face of Soviet architecture. This hexagon of glass and steel is planted in a broad pedestrian promenade in the heart of the city, and is illuminated like an alien spacecraft at night.

Some 10,000 tonnes of steel went into NDK's construction, which was completed in 1981. It was a popular year for grand openings, as the 1300-year anniversary of the dawn of the First Bulgarian Empire (a golden age of expansion and cultural growth). NDK was the pet project of Lyudmila Zhivkova, daughter of Todor Zhivkov, the last leader of socialist Bulgaria.

The People's Republic of Bulgaria was hardly renowned for freedom of expression, so there's a delicious irony that this centre, designed at the twilight of the era, now hosts a riotously varied range of performances. *www.ndk.bg; tel +359 2916 6300; Pl Bulgaria 1, Sofia*

03 SHIPKA MONUMENT

A 2.5-hour drive east of Sofia, Bulgaria's most incredible structures are littered across the Stara Planina

'The building narrowly escaped extinction at the end of Bulgaria's socialist regime; protesters tried to torch it'

01 Shumen's Monument to 1300 Years of Bulgaria

02 Vitosha Mountain looms behind an Orthodox Sofia church

03 Signs of abandonment as Cyrillic letters fall from a wall

04 Sci-fi Buzludzha Monument — also known as 'Bulgaria's UFO'

03-04 © Matt Munro / Lonely Planet

Mountains. Most visited is the Freedom Memorial, a 32m-tall granite tower that broods at the top of Mount Stoletov (1326m).

Heavily influenced by Stalinist style, the 1934 monument commemorates the Battles of Shipka Pass, which culminated in 1878. In this series of brutal conflicts, Russian soldiers and Bulgarian volunteers fended off Ottoman control of the strategic pass against incredible odds.

Experienced properly, getting to the memorial requires a strenuous hike. Visitors pace through woodland and up nearly 1000 stone steps. At the top, you are greeted with a stone lion clawing at the chains

of oppression, and a final set of stairs that rises to the memorial, flanked by cannons and topped with an even bigger lion (an 8m-high bronze statue).

The monument surveys a panorama of wind-blasted spruce forests and raw mountains. To truly capture the site's stark mood, hike 13km from Shipka village to reach it. *www.shipkamuseum.org; Shipka Pass; 9am-7pm summer, 9am-4.30pm winter*

04 BUZLUDZHA MONUMENT

Gazing out from the top of Shipka Monument on a clear day, you can see a strange object hovering on

the horizon. Shipka Monument is far from the strangest decoration in these hills: that honour goes to Buzludzha Monument, also known as Bulgaria's UFO. From Shipka Monument, it's a 30-minute drive east (or an uphill hike, taking three to four hours).

Formerly a socialist assembly hall, this saucer-shaped ark of concrete was constructed in the 1970s with all the typical Soviet hallmarks: an imposing location, epic scale, and sculptures to signify strength, such as fists and flaming torches.

After a grand opening in 1981 — the 1300-year anniversary of the First Bulgarian Empire — it became

a hallowed meeting place for the Bulgarian Communist Party.

After the fall of Bulgarian socialism, the building was left to rot. Looters seized seats, tore away crimson carpeting, and chiselled away at Socialist realist mosaics (the face of ousted Todor Zhivkov has been entirely hacked away).

A hammer and sickle still glow in gold on the ceiling; but dust hangs in the air, taunting graffiti scars the walls and broken glass coats the treacherous stairwells.

More than two decades of limbo may be coming to an end, as there are now plans on the cards to renovate the building into a museum. But for many visitors, decay is part of the building's magnetism.
Shipka; 24hr

05 DEFENDERS OF BULGARIA MONUMENT

Former trade town, modern business city and perennial road and rail connection point: most travellers expect Stara Zagora to be a nondescript masterclass in Soviet architecture's duller designs. But this surprisingly leafy city, an hour's drive south of Buzludzha, boasts Roman ruins, fountained parks and the impressive Defenders of Bulgaria Monument.

Like Shipka, Stara Zagora's monument commemorates the sacrifices of the Russo-Turkish Wars, erected in 1977 on the centenary of the battle for Stara Zagora. But unlike Shipka, the battle was a catastrophe and more than 14,000 Bulgarians were killed when Stara Zagora fell.

A 50m arm of concrete rises above the tomb-like monument. Seven Socialist realist-style statues of Bulgarian soldiers and a Russian officer are encased in concrete beneath it, casting a watchful eye over Stara Zagora.
Park Bulgarsko Opalchenie, Stara Zagora; 24hr

06 MONUMENT TO 1300 YEARS OF BULGARIA

Two and half hours' drive east of Stara Zagora stands Shumen's lofty Monument to 1300 Years of Bulgaria, built in 1981.

It signifies the end of an era, both politically and architecturally: an appropriate place to end your journey from west to east across Bulgaria. Within nine years of the monument

opening, the People's Republic of Bulgaria would be no more and the period's harsh design styles would fall out of favour.

But though its roots are firmly planted in Soviet style, the 1300 Years Monument was built for immortality. Bold, Cubist elements burst through its boxy Soviet walls.

Deified khans from Bulgaria's past, in gargantuan proportions, explode from stone alcoves. Helmeted warriors ride cyborg-like horses. Their deliberately angular features lend them a superhuman quality – as if they are machines in the engine of Bulgaria's unstoppable progress.

Shumensko Plato Nature Park; 8am-8pm May-Sep, 8.30am-5pm Oct-Apr
BY ANITA ISALSKA

05 Left to rack and ruin: inside the Buzludzha Monument

06 A military reminder in the mountains near Shipka, central Bulgaria

WHERE TO STAY
HOTEL IT SHIPKA
Combining a warm welcome, Bulgarian home cooking and unbeatable hiking advice, this family-run guesthouse in Shipka village is an ideal midway point for touring Bulgaria's Soviet architecture: a short hop by car to Buzludzha and Shipka monuments, or you can hike.
www.shipkaithotel.com; tel +359 4324 2112; Ul Kolyo Adzhara 12, Shipka

NIRVANA ART HOTEL
This architecturally intriguing hotel in lofty Shumen features columns and ornate trellises that evoke a Moorish-style palace; rooms feel crisp and contemporary.
www.hotelnirvana.bg; tel +359 5480 0127; Nezavisimost 25

WHERE TO EAT & DRINK
MOMA BULGARIAN FOOD & WINE
A traditional Bulgarian *mehana* (tavern) experience, updated for Sofia's jet set. MoMA serves Balkan comfort food with an upmarket twist: rabbit stew, honeyed pork ribs and

traditional desserts.
moma-restaurant.com; tel +359 885 622 020; Ul Solunska 28; 11am-10pm

UNIQATO
Refined Italian cuisine is on the menu at this restaurant in Stara Zagora – a refreshing change to Bulgarian grills. Wash it down with a little help from the sophisticated wine list.
www.uniqato.com; tel +359 4264 1164; Ul Sava Silov 36; 11am-midnight

CELEBRATIONS
ROSE FESTIVAL
This annual festival is held in the Valley of the Roses, 10km south of Shipka. The most elaborate festivities are in Kazanlâk on the first weekend of June. You'll be sprayed with rose water, offered rose liqueur, and led into fields to pluck a few lucky blooms.

SOFIA INTERNATIONAL FILM FESTIVAL
See the Bulgarian capital at its cosmopolitan best when movie buffs from around the country pour into Sofia for star-studded screenings of cutting-edge Bulgarian and international film in mid-March.
(siff.bg)

CANADA

Vancouver
Harbour

Burrard Inlet

04

05

WEST END

02 03

DOWNTOWN GASTOWN

English Bay

01

GRANVILLE ISLAND

KITSILANO

UNIVERSITY OF
BRITISH COLUMBIA

POINT GREY

FAIRVIEW

MAIN

06 WHISTLER

07

ARBUTUS

WEST SIDE

QUILCHENA

CAMBIE

BRITISH COLUMBIA

VANCOUVER

Canada

ABORIGINAL CULTURE IN BRITISH COLUMBIA

Canada's westernmost province embraces its aboriginal forefathers with monuments, museums and experiences designed to help visitors connect with First Nations cultures.

Aboriginal people have lived on Canada's west coast, in what is now the province of British Columbia, for more than 10,000 years. This region, which stretches from the Pacific Coast to the Rocky Mountains, from the border with the United States north to the Yukon, is still home to more than 200 different First Nations. Nearly 20 per cent of Canada's aboriginal population resides in BC.

Here on the northwest coast of North America, indigenous people drew on the region's abundant natural resources, catching salmon, crab, and other seafood from the surrounding waters. They built homes, carved dugout canoes and crafted totem poles from western red cedar and other native trees; using images of eagles, bears, and other wildlife, these poles marked milestones and told stories of their communities. For centuries, aboriginal artists from this region also created, and continue to create, masks, carvings,

NEED TO KNOW
Allow three days for this trail — two days in Vancouver and one in Whistler; reach the latter by car or bus.

jewellery and other works that are highly prized today. Starting from Vancouver, BC's largest city, where glass and steel towers rise up between the mountains and the sea, you can explore this native heritage and present-day culture. Stay in Canada's first aboriginal art hotel, explore traditional cultures at one of the country's best anthropology museums, check out contemporary aboriginal art and tour the city's vast rainforest park accompanied by a First Nations guide to bring the indigenous history to life.

From Vancouver, follow the scenic Sea-to-Sky Highway towards Whistler, a mountain resort community located a two-hour drive to the north. While Whistler is best known for its outdoor adventures, its aboriginal experiences may come as a surprise. Complete your trip with a visit to a modern cultural centre jointly operated by two First Nations, and a mountainside art museum with a significant aboriginal art collection.

01 © GerryRousseau / Alamy

02 © Michael Wheatley / Getty Images

01 MUSEUM OF ANTHROPOLOGY

Your first stop is at the University of British Columbia on Vancouver's west side, where the Museum of Anthropology's collections illuminate the culture of western Canada's aboriginal peoples, as well as other traditional cultures around the globe.

Highlights include the towering totem poles, canoes and other carvings in the window-lined Great Hall, dating from the 19th century to the present. While totem poles are considered a symbol of many Canadian aboriginal peoples, only six west-coast First Nations originally carved them.

The museum also holds a significant collection of works by BC aboriginal artist Bill Reid (1920-1998); look for

'Reid drew on indigenous tribal Haida traditions and imbued them with his own modern ideas, broadening their appeal'

his massive, intricately carved cedar sculpture, *The Raven and the First Men*. *moa.ubc.ca; tel +1 604 822 5087; 6393 NW Marine Dr; 10am-5pm Fri-Wed, to 9pm Thu mid-May–mid-Oct; closed Mon rest of yr*

02 BILL REID GALLERY OF NORTHWEST COAST ART

Reid, who was of mixed European and Haida First Nations ancestry, created more than 1500 sculptures, carvings,

and pieces of jewellery, most exploring Haida traditions and themes.

Born in Victoria, Reid was unaware of his native roots until he was a teen. As a young man, he travelled to the remote archipelago of Haida Gwaii where the work of his late uncle, Charles Edenshaw — a noted Haida carver and jewellery maker — inspired him. In his art, Reid drew on indigenous tribal Haida traditions and imbued them with his own modern

01 Totem poles in Vancouver's Stanley Park

02 The traditionally inspired exterior of the Museum of Anthropology

03 The historic neighbourhood of Gastown, Vancouver

04 Trails in Stanley Park

ideas, broadening their appeal outside the aboriginal community.

This gallery was opened by the Bill Reid Foundation in 2008 in downtown Vancouver to preserve the artist's work and legacy. As well as works by Reid, it exhibits native art from North America's northwest coastal regions. *www.billreidgallery.ca; tel +1 604 682 3455; 639 Hornby St; 10am–5pm late May–early Sep, 11am–5pm Wed–Sun rest of yr*

03 HILL'S NATIVE ART GALLERY

Lined with brick and stone buildings dating from the 1880s, Vancouver's Gastown neighbourhood is one of the city's oldest and designated a national historic site. Several commercial art galleries on Water Street, a 15-minute walk from the Bill Reid Gallery, show works by aboriginal artists.

One of the largest, multistorey Hill's Native Art Gallery, displays everything from inexpensive souvenirs to top-quality northwest coast aboriginal art, which retails for thousands of dollars. Look for carvings, stonework, jewellery, prints and even totem poles by native artists from across the region. *www.hills.ca; tel +1 604 685 4249; 165 Water St; 9am–9pm*

04 TALKING TREES WALK

The next day, explore Vancouver's Stanley Park, a 400-hectare rainforest green space at the end of the downtown peninsula. For generations, aboriginal peoples lived in the area that now encompasses this city park. To learn more about the park's aboriginal history and traditions, and its trees and plants, book a 90-minute 'Talking Trees Walk' with a First Nations guide. You might discover how the coast's indigenous people use particular plants for food or medicine, why they consider the red cedar to be 'the tree of life', and what legends the land and its flora have inspired. *www.talaysay.com; tel +1 604 628 8555; tours May–Oct*

05 STANLEY PARK

After you've finished with your guided walk through Stanley Park's interior, there's still more to explore. The best way to see the rest of the park's sights is by bicycle. Take a break for lunch (you'll find lots of places to

eat outside the park's Georgia St entrance), then rent your wheels from one of the nearby shops, or check out a bicycle using the Mobi bike-share system (www.mobibikes.ca).

Re-entering the park from West Georgia St, follow the Seawall, a 9km multi-use path that circles the park's perimeter. Stop first to see the nine totem poles at Brockton Point; they're replicas of originals that aboriginal carvers crafted between the early 1920s and the present.

Continue around the Seawall to the park's west side past Siwash Rock. According to native legends, this 18-metre-tall rock was created when the gods turned a young father to stone as he swam in Burrard Inlet to purify himself before his first

child was born. By transforming him into a rock, with a spirit that would never die, the gods honoured his commitment to 'clean fatherhood' and to protect his family.

At Third Beach, walk up the stairs to find a memorial honouring E Pauline Johnson (1861-1913) — the daughter of a Mohawk chief and an Englishwoman, she was an early feminist writer and performer, and one of the first indigenous authors to become broadly known in Canada. In her book, *Legends of Vancouver*, Johnson relayed aboriginal stories that she learned from a local Squamish First Nations chief. Johnson's ashes are buried at this Stanley Park site.

Keep following the Seawall to watch the sunset over English Bay, where the

stone sculpture *Inukshuk*, based on a traditional Inuit design, looks on. *vancouver.ca/parks-recreation-culture/stanley-park.aspx; tel +1 604 873 7000; park entrances at cnr West Georgia & Chilco Sts and cnr Beach Ave & English Bay; 6am-10pm*

06 SQUAMISH LIL'WAT CULTURAL CENTRE

A two-hour drive or bus ride along the scenic Sea-to-Sky Highway (Highway 99) brings you to the lofty resort town of Whistler, located on the traditional territory of several First Nations. If you're driving, stop at the 'Cultural Journey' roadside kiosks that introduce the region's indigenous peoples.

In Whistler Village, the Squamish Lil'Wat Cultural Centre provides

more details about these native communities, their histories and their present-day cultures. Squamish Nation are a coastal people numbering about 4000 today; the Lil'wat come from BC's mountains and now number 2500. Staff at this modern museum include cultural ambassadors from both communities, who can explain more about the exhibits.

The centre's small cafe serves dishes such as venison chilli, salmon chowder, and bannock (a native bread). *slcc.ca; tel +1 604 964 0990; 4584 Blackcomb Way; 10am-5pm Tue-Sun*

07 AUDAIN ART MUSEUM

Also in Whistler Village, the Audain Art Museum — new in 2016 — has an extensive collection of works by British Columbia artists. The carvings and other art by people of aboriginal heritage include dramatic northwest-coast masks, dating to the 19th century, used in ceremonial dances and rituals.

The museum also houses one of Canada's largest collections of works by BC artist Emily Carr (1871-1945). While not of aboriginal heritage herself, Carr is known for her artistic explorations of the region's native communities. *audainartmuseum.com; tel +1 604 962 0413; 4350 Blackcomb Way; 10am-5pm Wed-Mon*
BY CAROLYN B HELLER

05 Inuit sculpture, Whistler

06 Totem poles at the Museum of Anthropology

WHERE TO STAY

SKWACHÀYS LODGE
First Nations artists designed the 18 one-of-a-kind rooms at this lodge in Vancouver — Canada's first aboriginal arts hotel. Hotel profits help subsidise housing for First Nations artists, and the in-house gallery sells works by native Canadians. Arrange in advance to join a smudging or sweat-lodge ceremony. *skwachays.com; tel +1 604 687 3589; 29/31 W Pender St*

LISTEL HOTEL
This art-filled, 129-room downtown Vancouver property also has an aboriginal flavour. Choose a 'museum' room, designed in partnership with staff at the Museum of Anthropology, featuring works by First Nations artists. Original artworks feature throughout. *thelistelhotel.com; tel +1 604 684 8461; 1300 Robson St*

WHERE TO EAT & DRINK

SALMON N' BANNOCK
Sample salmon, elk and other traditional ingredients in modern preparations at this First Nations-owned bistro, not far from Toronto's Museum of Anthropology. Wines come from Nk'Mip Cellars, Canada's first aboriginal-owned winery. *www.salmonandbannock .net; tel +1 604 568 8971; 1128 W Broadway*

TIMBER
Start with a local craft beer or a Caesar (Canada's Bloody Mary) at this gastropub. Then dig into classic Canadian comfort foods such as bison burgers, deep-fried cheese curds or poutine — a Quebecois dish of potatoes, cheese curds and gravy. *timbervancouver.com; tel +1 604 661 2166; 1300 Robson St*

CELEBRATIONS

NATIONAL ABORIGINAL DAY
Canada celebrates its First Nation heritage the third weekend in June. Look for a variety of special events in Vancouver and elsewhere in British Columbia. *(www.aadnc-aandc.gc.ca)*

TALKING STICK FESTIVAL
In February, Vancouver's annual Talking Stick Festival features aboriginal performers and themes in theatre, storytelling, music and dance events. *(fullcircle.ca)*

Canada

ONTARIO WILDERNESS WITH THE GROUP OF SEVEN

One look at the vast forests, tranquil lakes and secret islands of Ontario and it's clear why the region's most beloved painters gained such respect for their classically Canadian art.

The early 20th-century landscape artists known as the Group of Seven made a unique mark on Canadian art history, capturing and promoting images of the country's wilderness. The painters worked primarily in Ontario, travelling from Toronto, Canada's largest city, to Algonquin Provincial Park, Georgian Bay, and more remote northern regions. They painted windblown pines, shimmering lakes and other outdoor images that remain Canadian icons today.

Most of the group's original members — Franklin Carmichael, Lawren Harris, A Y Jackson, Frank Johnston, Arthur Lismer, JEH MacDonald and Frederick Varley — met in Toronto between 1911 and 1913. Several became acquainted at a local design studio, others at the Arts and Letters Club — a social organisation for artists and other creatives. An eighth artist, Tom Thomson, who worked with these artists, died under mysterious circumstances

NEED TO KNOW
Spend four days on this trail: one in Toronto using public transport and three outside the city travelling by car.

before the group officially formed in 1920.

Harris, considered the group's founder, was from a wealthy background and helped finance the Group of Seven's work; his family ran a profitable farm equipment company. The artists worked until the mid- to late-1900s, but they held their final 'Group of Seven' show in 1931.

Begin this trail in Toronto, a multicultural metropolis of five million people on Lake Ontario. The city is both Canada's financial centre and its cultural heart, a vibrant mix of Victorian-era buildings and contemporary living. Trace the Group of Seven's artistic heritage in the wildernesses that surround the city; at the McMichael Canadian Art Collection, and in the vast forests of Algonquin Park, where you can explore scenes that members of this artistic circle painted. Finish off by visiting the islands of Georgian Bay to see more landscapes that inspired these legendary Ontario artists.

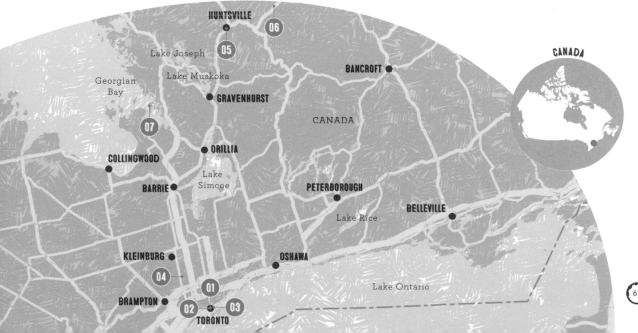

> 'Hike to Beausoleil Island's northern end, where the rocky shores and windblown forests most reflect the group's work'

01 ART GALLERY OF ONTARIO

The Group of Seven held their first public exhibition at this Toronto art gallery in 1920. Now one of North America's largest art museums, with a new building designed by Frank Gehry, the AGO is home to a significant collection of works by these landscape painters.

Its Canadian holdings include several of Tom Thomson's Algonquin Park paintings, such as *Evening: Canoe Lake* (1915-16) and *Sunset, Algonquin Park* (1914). Also look for works including Franklin Carmichael's *Light and Shadow* (1937) and JEH MacDonald's *Fall Evening* (1930). *www.ago.net; tel +1 416 979 6648; 317 Dundas St W; Subway: St Patrick; 10.30am-5pm Tues, Thurs, Sat & Sun, 10.30am-9pm Wed & Fri*

02 OCAD UNIVERSITY

Most of the Group of Seven were associated with Toronto's art school — now called OCAD (Ontario College of Art & Design) — at one time or another, be it as student, teacher or other staff. In 1919, Arthur Lismer became vice-principal; in 1929, JEH MacDonald took over as the college's principal.

Built long after the group's era, it's worth stopping by for a glimpse of the OCAD building that has become a widely recognised Toronto landmark. Constructed in 2004, the Sharp Centre for Design is a chequered box suspended in the sky, supported by vividly coloured 26-metre columns that resemble pencils. *www.ocadu.ca; tel +1 416 977 6000; 100 McCaul St; Subway: St Patrick*

03 THE ARTS AND LETTERS CLUB OF TORONTO

The Group of Seven socialised at this private club for Toronto artistic types, which is still going strong today.

03 © naibank / Getty Images; 04 © All Canada Photos / Alamy

01 Algonquin
Provincial Park,
beloved by the
Group of Seven

02 & 05 Scenes
from Georgian Bay
Islands National Park

03 Downtown
Toronto skyline

04 McMichael
Canadian Art
Collection entrance

MacDonald was particularly active in club life, serving several years as president and vice-president; he also designed the club's crest. Arthur Lismer sketched numerous caricatures of club members, which you can view on the club's website.

Established in 1908, the club moved to its current location in 1920. It's still members-only, so you'll have to satisfy yourself with a walk past the ornate brick and stone building — a designated historic landmark — to envision the group's meetings there. *www.artsandlettersclub.ca; tel +1 416 597 0223; 14 Elm St; Subway: Dundas*

04 MCMICHAEL CANADIAN ART COLLECTION

On day two, hire a car and head 45 minutes north of Toronto to this unique art museum set in the woods outside the city. Robert and Signe McMichael began collecting Canadian art in their country home in the 1950s. Their legacy, the McMichael Canadian Art Collection, now has more than 6000 works by aboriginal and contemporary artists, as well as pieces by the Group of Seven, displayed in 13 galleries throughout its stone and wood buildings.

The McMichaels loved the works of the Group of Seven and knew them personally. Jackson expressed his wish to the couple that he be buried on their peaceful land, and in 1968 they set aside a grassy knoll for a small cemetery.

Don't leave without visiting what is now known as the Artists' Cemetery, on the museum grounds: six members of the Group of Seven are laid to rest here, along with the McMichaels themselves. *www.mcmichael.com; tel +1 905 893 1121; 10365 Islington Ave, Kleinburg; 10am-5pm May-Oct, 10am-4pm Tue-Sun Nov-Apr*

05 © Bert Hoferichter / Alamy

05 GROUP OF SEVEN OUTDOOR GALLERY

Another two hours north, stop at the town of Huntsville — a small weekend-getaway town set between a chain of lakes — to explore this outdoor gallery of more than 90 murals inspired by the Group of Seven's works. Most of the paintings, on buildings and walls throughout Huntsville, are replicas of landscapes by group artists. Download a mural map online or pick one up at the Huntsville/Lake of Bays Chamber of Commerce Office on 37 Main St E.

As you leave Huntsville, take a break for a classic Ontario treat at long-popular Henrietta's Pine Bakery (www.henriettaspinebakery.net): a sticky bun, butter tart or 'Muskoka cloud' — similar to a cranberry scone. *thegroupofsevenoutdoorgallery.com*

06 ALGONQUIN PROVINCIAL PARK

You can easily spend days exploring Ontario's oldest provincial park, established in 1893 to protect 7500 sq km of thick pine forests, jagged cliffs, trickling crystal-clear streams, mossy bogs and thousands of lakes. In the early 1900s, Group of Seven members Jackson and Lismer were among the artists who began coming here to capture its landscapes on canvas.

The park is shrouded in intrigue, however, because of Tom Thomson, who worked with most of the Group of Seven members yet died under mysterious circumstances before the group officially formed in 1920. Thomson spent several years painting in Algonquin, primarily around Canoe Lake, and was last seen on July 8, 1917.

Several days later, his body was found in the lake. To this day, no one knows how the artist met his tragic end.

To discover for yourself the artistic appeal of Canoe Lake, rent a canoe or take a guided paddle from the lakeside Portage Store (www.portagestore. com, off Highway 60, Km14). One popular paddling excursion goes to the Tom Thomson memorial cairn, erected in 1930 on a Canoe Lake campsite that the artist favoured.

Algonquin continues to attract artists today. At the Algonquin Art Centre (www.algonquinartcentre. com, Highway 60, Km20), you can see exhibits by artists with Algonquin connections and even create your own artwork; the centre offers art classes for both kids and adults.

Algonquin Park is open year-

round, although many facilities and campgrounds close between mid-October and mid-May.
www.ontarioparks.com/park/algonquin; tel +1 705 633 5572; Highway 60, between Huntsville and Whitney

07 GEORGIAN BAY ISLANDS NATIONAL PARK

Before returning to Toronto, stop along Georgian Bay to explore the windswept landscapes that inspired some of the Group of Seven's paintings. One of the group's major patrons, Dr James MacCallum, had an island cottage on the bay where both Thomson and Jackson stayed and painted.

Georgian Bay Islands National Park encompasses 63 of the region's more than 30,000 islands. From the tiny town of Honey Harbour, take the park's DayTripper ferry for the 15-minute ride to Beausoleil Island, where most park services are located. Hike to the island's northern end, where the rocky shores and windblown pine and juniper forests are most reflective of the group's work.
www.pc.gc.ca; DayTripper ferry tel +1 705 526 8907; 2611 Honey Harbour Rd; 9.30am–5pm Fri–Tues mid-May–mid-Jun & early Sep–mid-Oct, 9.30am–5pm Sun–Thu, 9am–7pm Fri, to 6pm Sat mid-Jun–early Sep
BY CAROLYN B HELLER

06 OCAD's Sharp Centre of Design, a Toronto landmark

07 Frank Gehry designed the facade for Art Gallery of Ontario

08 Canoeing in Algonquin Provincial Park

09 Group of Seven exhibition, Art Gallery of Ontario

WHERE TO STAY

THE DRAKE HOTEL
If Group of Seven members were alive today, they might stay at The Drake, in Toronto's arty West Queen West neighbourhood. Its eclectic rooms feature original contemporary artworks, and the lounge hosts everything from trivia nights and poetry slams to dance parties.
www.thedrakehotel.ca; tel +1 416 531 5042; 1150 Queen St W

BARTLETT LODGE
At this 1917 Algonquin Park lodge, sleep in rooms named for AY Jackson or Lawren Harris (featuring the artists' works), or choose between old-time cottages and upscale platform tents. The resort is reached via a water taxi across Cache Lake.
www.bartlettlodge.com; tel +1 705 633 5543; mid-May–mid-Oct

WHERE TO EAT & DRINK

THE SENATOR
This old-time diner near downtown Toronto's Dundas Sq has been dishing up fresh home cooking, from bacon and eggs to chicken pot pie, fish 'n' chips and burgers, since 1920.
thesenator.com; tel +1 416 364 7517; 249 Victoria St

LIBRARY BAR
AY Jackson once spoke at Toronto's Fairmont Royal York Hotel, and you can enjoy the traditional ambience of this venerable property opposite Union Station in the downtown Financial District with drinks in its wood-panelled Library Bar. Known for its martinis, this classic lounge also offers whiskies sourced from Scotland to Sweden.
www.fairmont.com/royal-york-toronto; tel +1 416 368 2511; 100 Front St W

CELEBRATIONS

LUMINATO
Toronto's arts community kicks off the summer with this 10-day June festival of visual art, theatre, music, dance and other performances.
(luminatofestival.com)

TORONTO INTERNATIONAL FILM FESTIVAL
Toronto's top art event screens scores of movies and brings celebrities to town every September.
(www.tiff.net)

Map labels

INDEPENDENCIA

RECOLETA

SAN FELIPE

07

QUILLOTA

VALPARAÍSO

CHILE

08

SANTIAGO

CHILE

PATRONATO

Río Mapocho

04

BARRIO BELLAVISTA

BARRIO BRASIL

BARRIO LASTARRIA

01

03

05

SANTIAGO CENTRO

02

BARRIO PARÍS LONDRES

Chile

A LATIN AMERICAN LITERARY LEGACY

The spirit of boundary-pushing Chilean writers that thrived before the Pinochet regime has been revived in Santiago and nearby Valparaíso, where literary heroes loom large.

Santiago, a modern city of seven million on the edge of the Andes Mountains, is now vibrant again after decades of repression that followed the country's 1973 military coup. Vividly painted street murals colour its neighbourhoods, and writers, artists and other bohemians fill its cafes once more. The thriving capital is Chile's present-day cultural heart, but it's also where the country's three most important writers left an indelible mark.

Chile's most famous contemporary writer, Isabel Allende (b1942), lived in the country just a short time, yet her historic — and at-times magic realist — fictional depictions of South America, and in particular Chile, have made her one of the continent's most prized literary voices. In the 1960s, she worked in Santiago as a journalist before beginning a prolific novelist career that so far numbers more than 20 books, including the modern classic *The House of the Spirits* (1982).

> **NEED TO KNOW**
> Allow two days in Santiago and one in Valparaíso for this trail, which you can cover on foot and by public transport.

Like many writers and artists, Allende fled Chile after the 1973 military coup that brought General Pinochet to power. Pinochet dissolved Congress, discarded the country's constitution and censored the press; many who objected were tortured or 'disappeared'. He may have even played a role in the demise of Pablo Neruda (1904-1973), beloved for his prolific output of love poems, who won the 1971 Nobel Prize in Literature and influenced Allende. His homes in Santiago and the nearby port town of Valparaíso are now museums celebrating his life.

But Neruda wasn't the first Chilean to be awarded the Noble prize in Literature; that was the powerful and emotional female poet Gabriela Mistral (1889-1957). A teacher and educational reformer, one student Mistral influenced was a teenage Pablo Neruda. One after the other, these three literary giants helped shape Chile's popular consciousness, and their presence can still be felt.

01 TEATRO OPERA

Begin your tour in downtown Santiago, where one of Isabel Allende's memorable journalistic endeavours took place inside this former theatre that once housed the Bim Bam Bum burlesque club.

In the early 1970s, on assignment for the feminist magazine *Paula* — one of the first Chilean publications to address topics such as divorce, contraception and prostitution — brazen reporter Allende responded to an ad for exotic dancers at the club. She wrote a widely publicised article about the experience: how she prepared for her audition, what she wore, and how she dealt with taking her clothes off.

Interestingly, Neruda crossed paths with Allende during her Santiago

'Neruda called Allende a terrible journalist and advised her to write fiction, where, the poet said, making things up is a virtue'

journalistic career in a way that altered the younger author's writing life. She requested an interview but Neruda refused, calling her a terrible journalist who was loose with the facts. Instead, he advised her to write fiction, where, the poet said, making things up is a virtue.

The Bim Bam Bum closed in 1978, so you'll have to settle for a walk by its arched stone façade.
Huérfanos 837, Santiago

02 GABRIELA MISTRAL MURAL

A short stroll brings you to the entrance to Cerro Santa Lucía, a hillside park in the city centre, and nearby it this mural honouring early 20th-century poet Gabriela Mistral. In 1970, Santiago artist Fernando Daza Osorio (1930-2016) crafted the 10x5.5-metre ceramic-tile mosaic, *Homenaje a Gabriela Mistral*, to be installed here after winning a local government contest.

In muted beiges and blues, it shows

01 Colourful rooftops
of Valparaíso

02 Skyline of Santiago
de Chile

03 Gabriela Mistral
mural in Santa Lucía park

04 Monument to
Chilean poet Pablo
Neruda in Valparaíso

the poet — who is recognised for her work in education as much as for her literary output — dressed in a flowing cape, greeting a group of Indigenous children.
Cnr Av Libertador Bernardo O'Higgins & Miraflores

03 CENTRE GABRIELA MISTRAL

A few blocks from the Mistral mural, this modern central Santiago cultural centre also honours the poet's work in education and the arts. It's a busy arts destination, with theatre, dance and musical performances, lectures and art classes.

On the lower level, the Museo de Arte Popular Americano (MAPA) shows changing exhibits of folk art from across the Americas; Pablo Neruda helped establish this museum back in the 1940s.
www.gam.cl; tel +56 2 2566 5500; Av Libertador Bernardo O'Higgins 227; MAPA 10am-8pm Tues-Fri, from 11am Sat & Sun

04 LA CHASCONA

Neruda named his 1950s Santiago home for Matilde Urrutia, who became his third wife; 'La Chascona' refers to her wild red hair. This quirky multi-level house on a steep hill reflects the poet's far-flung travels and his sense of humour. On his dining table, the salt and pepper shakers were labelled 'marijuana' and 'morphine.'

The house was damaged in the 1973 coup, but Urrutia insisted on holding Neruda's wake here. The poet died 12 days after Pinochet took power.

After you've toured La Chascona, a 20-minute walk from the Centre Gabriela Mistral, wander through the surrounding Bellavista neighbourhood — it's an open-air gallery for street art.
www.fundacionneruda.org; tel +56 2 2777 8741; Fernando Márquez de la Plata 0192, Barrio Bellavista; 10am-7pm Tues-Sun Jan-Feb, to 6pm Tues-Sun Mar-Dec

05 MUSEO DE LA MEMORIA Y LOS DERECHOS HUMANOS

In a stark stone and glass structure, this Santiago museum of remembrance, west of the city centre (take the metro from La Chascona), documents the human rights abuses that took place in Chile following the 1973 coup. Writers

and artists were among those targeted by the military, and nearly 200,000 Chileans, including Isabel Allende, escaped or were forced to leave.

Grim exhibits document the 1000-plus torture centres that the Chilean military established, and a wall of black-and-white photos remembers many of the more than 3100 Chileans who disappeared or were killed. *www.museodelamemoria.cl; tel +56 2 2597 9600; Av Matucana 501; 10am-8pm Tues-Sun Jan-Feb, 10am-6pm Tues-Sun Mar-Dec*

06 CERRO ALEGRE AND CERRO CONCEPCIÓN

Today's excursion takes you to Valparaíso, a coastal city of nearly one million, a 90-minute drive northwest

of Santiago. Isabel Allende's novel *Daughter of Fortune* (1999) begins in 1840s Valparaíso, where many British and German immigrants settled in the colourful houses along Cerro Alegre and Cerro Concepción, two of the 30-plus hills that rise precipitously up from the rough-and-ready port.

The neighbourhood atop Cerro Alegre was given the moniker 'Happy Hill' for the bars and prostitutes that once frequented its lanes. Today, artists have painted murals and other art along its steep narrow streets. One tongue-in-cheek work on Calle Templeman proclaims: 'We are not hippies. We are happies.'

There are a handful of old funiculars scaling Valparaíso's hills, and the city's eldest — Ascensor

Concepción, built in 1883 — runs from the port area to Paseo Gervasoni at the lower end of Cerro Concepción, adjacent to Cerro Alegre. *Paseo Gervasoni*

07 MUSEO LUKAS

For another take on Chile's political and literary history, stop into this small free gallery that shows the work of cartoonist and political satirist Renzo Pecchenino Raggi (1934-1988), known by his pen name 'Lukas'.

Born in Italy, he immigrated to Chile with his family as a young child; his first cartoons appeared in 1958 in the Valparaíso newspaper *La Union*. Lukas continued commenting on Chilean society into the 1980s through his sketches and satirical

cartoons, many of which are on view in this Victorian-era Valparaíso house-turned-museum.
www.lukas.cl; tel +56 3 2222 1344; Paseo Gervasoni 448, Cerro Concepción; 11am-6pm Tues-Sun

08 LA SEBASTIANA

Pablo Neruda bought this house, now a museum, high on a Valparaíso hill to use as a writing retreat. When he moved in, in 1961, he hosted a legendary party and wrote a poem, 'La Sebastiana', to mark the occasion. Neruda often celebrated New Year's Eve here — a spectacular vantage point for the holiday fireworks.

Neruda was affiliated with the Communist Party and had close ties to Salvador Allende, the socialist president (and relative of Isabel) whom the Pinochet coup deposed. Although the poet officially died of prostate cancer, it was widely speculated that Pinochet's government had him poisoned. A 2015 statement following an investigation by Chile's Interior Ministry called it 'highly probable' that the Nobel laureate had not died of natural causes.
www.fundacionneruda.org; tel +56 3 2225 6606; Ferrari 692, Cerro Florida; 10am-7pm Tues-Sun Jan-Feb, 10:10am-6pm Tues-Sun Mar-Dec
BY CAROLYN B HELLER

05 Street art atop Cerro Alegre

06 Museum of Memory, Santiago

WHERE TO STAY
HOTEL LUCIANO K
In a 1928 building in Santiago's Barrio Lastarria, this boutique lodging retains its tiny cage elevator, ornate ironwork and other original features. On the rooftop overlooking the city, you can swim in the narrow lap pool or sup in the stylish restaurant.
www.lucianokhotel.com; tel +56 2 2620 0900; Merced 84

HOTEL MAGNOLIA
A grand 1920s stone mansion on a quiet city-centre street houses this 42-room Santiago inn. The guest rooms are minimalist and contemporary, while the public spaces feature grand spiral staircases, a brick-walled library and smart lobby bar.
hotelmagnolia.cl; tel +56 2 2664 4043; Huérfanos 539

WHERE TO EAT & DRINK
COMO AGUA PARA CHOCOLATE
Walking into this restaurant near Neruda's Santiago home is like stepping into a magic realist novel. With its courtyard built around a bubbling fountain and tables scattered

with flower petals, it's a romantic backdrop for a traditional menu of seafood, steaks and pastas. The signature dessert is a three-layer mousse cake.
comoaguaparachocolate. cl; tel +56 2 2777 8740; Constitución 88, Barrio Bellavista

EL INTERNADO
The terrace at this Valparaíso gastropub has great views of the twinkling hillside lights. It's a good place to try the classic Chilean bar food *chorrillana* — a pile of potato wedges topped with steak, eggs and fried onions.
www.elinternado.cl; tel +56 3 2335 4153; Paseo Dimalow 167, Cerro Alegre

CELEBRATIONS
FIESTAS PATRIAS
Chileans celebrate the country's independence with a week of barbecues and other festivities every September.

SANTIAGO A MIL
In January, this annual festival hosts three weeks of theatre, dance, music and other performances around the capital.
(www.fundacionteatro amil.cl)

CHINA

Map labels:

STONECUTTERS ISLAND

01 — KOWLOON CITY

MA TAU WAI

MONG KOK

02 — 03

YAU MA TEI

TSIM SHA TSUI

Kowloon Bay

CHINA

05 — Victoria Harbour

SAI YING PUN

04 — CENTRAL

CAUSEWAY BAY

WAN CHAI

HAPPY VALLEY

THE PEAK

HONG KONG ISLAND

ABERDEEN

SHOUSON HILL

06 — WONG CHUK HANG

AP LEI CHAU

China

MYTHS & LEGENDS OF OLD HONG KONG

Today this former British territory is synonymous with skyscrapers and light shows, but beneath its steely glint the city is beholden to deities, rituals and urban legends of old.

Deities, filial offsprings, fantastical creatures and more — Hong Kong has inherited China's enormous wealth of myths and legends. Alongside this dazzling collection of stories are the unique tales spun from major events in the city's modern history.

Ghostly anecdotes about Sheung Wan and Western District are often found to have roots in the Bubonic Plague that swept through these parts in 1894, killing tens of thousands, and in the early public health facilities that appeared as a result — stark, confining and with undertones of bleach; a far cry from the Chinese herbal or bone-setting clinics most of the population was used to.

Reports of mystery wailings and poltergeist sightings are de rigueur at sites where people had been executed by the Japanese military in WWII, such as Murray House and St Stephen's College in Stanley. Then there

NEED TO KNOW
Metro and bus combined with walking is the best way to negotiate this two-day city trail.

are the universal accounts of paranormal happenings in crime and suicide scenes, prisons and cemeteries that no city is immune to.

But the most fascinating narratives in Hong Kong, arguably, are the urban legends, born of the fantasies, obsessions and taboos of ordinary Hong Kongers, and made wilder through decades of retelling, often outliving the circumstances that inspired them. Opium dens may be a thing of the past, but the tales of squandered fortunes and thwarted love may live on in an ancient operatic aria faintly heard on a minibus.

And new legends take shape as we speak. In the city's never-ending process of construction and destruction, repressed anxieties trickle like sugar into a spinner, and emerge coloured and flamboyant, to be paraded over morning tea or savoured in torchlight from generation to generation.

> 'Dragon-boat racing is one of many ritual-rich engagements of a people whose patron deity is Tin Hau, Goddess of the Sea'

01 JL CERAMICS

Blindman Nanyin is a soulful music that features singing and narration in colloquial Cantonese. Originating in Guangdong during the Qing dynasty, it was performed by blind beggars all over Hong Kong in the early 20th century, notably in the opium dens, brothels and teahouses of the old red-light district. The beggars spoke and sang of doomed love between courtesans and customers, life on the streets, suicide by opium swallowing — realities of an era that are romanticised by posterity.

Make your first stop on this trail the antique shop JL Ceramics, which holds a Nanyin concert on the third Saturday of every month from 6.30pm to 9.30pm. It is one of the new tenants occupying the restored art deco buildings at 190 to 212 Prince Edward Road in Mong Kok. Concerts might include pieces such as 'Man Burning Funerary Goods', in which the lover of a debt-ridden courtesan who hanged herself burns paper offerings while describing the items in moving detail.

If you can't make a concert, you can still visit to check out the goods and the decor — floor tiles and French doors from the 1930s, and the original terrazzo stairwell.
Tel +852 9658 9959; 2nd floor, 202 Prince Edward Road West

02 YAU MA TEI THEATRE

Mention Yau Ma Tei Theatre to any Hong Konger and you'll get a knowing smile, or they might tell you about someone's uncle who had a stroke after a marathon session in there. It's unfair, but YMT Theatre (c1930) is best known for its sordid years as a porn cinema. The working-class facility featuring an eclectic mix of classical, art deco and Chinese styles of architecture began its life showing silent films to hawkers and fishermen. As the film industry flourished in the 1960s, so did its business.

In the 1980s, it imported low-budget porn and promoted an 'all-you-can-watch' policy to stay afloat, before going under in 1998. Despite this, the translations of the titles — legendary in their wit and irreverence — stuck in the city's memory. Imagine being greeted with the likes of *Horny Planet: Wild Cuntry Revealed* every

01 A traditional boat glides across mist-shrouded Hong Kong harbour

02 Luk Yu Tea House

03 Dragon boat race at Stanley Beach

04 Old Central Police Station is being converted into an arts hub

05 Wholesale Fruit Market, once a Triad hang-out

time you emerge from Yau Ma Tei metro station. The theatre is now a Cantonese opera training and performance centre — tickets can be booked online.
www.lcsd.gov.hk; tel +852 2264 8108; 6 Waterloo Rd

03 WHOLESALE FRUIT MARKET

Behind YMT Theatre is the century-old Wholesale Fruit Market, a once-mysterious labyrinth that was a popular backdrop for crime thrillers. In the 1980s and 1990s, Triads exploited its shadowy layout to run gambling dens and drug-trafficking businesses; and gang fights were frequent. Now peace (and CCTV) reign.

Though you may run into a few sinewy uncles who know martial arts, or spot a training dummy or two behind mounds of citrus, it's a very safe — not to mention, very charming — place in which to lose yourself.

The one- or two-storey stone buildings in the 1.5-hectare sprawl sport gables and pediments of a Dutch Colonial style, on which are carved the traders' names in Chinese calligraphic font. Trees sprout from the speckled parapet walls, and smells of fruit, both fresh and rotting, permeate the arcades.

The market began as straw-bale sheds in 1913. The earliest stone structures appeared in the 1920s — see them on Reclamation St. The row on Shek Lung St was built in 1952. Many stalls are open for retail from around noon, selling top-notch goods at reasonable prices, but the market is busiest in the wee hours, when it bustles with potential buyers and barebacked workers bargaining and handling boxes fat with fruit.
Bounded by Waterloo Rd, Reclamation St, Ferry St & Shek Lung St; busiest 2–6am

04 LUK YU TEA HOUSE

Arguably Hong Kong's most beautiful teahouse, 80-year-old Luk Yu was where illustrious painters and writers, as well as iconic figures in Cantonese opera, used to come for dim sum. Up until the late 1970s, this cultured circle held legendary soirées during which poetry was composed, and

04 © GerryRousseau / Alamy; 05 © Lewis Tse Pui Lung / Shutterstock

calligraphy and music made over white peony tea surrounded by fine scrolls. It wasn't until burglars made away with 18 paintings in 1996 that the rest of Hong Kong realised the exorbitant value of Luk Yu's art collection. 'Oh, it's just the tip of the iceberg,' a regular famously remarked.

Today Luk Yu is known for its old-school Cantonese cooking that includes nostalgic selections such as *siu mai* dumplings with pork liver. Some of the waiters who poured tea for the literati as boys are still here, as are the lovely ceiling fans, folding screens and stained windows that together make up the finest example of Eastern art deco in Hong Kong. Luk Yu Tea House is very close to the Central metro station. *Tel + 852 2523 5464; 24-26 Stanley St; 7am-10pm*

05 CENTRAL POLICE STATION

Hong Kong's oldest symbol of law and order has been turned into an arts hub called Tai Kwun ('Big Station') by a team starring Swiss architect firm Herzog & de Meuron, which recently completed the Tate Modern extension in London, UK. The 19th-century complex, 10 minutes from Central metro station, comprises the former police headquarters, a magistrate's court and Victoria Prison.

Fleeing rebels, exiled writers and prisoners of the Japanese military police did time here, and public executions were also conducted on site. More than 2000 spectators attended the first one (in 1859) of two Englishmen convicted of murder. The facility is rife with ghost stories.

One account tells of a worker struck dumb by an uncanny sighting. The poor man slept in the hall near a connecting bridge between the prison block and the magistracy. One night, dozing off, he saw dead prisoners floating into his makeshift bedroom, and from then on lost the ability to speak.

In 2016, as the restoration was nearing completion, part of a block collapsed – officially due to weak masonry, but who knows? Tai Kwun, opening in summer 2017, will feature galleries, boutiques and a cinema. *www.taikwun.hk; 10 Hollywood Rd*

06 ABERDEEN TYPHOON SHELTER

A tour in a small traditional sampan boat is an awesome way to see the harbour where Hong Kong's boat-dwelling fisherfolk used to moor. Sampan operators mill around the eastern end of Aberdeen Promenade, a 40-minute bus ride from Central.

In the 1960s, the water was covered by a blanket of boats; now you'll see fishing junks next to luxury yachts; temples and shipyards side by side luxury high rises. Go at dusk and you may spot vigorous dragon-boat action — one of many ritual-rich engagements of a people whose patron deity is Tin Hau, Goddess of the Sea.

'On Tin Hau's birthday we pay our respects at her temples,' says boatman Leung Ka-lung. 'Then we collect the partially burnt incense sticks and stash them away on our boats. If we need protection during a fishing trip, we light incense. Say we haul in a [human] corpse. Either we find an island to bury it or, failing that, we light incense and bury it when we get home. People who throw it overboard are plagued by misfortune. When a spirit approaches you in search of release, a proper burial is the only way.'
Aberdeen Praya Rd
BY PIERA CHEN

06 © Ian Macpherson Hong Kong / Alamy

06 Hong Kong skyline from atop Victoria Peak

07 Festival dragon boat figurehead

WHERE TO STAY

HYATT REGENCY TSIM SHA TSUI
This classic is all about understated elegance and composure. Rooms are plush and upper floors have views over the city. The black-and-white photos of old Tsim Sha Tsui district are a bonus. *hongkong.tsimshatsui. hyatt.com; tel +852 2311 1234; 18 Hanoi Rd, Tsim Sha Tsui*

T HOTEL
The low-key but fabulous T in Pok Fu Lam is run by hospitality students, and they are attentive, cheerful and eager to hone their skills. The 30 rooms are sparkling and spacious, offering sea or hill views. The suites are larger than many serviced apartments. *www.vtc.edu.hk/thotel; tel +852 3717 7388; VTC Pokfulam Complex, 145 Pok Fu Lam Rd*

WHERE TO EAT & DRINK

PING PONG GINTONERIA
Located in a subterranean former ping-pong hall, this hip place stocks more than 50 types of gin, served in a variety of cocktails. The old Hong Kong-inspired decor goes well with the cavernous, pillared hall. *www.pingpong129.com; 852-9835-5061; 135 Second St; Sai Ying Pun; 6-11.30pm*

AP LEI CHAU COOKED FOOD CENTRE
Above a luscious seafood market, this lively sprawl of tables and food stalls cooks up a storm every evening. Buy seafood from the market downstairs and pay one of the operators to prepare it the way you want. *1st fl, Ap Lei Chau Municipal Services Bldg, 8 Hung Shing St*

CELEBRATIONS

DRAGON BOAT FESTIVAL
Around the fifth day of the fifth lunar month (usually in June), dragon-boaters race in waterways all over Hong Kong, including thousands of international participants who descend for the Hong Kong International Dragon Boat Races at Victoria Harbour. Smaller competitions take place all over the city from March to October. *(www.hkdba.com.hk).*

China

PEEKING INTO PEKING OPERA

Beijing is the nerve centre of China's cultural scene and no art form is more beloved by the city than mysterious Peking Opera, with its theatrical costumes and unique sound.

Big and boisterous, yet magically beguiling, Beijing (once known in the West as Peking) is one of those exceptional cities that manages to display its mighty history and deep-rooted cultural traditions while simultaneously racing headfirst into the future. This is the capital of the country that will surely dominate the next century, and its iconic modern architecture, gleaming malls and crazy-quick bullet trains offer a glimpse into what the rest of China — and perhaps the world — will one day look like. But this is also one of Asia's true ancient citadels, and it is laden with historical marvels; visitors can spend days ticking off its impressive array of top-drawer attractions.

Not content with just being China's political nerve centre, economic powerhouse and main tourism hub, Beijing is also the cultural heart of the country. The nation's top artists, writers, movie-makers and musicians converge here, making Beijing the place to

NEED TO KNOW
Use the subway when in Beijing itself, but you'll need the bullet train for Tianjin to complete this two-day trail.

take the pulse of China's rapidly evolving cultural scene. And the undisputed king of that scene is Peking Opera.

China's national art form is, for foreign audiences, a mysterious, sometimes incomprehensible blend of shrill sounds and heavily painted faces, but the journey to understand it is often its own reward. Its roots in local Chinese folk opera can be traced to the Tang Dynasty (618-907), although Peking Opera itself dates from the late 18th century after an opera troupe from far-off Anhui province performed at Emperor Qianlong's 80th birthday celebrations, and decided to stay put in the capital.

The troupe spawned a new blend of opera, using a Beijing dialect and capital-centric themes. It's this opera style in particular that grew from street-side skits into informal teahouse shows and eventually into the full-blown theatrical productions adored by opera fans nationwide.

01 © hxdbl / Getty Images

Qiánhai Lake

Beihai Lake

XIDAN

XICHÉNG

Zhonghai Lake

FORBIDDEN PALACE

ZHONGNÁNHAI

DONGCHÉNG

DASHILAR

CHINA

BEIJING

LANGFANG

TIANJIN

❶ MEI LANFANG'S FORMER RESIDENCE

This traditional Beijing *siheyuan* (courtyard home) was the former residence of one of the most revered Peking opera stars of all time. Mei Lanfang (1894–1961) is largely credited with taking Peking opera to the west, forming friendships during his world tours with contemporaries such as Charlie Chaplin. He was best known for his graceful *dan* (female lead) roles, and his small courtyard home is fittingly refined, located in a charming hutong (narrow lane) neighbourhood, close to the willow tree-lined Houhai Lake.

Rub shoulders with fellow opera pilgrims as you peruse Mei's old costumes, furniture, photographs and posters. Note how elaborate and colourful Peking opera costumes are.

Traditionally, opera troupes would travel from show to show by caravan so had to limit their on-stage sets. Instead, they saved the detail for the elaborate costumes. Tuned-in audiences can tell a character's gender, role, occupation, social status, and even personality, just from the colour of their robe, or the style of their shoes, hat or make up.

See if you can recognise which parts of the house were used in Chen Kaige's award-winning 1993 Peking opera film *Farewell My Concubine*. The house is walking distance from Ping'an Li subway station. *www.meilanfang.com.cn; tel +86 10 8322 3598; 9 Huguosi Lu, Xicheng District; 9am-4pm Tue-Sun*

❷ THE PAVILION OF CHEERFUL MELODIES

It's unlikely that you'll come all the way to Beijing without paying a visit to the magnificent Forbidden City, the world's largest palace complex and home to emperors of China for more than 500 years. While you're inside, though, don't miss sidling off to the eastern wing of this one-time royal residence to hunt down one of the few remaining open-air opera stages left in Beijing.

02 © Hung Chung Chih / Shutterstock

'Opera troupes would travel by caravan so had to limit their on-stage sets; they saved the detail for elaborate costumes'

01 Old and new clash in Beijing

02 Opera at Huguang Guild Hall: a feast for the eyes and ears

03 A Peking opera performer prepares to go on stage

04 Beijing's Temple of Heaven complex

The beautifully named Pavilion of Cheerful Melodies is a three-storey wooden opera house dating from 1776. It was the largest opera stage in the Forbidden City and is the only one that still remains. Note the trap doors that allowed actors to make dramatic stage entrances, and look out for the Hall for Viewing Opera, a modest-sized room across the courtyard from the stage, where the emperor once watched performances and where today you'll find a small collection of opera artefacts and clothing.

The Forbidden City must be entered through its southern Meridian Gate, which is walking distance from Tiananmen East subway station.

www.en.dpm.org.cn; tel +86 10 8500 7114; The Forbidden City, Chang'an Jie, Dongcheng District; 8.30am-5pm Tue-Sun

03 LAO SHE TEAHOUSE

Long before it was allowed to grace the best theatres in the land, Peking opera was the domain of the capital's teahouses, played out to chatting audiences who would slurp tea and crack open sunflower seeds as they kept one eye on the show. This form of opera's signature singing style features a shrill upper register, which ensures that stories can be heard over the orchestra and the noisy teahouse crowd.

Performances at this famed teahouse remain refreshingly informal, and showcase a variety of traditional Chinese artistic skills, from Peking Opera and Sichuan bianlian (face-changing) to shadow puppetry and kungfu. Even the tea pourers put on a show for you, twisting this way and that before pouring tea into your cups from metre-long tea spouts held behind their shoulders.

The teahouse is walking distance from Tian'anmen Square. Book your tickets a day in advance if possible. www.laosheteahouse.com; tel +86 10 6303 6830; 3rd fl, 3 Qianmenxi Dajie, Xicheng District; 10am-10pm

(05)

04 LAO SHE'S FORMER HOME

Ease your way into day two of this trail with a morning visit to this peaceful courtyard home. The teahouse you visited on day one was named after one of China's best-known novelists and dramatists — Lao She — and this courtyard home is his former residence.

Wander its small quadrangles and peek inside the modestly decorated rooms before slipping into the attached bookshop to track down an English translation of his famous play *Tea House*, a social and cultural commentary on early 20th-century China.

Lao She's former residence is a stone's throw from the malls and street-food stalls of Wangfujing, Beijing's premier shopping strip.

Perhaps grab a bite here, before catching the train to Tianjin. *www.bjlsjng.com; tel +86 10 6514 2612; 19 Fengfu Hutong, Dongcheng District; 9am-4pm Tue-Sun*

05 TIANJIN'S GUANGDONG GUILD HALL

Time for a change of scene. Catch the subway to Beijing South train station then hop on a super-slick bullet train to the nearby city of Tianjin. Trains leave every 15 minutes — no need to book — and make the 140km trip in just 29 minutes. Once there, head to Tianjin's Old Town and, 100 metres or so from the easy-to-find Drum Tower, sneak into the lesser-known Guangdong Guild Hall.

This creaky old building contains one of north China's best-preserved

teahouse theatres; a salt-of-the-earth establishment where the city's more traditional folk meet for some tea, a natter and a spot of Peking opera. It's open all day, although opera performances are only held on Sunday afternoons (2-4pm). *Tel +86 22 2727 3443; Gulou Dong Jie, Tianjin Old Town, Nankai District; 9am-4.30pm*

06 HUGUANG GUILD HALL THEATRE

For a fittingly grand finale, zip back to Beijing to watch a full-blown Peking opera show inside this beautiful 200-year-old wooden theatre. Most Peking opera stories fall into two categories: civilian (wen) or military (wu). The latter includes plenty of martial-arts action, but both tend

to weave in elements from history, mythology, literature and legends.

If you're worried about not being able to keep up with the Chinese-language plot lines, fear not; the 90-minute performances at this theatre come with handy English subtitles on digital displays beside the stage.

There's a small opera museum here too, so it's worth coming along a little early for full immersion before diving into the main show. The theatre's right outside Hufangqiao subway station. As with the show at Lao She Teahouse, it's worth booking tickets a day in advance. *en.beijinghuguang.com; tel +86 10 6352 9140; 3 Hufangqiao Dajie, Xicheng District; 9am-5pm & 6.30pm-10pm*

BY DANIEL MCCROHAN

06 © Daniel McCrohan

05 Guangdong Guild Hall's well-preserve teahouse theatre

06 A performance at Lao She Teahouse

WHERE TO STAY

SHICHAHAI SHADOW ART PERFORMANCE HOTEL
This quirky hutong hotel near willow tree-lined Houhai Lake has a small stage in the teahouse-lookalike lobby, where shadow-puppet shows are performed. Rooms are modern, but with traditional-style furnishings. *www.shichahaitour.com; tel +86 10 8401 8677; 24 Songshu Jie, Dongcheng District*

COURTYARD 7
Bed down in this graceful courtyard hotel off trendy Nanluogu Xiang hutong. The 300-year-old complex includes Qing-style rooms dotted around a series of pleasant courtyards. Nanluogu Xiang has a lively street market with cafes, shops and restaurants. *www.courtyard7.com; tel +86 10 6406 0777; 7 Qiangulouyuan Hutong, Dongcheng District*

WHERE TO EAT & DRINK

TEMPLE RESTAURANT BEIJING (TRB)
Worth saving for a treat, this stunning heritage restaurant serving contemporary European cuisine is housed within the 250-year-old grounds of a former Buddhist temple. The wine list runs to 68 pages. *www.trb-cn.com; tel +86 10 8400 2232; 23 Shatan Beijie, off Wusi Dajie, Dongcheng District; 11.30am-2.30pm & 5.30-10pm*

MR SHI'S DUMPLINGS
For something more down to earth, try this popular dumplings joint tucked down a hutong close to the historic Drum & Bell Towers. No fine wines, but plenty of Beijing's locally brewed Yanjing beer. *Tel +86 10 8405 0399; 74 Baochao Hutong, Dongcheng District; 10am-11pm*

CELEBRATIONS

It's well worth tracking down some of temple fairs that spring up around Beijing during Chinese New Year (late January or February, depending on the lunar calendar). The more traditional ones include small puppet-show performances or even, if you're very lucky, a taster show from a local operatic troupe. Try the fairs at Dongyue Temple or White Cloud Temple.

CUBA

04

05

CAYO HUESO

02

CENTRO HABANA

03

EL BARRIO CHINO

06

01

VEDADO

NUEVO VEDADO

Cuba

HAVANA'S MUSIC SCENE

Cuba's sizzling capital is a round-the-clock jam session of staggering diversity thanks to centuries of cross-cultural influences. Rumba, jazz, son, thrash metal... it's all here.

Cuba may have endured shortages and sacrifice over the past 50 years, but it's never lacked culture. While the economy has spluttered and stalled, the arts — in particular music — have prospered, spurred on by government patronage, local talent and a remarkably fertile culture. The fertility is particularly rife in Havana, a city of faded grandeur and animated street life that has recently started to rediscover its entrepreneurial spirit. The Cuban capital practically bleeds music; a simmering stew of Spanish, African, French, North American and indigenous influences that have combined to create a beautifully syncopated whole.

To hear it, you don't have to walk far. The city bubbles over with a maelstrom of sounds that swing, dance and rock out of every nook and cranny. There's the jazz trombonist standing on the sea wall practising his scales; the rumba drummers engrossed in an all-day Santería

NEED TO KNOW
Four days is best for this trail. Travel mostly on foot to soak up the street life, with a couple of taxis to make life easier.

ritual; the wandering troubadour seducing tourists with songs about Che Guevara; the octogenarian crooner belting out a plaintive Besame Mucho; and the thrash metal quartet screaming something in Spanish about revolution. The music never stops. Even better, it's nearly always live. In Havana, guitars are as common as mobile phones, and singing and dancing as natural as walking and breathing.

Enriched by centuries of cross-fertilisation, the city's musical variety is astounding. Popular exports son and salsa are merely a warm-up act. Dip your sonic barometer into some of the city's less heralded corners and the Grammy-winning Buena Vista Social Club album looks like a small groove in a much bigger record.

Havana has been pushing the musical envelope for decades, packing a punch way out of proportion to its size. You can walk through the city and plot the path, from Benny Moré to hip hop, via jazz, charanga, rumba, salsa, timba and cha-cha-chá. Take a deep breath and dive in.

01 EL GUAJIRITO

In the mid-1990s, legendary American slide guitarist Ry Cooder resurrected a group of half-forgotten Cuban musicians on the streets of Havana and funnelled them into an extraordinary musical collective called the Buena Vista Social Club. The band made a self-titled record, sold out a tour and won a Grammy, while Cooder, bizarrely, got stung with a US$25,000 fine for doing 'illegal business' with Cuba. Yet the group left its mark and its name has stood the test of time.

Many of Cooder's band were so old that they've since passed away, but the salsa-ing spirit of the Buena Vista Social Club still lives on in El Guajirito, a cosy restaurant and live music venue hidden inside a grotty-

'Rumba is a building block of Cuban music, a mixture of athletic dancing and ritual drumming associated with religions of African origin'

on-the-outside tenement in the district of Centro Habana.

Sure, the place is popular with tourists (why wouldn't it be?), but, once the chatter dies down it's hard not to be seduced by the energy of the pensionable-age singers and musicians running through 90-minute sets of old Cuban classics.
Tel +53 7 863 3009; Calle Agramonte 660, btwn Gloria & Apodaca; shows 9.30pm

02 CALLE OBISPO

By day, Calle Obispo, a five-minute stroll from El Guajirito, is the main shopping street in Habana Vieja — Havana's gloriously crumbling old town. By night, it's a beautiful din of competing live music with guitars, flutes, bongos and trumpets filling the air and reminding you that, even with your eyes closed, you couldn't be anywhere else but Cuba.

02 © James Quine / Alamy

Some musicians play for love, others pass the hat for money. In a few of the more clamorous bars, the band is squeezed in so tight, the bass player is virtually French-kissing the guitarist.

With so much going on, the real joy of Obispo is deciding where to pause. In La Dichosa, the band is often bigger than the audience. Hotel Ambos Mundos always has a pianist tinkling on the ivories. Café Paris is a more animated scene packed with tourists dancing.

If you're lucky you might spot a star. Last November, trova legend Silvio Rodríguez sang live in nearby Plaza del Cristo — for free. That's Obispo for you — music of the people, by the people, for the people.

03 © Fabrizio Proietto / Alamy; 04 © Antony SOUTER / Alamy

03 CALLEJÓN DE HAMEL

This community art project in Centro Habana, a half-hour walk from Calle Obispo (stroll along the Malecón sea-drive), is a living manifestation of the city's Afro-Cuban soul — a paint-splattered back alley filled with strange murals, sacred Santería shrines and the rhythmic beat of rumba.

Rumba is one of the building blocks of Cuban music, a mixture of athletic dancing and ritual drumming that is closely associated with syncretised religions of African origin. Some have called it a national sport; others claim Cuba wouldn't be Cuba without it. Of all the places to hear it, the Callejón de Hamel is the most spontaneous and rootsy. Live rumba, with its interlocking rhythms and Yoruba chants, kicks off in the street every Sunday around noon and pretty much closes down all other business. Follow the crowds.

Hamel btwn Aramburu & Hospital

04 CABARET PARISIEN

Cabaret is one of the few aspects of Havana's pre-1959 nightlife that survived the revolution. When Fidel Castro closed down the casinos and the mafia retreated back to the US, tail between its legs, Havana's most renowned cabarets kept on going, knocking out their famously flamboyant shows replete with spectacular dance routines and multiple costume changes.

While the Tropicana, in business

since 1939, is Havana's best-known cabaret venue, savvy travellers on limited budgets often opt for the cheaper, easier to reach – but no less ostentatious – Parisien held nightly in the iconic Hotel Nacional, a short 15-minute walk from Callejón de Hamel.

True, there's a hint of Vegas in the show's unashamed glitz. But, underneath the outrageous headgear, this is an inherently Cuban show celebrating practically every old-school music genre from son through rumba to cha-cha-chá. Grab a mojito and a front-row seat, and prepare to be entertained.
www.hotelnacionaldecuba.com; tel +53 7 836 3564; Hotel Nacional, cnr Calle 21 & O; 9pm-2am

05 JAZZ CAFÉ

There's jazz, and there's Cuban jazz — a distinctly Africanised version of the genre augmented with *batá* drums, maracas and claves that was first pioneered by piano maestro Chucho Valdés and his band Irakere in the 1970s.

Supported by Havana's annual jazz festival, one of the city's most anticipated musical events, Cuban jazz has never been healthier. Of the several places in the city that swing nightly to its improvised sounds, the Jazz Café in Vedado, 1km west of the Hotel Nacional, is by far the most suave and sophisticated.

Cocooned on the upper floor of a once-modern, now kitschy shopping mall, it serves decent food and

perfect cocktails. Sure, there are more frenetic jazz clubs in Havana, but nothing is quite as cool and classy as this one.
Tel +53 7 838 3302; cnr Calle 3 & Paseo; noon-2am

06 FÁBRICA DE ARTE CUBANO

Anyone who thinks that Cuba is on the verge of selling its soul wholesale to US consumerism needs to visit this nascent art 'factory' in Vedado, a 20-minute walk from the Jazz Café. Welcome to the vortex of Havana's contemporary art and music scene, where cultural interchange has stimulated a breeding ground for creativity and ideas.

Founded by Cuban fusion musician X Alfonso in 2014, the Fábrica de Arte

Cubano is encased in an old olive oil factory and opens its doors four nights a week for a full programme of electrifying happenings, including *mucho* music. Inside, you can wander at will between different interactive spaces lingering whenever and wherever you wish. Serendipity might cough up tango dancing lessons, a throbbing DJ set, an avant-garde art expo, an a capella singing group, a film about Cuba's music heritage, or a late-night jazz jam.

There are bars, terraces, beautiful design features and even a mini eat-street. It's more than exciting. *www.fabricadeartecubano.com; tel +53 7 838 2260; Calle 26 cnr 11; 8pm-3am Thu-Sun*
BY BRENDAN SAINSBURY

05 Band playing on street

06 El Capitol, the former seat of government in Cuba

06 © Toniflap / Shutterstock

WHERE TO STAY
HOTEL SARATOGA
The Saratoga inhabits a beautifully restored neoclassical building in Centro Habana. Inside, tip-top international service coexists seamlessly with the ghosts of Havana's colonial past. *www.hotel-saratoga.com; tel +53 7 868 1000; Paseo de Martí 603*

HOSTAL CALLE HABANA
A shining example of Havana's new private sector, here is a *casa particular* (homestay) that has morphed into something closer to a mini-hotel without losing that charming Cuban bonhomie. Squeezed into one of Habana Vieja's gritty, unrestored streets, it has four rooms. *www.hostalcallehabana. com; tel +53 7 867 4081; Habana 559 btwn Brasil & Amargura*

WHERE TO EAT & DRINK
EL RUM RUM DE LA HABANA
This restaurant in Habana Vieja is named not for the drink (though they serve plenty of that!), but the slang Cuban term for gossip (*rum rum*). True to form, El Rum Rum is a name on everyone's lips thanks to its inventive Spanish-style seafood. *Tel +53 7 861 0806; Empedrado 256 btwn Cuba & Aguiar*

LAMPARILLA 361 TAPAS & CERVEZAS
This hip but friendly bar-restaurant serves up wonders such as tapa-sized lasagne and a rich espresso-flavoured crème brûlée. Menus are written on dried palm leaves. *Tel +53 5 289 5324; Lamparilla 361 btwn Aguacate & Villegas*

CELEBRATIONS
JAZZ FESTIVAL
The cream of Cuban music festivals arrives every December like a Christmas present. In the past it has attracted the greats — Dizzy Gillespie and Max Roach among them — along with a perfect storm of Cuban talent.

BOLEROS DE ORO
Organised by Cuba's Writers' Union, this is a global celebration of the slow, lyrical ballads known as *boleros,* by crooners from Havana and beyond.

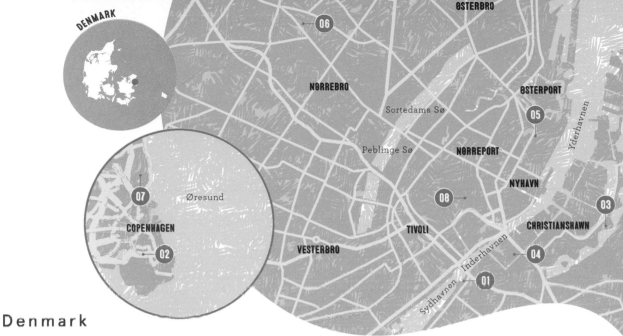

The map shows Copenhagen, Denmark, with numbered locations 01–08 across districts including ØSTERBRO, NØRREBRO, ØSTERPORT, NØRREPORT, NYHAVN, CHRISTIANSHAWN, TIVOLI, and VESTERBRO. Water features labelled include Sortedams Sø, Peblinge Sø, Øresund, Yderhavnen, Inderhavnen, and Sydhavnen.

Denmark
COPENHAGEN'S DESIGN CULTURE

Denmark's distinctive design ethic extends way beyond its impressive buildings and classic furniture; head to Copenhagen to see how the urban environment is being redesigned, too.

Danish design casts a long shadow over contemporary culture, influencing everything from furniture to fashion. With its emphasis on clean lines and natural materials, and its seamless marriage of form and function, it is instantly recognisable. And there's no better place to explore its tradition or grasp its timeless appeal than in Copenhagen — Denmark's design-conscious capital.

Start with the skyline. From the rococo elegance of the royal palace to the sleek modernism of the Black Diamond library, Copenhagen has a rich architectural portfolio, especially around its revitalised harbourfront. But good design isn't just about impressive buildings. What distinguishes Copenhagen, says Christian Bason, chief executive of the Danish Design Center, is 'its focus on the development of excellent urban living spaces, human-centred urban design and sustainability'.

Copenhagen is redesigning the urban environment by putting people first — and the results are remarkable. Think vibrant public spaces, clean harbour baths, and a network of bicycle lanes and award-winning bridges.

NEED TO KNOW
You can easily do this trail in two or three days. Walk or cycle — Copenhagen was designed for exploring on two wheels.

The city is also the birthplace of design icons such as the Christiania bike, the Wishbone chair and the Artichoke lamp.

The evergreen appeal of these objects lies in their simplicity, accessibility and functionality — the hallmarks of Danish design.

To learn more about Denmark's rich design tradition, culture vultures should flock to its first-class design museum, architecture centre and shops for design enthusiasts. And if all this sounds like hungry work, don't worry. Copenhagen is home not only to some of the world's best restaurants but to some of the best-looking ones too.

Despite its 20th-century roots, Danish design feels as modern as ever. The world can't seem to get enough of it — and neither will visitors to Copenhagen.

> 'Christiania's residents have created an architectural style that could be described as Steampunk Hobbit'

01 GOBOAT

Get your bearings by sailing around Copenhagen harbour in a self-drive solar-powered GoBoat — a design marvel in itself with its wave-piercing hull, smooth edges and silent engine. No sailing experience is required, but pack a picnic: each boat has a built-in table for on-water dining.

Harbour highlights include Christiansborg Slot — a series of castles for which construction began in 1167, home to the Danish parliament — and some of Copenhagen's most striking contemporary buildings, such as the Henning Larsen-designed Opera House (2005) and the Black Diamond (1999), with its shiny granite surface.

You'll also sail under Olafur Eliasson's distinctive Circle Bridge, the wire masts of which resemble ship rigging. And look out for the Cycle Snake, a 220-metre-long elevated cycle path. A pedal push from the GoBoat docking station, it typifies human-centred urban design and is a joy to ride.
goboat.dk/en/; Islands Brygge 10; tel +45 40 26 10 25; 9.30am-sunset

02 ØRESTAD

Back on dry land, head to Ørestad — a new suburb in southern Copenhagen — to see three of the world's most startling residential buildings, all designed by Copenhagen-born starchitect Bjarke Ingels. From Islands Brygge, take the metro to Vestamager, where you'll find 8-Tallet — aka the 8 Building. Denmark's biggest residential building, it's shaped like the figure 8 and is a jaw-dropping expression of what Ingels calls 'architectural alchemy' — a magic that happens when designers aren't restricted by a single notion of what a building could be.

Just north are two other buildings that Ingels built. VM Bjerget (aka Mountain Dwelling) is distinguished by its terraced roof gardens, VH Houses by its glass facade and jutting balconies.
www.8tallet.dk; Richard Mortensens Vej

03 CHRISTIANIA

Few visitors to Freetown Christiania — the legendary commune set up by squatters in the 1970s — are aware of the remarkable DIY houses nestled in the woods. Repurposing old buildings

01 Residential
architecture in
Ørestad

02 Olafur Eliasson's
Circle Bridge

03 Boats along
Nyhavn

04 Classic Danish
chairs at the
Designmuseum

05 Inside
Illums Bolighus

and using recycled materials, Christiania's residents have created an architectural style that could be described as Steampunk Hobbit.

Head northeast through the commune until you hit a stretch of water, wander along either side and you'll soon spot the DIY houses, which run the gamut from quasi-spaceships to moss-roofed cottages. On your return, stop at Christiania Smithy, where the iconic Christiania cargo bike — designed to carry everything from boxes to children — was born.

04 KADEAU

End the day with dinner at Kadeau, a Michelin-starred restaurant that was redesigned in 2016 and whose seasonal menu is inspired by ingredients from the Baltic island of Bornholm.

'We wanted to create a room that would feel more homely than most restaurants — and to keep guests in our world from start to finish,' says head chef Nicolai Nørregaard.

And what a world it is. To create a space that's sophisticated yet cosy, design studio OeO put an open kitchen in the centre of the restaurant and added low-key lighting, a herringbone floor pattern and a book-lined lounge. *www.kadeau.dk; Wildersgade 10b; tel +45 33 25 22 23; 6.30pm-midnight Mon-Sat, plus noon-4pm Sat*

05 DESIGNMUSEUM DANMARK

Start day two at this magnificent museum, housed in one of Copenhagen's finest rococo buildings, an 18th-century hospital.

There's a top-drawer display of Danish silver, porcelain and textiles, but the chief attraction is its collection of 20th-century Danish design icons, including works by Kaare Klint, Poul Henningsen and Arne Jacobsen.

The museum lies just northeast of Nyhavn, and there's also a lovely garden, cafe and shop. *designmuseum.dk/en; Bredgade 68, 1260 Copenhagen K; tel +45 33 18 56 56; 10am-6pm Tue & Thu-Sun, to 9pm Wed May-Oct, shorter hrs Nov-Apr*

06 SUPERKILEN

Palm trees from China. Neon signs from Russia. Gym equipment from California. And three tonnes of soil from the Palestinian territories. Welcome to Superkilen — a unique public park in Nørrebro, a diverse neighbourhood just north of the city centre.

The winner of the Geneva-based Aga Khan Award for Architecture, Superkilen snakes for almost a kilometre, its path dotted with 108 objects gathered from more than 50 countries, to represent the nationalities of all those who call Nørrebro home. Many objects are functional — you'll spot benches from Cuba, bollards from Uganda, bins from Blackpool. Others are playful, like the basketball hoop from California and the swings from Baghdad. Use the free app (available in English) to find out about each of the objects.

To find the park, go to Nørrebrogade 210 and head north along the bicycle lane and pedestrian path.
www.superflex.net/superkilen

07 FINN JUHL'S HOUSE

'One cannot create happiness with beautiful objects,' Finn Juhl said, 'but one can spoil quite a lot of happiness with bad ones.' The Dane dedicated his life to designing beautiful objects, many of which furnish the house that he designed, built and lived in until his death in 1989.

Finn was one of the leading lights of Danish Modern – the style of furniture and homewares that emerged from Denmark midway through the 20th century. With its seamless marriage of form and function and its emphasis on natural materials and minimalist design, Danish Modern is often instantly recognisable today. A trip to Finn's house can transport you into this iconic design era.

Located five miles north of Copenhagen (catch a train to Ordrup and cycle the rest of the way), it's laid out as it was when Juhl lived there. From the open-plan layout — unusual in its day — to the surrealist-influenced Poet Sofa, there's beauty in abundance and a sense of harmony. 'All the details seem to work together and complement each other,' says Mille Maria

Steffen-Nielsen, who works there. *ordrupgaard.dk/en/finn-juhls-house; Ordrupgaard, Vilvordevej 110, 2920 Charlottenlund; tel +45 39 64 11 83; 11am-4.45pm Sat-Sun, plus Tue-Fri 1pm-4.45pm, to 8.45pm Wed Jul-Aug*

08 ILLUMS BOLIGHUS

End your trail at this 10,000-sq-metre design temple in central Copenhagen, which showcases top brands such as Fritz Hansen furniture, Louis Poulsen lighting (both Danish-designed), and Marimekko, the Finnish homewares company, as well as up-and-coming Scandinavian designers. This department store is a shrine to Scandinavian design.

Head to the top floor to see the shop's collection of iconic Danish chairs, such as the Wishbone, designed by Hans J Wegner for Carl Hansen & Søn in 1949 and instantly recognisable thanks to its elegant Y-shaped back. Then return to the ground floor, where you'll find plenty of smaller items you can squeeze into your luggage, including ceramics, jewellery and stationery. *www.illumsbolighus.com; 10 Amagertorv, 1160 Copenhagen K; tel +45 33 14 19 41; Mon-Sat 10am-7pm Mon-Thu & Sat, to 8pm Fri, 11am-6pm Sun*
BY JAMES CLASPER

06 Bjarke Ingels' 8 Building in Ørestad

07 A DIY house in the Christiania commune

WHERE TO STAY
RADISSON BLU ROYAL
Arne Jacobsen designed the building and almost everything in it, such as the curved door handles and the Egg chairs that grace the lobby. Room 606 maintains his original aesthetic, including a wenge-wood desk and pale-blue Royal floor lamp; a shrine to Danish Modern. *www.radissonblu.com; Hammerichsgade 1, 1611 Copenhagen V; tel +45 33 42 60 00*

HOTEL ALEXANDRA
The Alexandra has amassed a huge collection of Danish Modern furniture, making a stay here more like time travel than tourism. Its 61 rooms feature midcentury styling, with several decorated in tribute to particular designers. *hotelalexandra.dk; H C Andersens Blvd 8, 1553 Copenhagen V; tel +45 33 74 44 44*

WHERE TO EAT & DRINK
HÖST
This stylish spot was the first Danish restaurant to win a Restaurant & Bar Design Award, thanks to its rough-hewn wooden frames, industrial lamps and elegant tableware. The cooking celebrates the seasons, executing dishes with flair. The results are spectacular, and superb value. *hostvakst.dk/host; Nørre Farimagsgade 41, 1364 Kobenhavn K; tel +45 89 93 84 09*

108
SPACE Copenhagen designed renowned restaurant Noma, making it the clear choice to convert an industrial warehouse into 108, dubbed Noma's baby brother when it opened in 2016. Tall and light, the space is stunning, the original materials — concrete, bricks, metal — suitably minimalist. *108.dk; Strangade 108, 1401 Kobenhavn K; tel +45 32 96 32 92*

CELEBRATIONS
3 DAYS OF DESIGN
Design fans shouldn't miss this 72-hour celebration of Danish design and Copenhagen's status as a global design capital. The free festival is a fantastic opportunity to mingle with designers, buyers and other design devotees. *(3daysofdesign.dk)*

England

ROCK STAR LONDON

Enduring mega hits, global rock idols and pioneering artists have turned London into a mythical destination for music fans, tracing rock history in hallowed footsteps.

The sound of London and its music history reverberates in everyone who has sung a song, played a tune or turned on a radio station. If you feel your heartbeat quicken at the opening chords of The Clash's 'London Calling', get goosebumps as David Bowie's 'Space Oddity' looms louder, a little wistful at The Kinks' 'Days' or downright teary at The Beatles' 'While My Guitar Gently Weeps', this trail is for you.

The British are not immune to their home-grown musical heroes, but London as a mythical destination, a magnet for music fans far and wide, is something that can really only be appreciated by those not born and raised here. In his 2016 autobiography, *Born to Run*, Bruce Springsteen captured it best: 'The Beatles, the Stones, the Animals, the Yardbirds, the Kinks, Jeff Beck, Clapton, Hendrix, the Who — we were heading for the isle of our heroes. Rock's second

generation of Beat groups had pulled off a Herculean task. They'd reinvented some of the greatest music that had ever been made. I still feel I owe all of these groups, these young Englishmen, an enormous debt of gratitude...'

As you walk the streets of London, the clues might be as blatantly obvious as Abbey Road or one of the English Heritage blue plaques denoting a famous site, or musical memories may simply sneak up on you, courtesy of a sudden sighting (Baker Street, Victoria, or a Waterloo sunset).

England's capital was where rock music was reborn. Nothing has come close to the excitement of the swinging '60s, the likes of Beatlemania, or the mayhem of a Rolling Stones tour. But rising above all the hype is the simple fact that some of the world's very best music was written and recorded here, and continues to influence all musicians and music-lovers today.

ENGLAND

ISLINGTON

CAMDEN TOWN

ST JOHN'S WOOD

01

FINSBURY

MARYLEBONE

BLOOMSBURY

02

04

COVENT GARDEN

SOHO

05

BAYSWATER

03

Thames

MAYFAIR

06

ST JAMES'S

THE SOUTH BANK

02 © Anna Moskvina / Shutterstock

01 ABBEY ROAD STUDIOS

Celebrating 86 years of music in 2017, the world's most renowned recording studio is synonymous not just with the Beatles (though Paul McCartney still records here); a who's who of recording artists are still cutting tracks at this spot today. The studios themselves aren't open to the public, but you can join the throng making a pilgrimage to follow in some famous footsteps; it's all about THAT pedestrian crossing and fans recreating the Beatles' 1969 Abbey Road album cover.

'People get really emotional,' says Richard Porter, co-owner of the nearby Beatles Coffee Shop and also a tour guide. Richard recalls one fan who had managed to get out of North Korea and made it to Abbey Road three years ago. 'He dissolved into tears when he got here.

'Then there was the guy who came out of the station and tapped a stranger on a shoulder to ask where Abbey Road was: that stranger turned around and it was only Paul McCartney himself!' *www.abbeyroad.com; tel +44 20 7266 7000; 3 Abbey Rd, St John's Wood, NW8*

'It was here that the cover of John and Yoko's *Two Virgins* album was photographed, and where Ringo told John he was quitting The Beatles'

02 34 MONTAGU SQUARE

If these walls could talk... Within the space of three years in the 1960s, this address, a short hop on the tube from Abbey Road into central London, was a revolving door of some of music's biggest names. Ringo Starr lived here in 1965 and took out a lease on the flat, then Paul McCartney moved in and set up a demo studio here in 1966 (notably working on 'Eleanor Rigby', but

01 The view to St
Paul's and Waterloo
Bridge

03 A guitar leans
against the wall at the
legendary 100 Club

02 Piccadilly Circus,
birthplace of David
Bowie's Ziggy Stardust

04 Outside the Savoy,
where Bob Dylan filmed

American poet William Burroughs also visited to do some spoken word recordings). Jimi Hendrix arrived in 1966 and wrote 'The Wind Cries Mary', moving out just four months later because people were complaining about the noise (undoubtedly an occupational hazard for guitar legends). Then in 1968, when John Lennon and Yoko Ono moved in, things got really interesting.

Apart from the recording of *The White Album* going on during this time, it was here that the cover of John and Yoko's *Two Virgins* album was photographed, where Ringo told John he was quitting The Beatles, and where, a few months later, John and Yoko were arrested for possessing hashish after a police raid. This was the final straw for the other long-suffering building residents, not to mention the landlord who sought an injunction against Ringo to try to prevent the flat being the scene of any further dodgy dealings. By 1969 Ringo had to sell his lease, thus shutting the door on a tumultuous yet memorable time in rock. *www.34montagusquare.com; 34 Montagu Sq, W1*

03 23 HEDDON ST

From Montagu Sq, grab another tube to Piccadilly Circus and the birthplace of David Bowie's Ziggy Stardust. This dead-end street has become all the more significant following the sad and sudden passing of the singer in 2016. A plaque marks this spot as the location for the cover photo of Bowie's 1972 masterpiece *The Rise and Fall of Ziggy Stardust and the Spiders From Mars*.

While the shoot for the album initially took place indoors, it was the final shot featuring Bowie posing beside a doorway outside 23 Heddon St that made the cover — the other band members felt it was too cold to hang about and left him to it. And while Heddon St looks totally different today as a result of nearby Regent St's regeneration, a plaque marks a special spot: where The Starman first landed. *23 Heddon St, Mayfair, W1*

04 100 CLUB

Take a 10-minute walk northeast to this rock 'n' roll institution. In September 1976, the 100 Club hosted the first international punk festival,

03 © Seb Agudelo / Alamy; 04 © Roger Cracknell 05/London / Alamy

with the Sex Pistols, Siouxsie & the Banshees, The Stranglers, The Jam and The Clash all on the bill. While it may have close associations with the early punk movement, it was also where The Rolling Stones played a secret warm-up gig in 1982 — and also a tribute show in 1986 for their deceased pianist, Ian Stewart.

The 100 Club almost closed in 2010, but remains open thanks to a campaign supported by the likes of Sir Paul McCartney. It's a great spot to catch some live music, especially tribute bands (think: Sex Pistols, The Who, The Clash), not to mention the occasional big name dropping a 'secret gig'. *www.the100club.co.uk; tel +44 20 7636 0933; 100 Oxford St, Soho, London W1; check website for gig times*

05 SAVOY STEPS

Take the tube to Embankment then stroll to this famous alley where one of Bob Dylan's classic videos was filmed in 1965; indeed, 'Subterranean Homesick Blues' is recognised as being one of rock's first music videos.

It won't take long to recognise the backdrop to Dylan flipping through cue cards of his lyrics (a concept all his idea), and the spot where poet Allen Ginsberg stood in the background during the shoot.

Dylan stayed at the Savoy Hotel while shooting this as part of the *Don't Look Back* documentary on his tour of England. Two alternate takes were also filmed, one behind the hotel in Victoria Embankment

Gardens and one on the roof of the hotel itself. The Savoy, with impeccable British discretion, refuses to be drawn into discussing this, or Dylan's jamming sessions in his room with Joan Baez and Donovan. Shame. *Savoy Hotel; Strand, London WC2*

06 WATERLOO BRIDGE

From The Strand it's a two-minute walk to the River Thames and Waterloo Bridge, the setting for possibly The Kinks' best-known song. In 1967 The Kinks' singer Ray Davies declared that his song 'Waterloo Sunset' was so personal it was 'like an extract from a diary nobody was allowed to read'. Pay him no regard — you'll find you can't help humming the uplifting tune as you stroll the

24m-wide Waterloo Bridge with spectacular views wherever you look: take your pick of Big Ben, the Houses of Parliament and London Eye on one side, or St Paul's Cathedral and distinctive contemporary buildings such as the Gherkin and the Walkie Talkie on the other.

It's a fitting spot to reflect on all the rock icons who have come before and those who have recently departed (notably Bowie, who covered 'Waterloo Sunset', and also duetted with Davies on this song at a Tibet House benefit concert in 2003). And, if you time it right, maybe, just maybe, you'll get a magical London sunset. Then you'll be in paradise.
A301, Lambeth, SE1
BY KARYN NOBLE

05 Victoria Embankment Gardens, behind the Savoy

06 John Lennon graffiti outside Abbey Road Studios

WHERE TO STAY

CUMBERLAND HOTEL
This West End hotel includes a plush suite with flamboyant rock touches dedicated to the memory of guitar hero Jimi Hendrix (who regularly stayed here). You'll feel like you've time-travelled to the '60s, man. *www.guoman.com; tel +44 20 7523 5053; Great Cumberland Pl, W1*

SANCTUM SOHO HOTEL
Look no further for your rock crash pad. The rooms at Sanctum have Onkyo sound systems and triple-soundproofed walls. Guitars and amps are available on the room-service menu, and the 24-hour rooftop bar is the place to chill with your entourage. *www.sanctumsoho.com; tel +44 20 7292 6100; 20 Warwick St, W1*

WHERE TO EAT & DRINK

STICKY FINGERS
The reference to a Rolling Stones album is no accident; Sticky Fingers is a burger restaurant owned by former Stones bass player Bill Wyman. Revel in all the band memorabilia lining the walls, such as Wyman's bass, gold discs, and Brian Jones's guitar. *www.stickyfingers.co.uk; tel +44 20 7938 5338; 1A Phillimore Gardens, W8*

HARD ROCK CAFE
Put any chain-restaurant preconceptions aside — London's Hard Rock Cafe is your best excuse to visit the largest collection of rock memorabilia: John Lennon's glasses, Bob Dylan's USA-shaped guitar, and more. *www.hardrock.com; tel +44 20 7514 1700; 150 Old Park Ln, London W1*

CELEBRATIONS

ANNUAL KINKS CONVENTION
You have to join the Kinks Fan Club to be able to attend this gathering in November, but the membership fee is more than worth it. Ray Davies himself makes a special appearance, as do past band members. *(www.officialkinksfanclub.co.uk/news)*

LONDON BEATLES DAYS
Looking to buy/sell Beatles memorabilia and meet like-minded people? This is the place. Not so much 'a day' but an event held four times a year, it's fab and it's free. *(www.beatlesdays.com)*

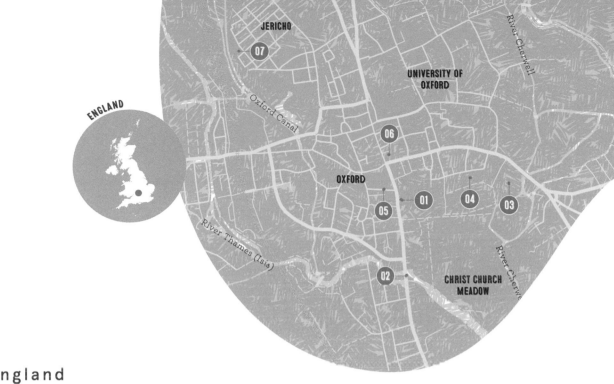

Oxford Canal · JERICHO 07 · ENGLAND · UNIVERSITY OF OXFORD · River Cherwell · 06 · OXFORD · 01 · 04 · 03 · 05 · River Thames (Isis) · 02 · CHRIST CHURCH MEADOW · River Cherwe

England
OXFORD'S STORYTELLERS

There's something in the air around Oxford's medieval lanes, where gargoyled buildings and time-warp colleges have tickled many of England's wildest literary fantasies.

A breeding ground for greatness, Oxford is an august and erudite place where medieval buildings flank hushed quads and future world leaders hone the art of oratory in hallowed halls. Some of the world's most famous names have studied here, from presidents and prime ministers to economists and industrialists, media moguls and Nobel laureates.

It's an otherworldly kind of place trapped in a time warp, where bizarre traditions are still upheld and an archaic argot bewilders outsiders. Bookish hordes wander down cobbled laneways, gowned cyclists are watched by grotesque gargoyles and children in cassocks scurry to choir practice in ancient chapels. In essence, the perfect fodder for storytellers.

Over the years Oxford has churned out a litany of world-renowned writers, its medieval libraries, mysterious laneways and weird goings-on a rich source of inspiration for creative minds and imaginative souls. It's a

NEED TO KNOW
To do the trail justice you'll need about three days in Oxford, which is about an hour west of London by road or train.

place where secret doors reveal hidden gardens, where baroque churches inspired poets and tiny pubs hosted those who became the most famous storytellers of all. Shakespeare, Tolkien and WH Auden all passed through, Oscar Wilde wowed his examiners with wit and wisdom and CS Lewis was inspired by the city's ornately carved doors and stone statues. Numerous others set their fiction here: Oxford passed as Christminster in Thomas Hardy's *Jude the Obscure*; an alternative Oxford provided the setting for Philip Pullman's *His Dark Materials*; and Philip Larkin and Dorothy L Sayers described a more recognisable Oxford world in their work.

The city's historic heart remains largely untouched, and it's easy to imagine Oxford's celebrated storytellers wandering the laneways exactly as you see them today. Who knows — you may even rub shoulders with the next generation of greats as they shuffle between lectures and libraries.

‘Lewis Carroll and the stories of *Alice in Wonderland* are particularly synonymous with the River Thames’

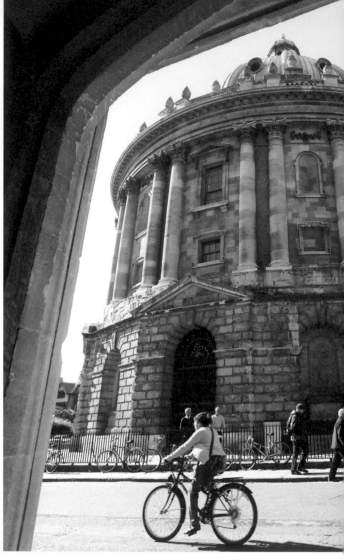

01 CHRIST CHURCH

The grandest of all Oxford colleges, Christ Church played a central role in the life of one of the city's greatest storytellers. Charles Dodgson, better known as Lewis Carroll, studied maths and then lectured here, and was inspired by Alice Liddell, daughter of the dean, to write *Alice's Adventures in Wonderland* in 1865.

He used many details of college life as inspiration, modelling Alice's long neck on the brass fire dogs in the Great Hall, the mock turtle on the shells on the kitchen wall, and the little door to another world on a locked door in the deanery garden that supposedly fascinated the real-life Alice. From Christ Church, head down St Aldate's to the river. *www.chch.ox.ac.uk; tel +44 1865 276 150; St Aldate's; 10am-5pm Mon-Sat, 2-5pm Sun*

02 RIVER THAMES

As Carroll became friends with Alice and her sisters he took them on a boat trip to Godstow when he told the Alice stories for the first time. You can recreate their trip on an Edwardian-style river launch that passes bucolic Port Meadow, said to have inspired Carroll as well as CS Lewis, Evelyn Waugh and Gerard Manley Hopkins, before arriving at the quaint village of Binsey where St Frideswide's Well served as a model for the well in Alice's adventures.

Giles Dobson of Oxford River Cruises says: 'Many of the famous names [in children's literature] — Tolkien, CS Lewis, Philip Pullman — have had some connection to the city's waterways. Lewis Carroll and the stories of *Alice in Wonderland* are particularly synonymous with the River Thames.'

From here it is a tranquil cruise to Godstow with its ruined abbey, which

01 Oxford's well-preserved historic core

02 The River Thames has inspired writers for centuries

03 Grand university buildings are a symbol of Oxford

04 An actor dressed as an *Alice in Wonderland* character performs at the Story Museum

05 The Bodleian Library entrance

sits opposite Trout Island, home to a large statue of a lion supposedly inspired CS Lewis's fabled land of Narnia. Once back in town, look for the gate behind the Head of the River pub that leads to Christ Church Meadow, where you can meander along tree-lined paths to Oxford's Botanic Garden. *www.oxfordrivercruises.com; tel +44 8452 269396; Folly Bridge; Apr–Oct, book in advance*

03 BOTANIC GARDEN

Embraced by a curve in the River Cherwell, Oxford's Botanic Garden was first planted in 1621 and has provided inspiration for a host of Oxford storytellers. Carroll used it as a basis for the queen's garden in Alice's adventures; Tolkien used to sit here writing under a pine tree that was said to have inspired the 'ents' in *Lord of the Rings*; Charles and Sebastian first got to know each other as they walked through this garden in Evelyn Waugh's *Brideshead Revisited*; and Will and Lyra, from Philip Pullman's *His Dark Materials*, meet on a bench here, each in their own separate worlds, at noon on midsummer's day. *www. botanic-garden.ox.ac.uk; +44 1865 286690; Rose Lane; 9am–5pm*

04 MERTON COLLEGE

Established in 1264, nearby Merton is one of Oxford's oldest colleges and many of its medieval buildings with their mullioned windows and Gothic doorways still survive. The 14th-century library retains some of its original fittings and Tolkien, who was professor of Anglo-Saxon at Merton, would undoubtedly have spent many hours leafing through ancient books and medieval manuscripts in search of images and ideas that helped shape *The Lord of the Rings*.

If you can, stay for the choral evensong in the beautiful chapel

(usually Tue-Thu & Sun). From here continue along cobbled Merton St into higgledy-piggledy Bear Lane and Blue Boar St towards the Story Museum. www.merton.ox.ac.uk; tel +44 1865 276310; Merton St; 2-5pm Mon-Fri, 10am-5pm Sat & Sun

05 STORY MUSEUM

Tucked away in a courtyard off a quiet side street in the city centre, the Story Museum is a wonderful celebration of storytelling of all kinds.

Immersive exhibitions feature multisensory displays about much-loved writers, stories or fictional characters, while a rolling programme of events provides a fascinating exploration of storytelling for both children and adults. You might catch a comic book or poetry workshop, quiz night or talks by authors — it's a place where reality is temporarily suspended and you can enter the wildest fictional worlds of your childhood.
www.storymuseum.org.uk; tel +44 1865 790050; 42 Pembroke St; 10am-5pm Mon-Sat, 11am-4pm Sun during school holidays, 10am-5pm Fri-Sat & 11am-4pm Sun during term time

06 GOLDEN CROSS

Shakespeare was a regular visitor to Oxford, staying here overnight on the journey between his home in Stratford and the Globe Theatre in London. His theatre company performed here regularly and the courtyard of the Golden Cross Inn, five minutes from the Story Museum, is where Hamlet is thought to have been first performed.

Today, the 15th-century inn has been converted into shops and restaurants, but the original timberwork remains and early wall paintings and hand-painted wallpaper can easily be seen on the upper floor of the restaurant on the northern side. Shakespeare supposedly preferred the Crown Tavern a few doors down for his overnight stays. He was a family friend of the owner and is suspected of fathering the innkeeper's son.
5 Cornmarket St

07 ST BARNABAS CHURCH

Subject of a poem by Sir John Betjeman, St Barnabas Church in Jericho is surrounded by rows of Victorian workers' houses in what is now a quietly hip part of town, about a 15-minute walk northwest of the

08 © Jon Bower Oxford / Alamy

Golden Cross. Thomas Hardy worked as an assistant to Sir Arthur Blomfield, who designed the church, and Hardy used it as a location in *Jude the Obscure*.

Most famously, the 19th-century church with its striking Venetian style bell tower became the Oratory of St Barnabas the Chymist in Philip Pullman's fantasy novels. The parallel universe in which *His Dark Materials* characters Lyra and Will exist is based on Oxford; the Oxford Canal, home to the fictional Gyptians, runs behind the church, the Eagle Iron Works (now apartments) is nearby and the Fell Press (the real-life Oxford University Press building) is just up the road. *www.sbarnabas.org.uk; tel +44 1865 557 530; St Barnabas St; 8.30am-11am Tues & Fri, 7.30am-noon & 6-7.30pm Sun*
BY ETAIN O'CARROLL

06 A fat cherub performs over the counter at The Eagle & Child pub

07 *Alice in Wonderland* characters outside Alice's Shop

08 The Great Hall at Christ Church College

WHERE TO STAY
OLD PARSONAGE
Thrown out of his college rooms, Oscar Wilde took refuge in the Old Parsonage, now one of Oxford's top hotels. Expect heavy oak doors, arched fireplaces, Queen Anne panelling, eclectic art and sleek and stylish rooms. *www.oldparsonage-hotel.co.uk; tel +44 1865 3102101; Banbury Rd*

BATH PLACE HOTEL
In the heart of the city, this 17th-century hotel has floors that slope at disconcerting angles and stairs that are fit for a hobbit. Its creaking, crooked rooms are full of character. *www.bathplace.co.uk; tel +44 1865 791812, 4-5 Bath Pl*

WHERE TO EAT & DRINK
THE OLD BOOKBINDERS
Down a back street in Jericho, this quirky pub is a charming spot to nurse a pint, join a pub quiz and enjoy some remarkable French food. It's warm and cosy, and usually packed. *www.oldbookbinders. co.uk; tel +44 1865 553549; 17-18 Victor St*

THE EAGLE & CHILD
This 17th-century watering hole was a favourite of JRR Tolkien, CS Lewis and their literary mates ('The Inklings'). They met here to discuss their work and the tiny snugs, uneven floor, real ale and traditional grub have changed little since. *www.nicholsonspubs .co.uk; tel +44 1865 302925; 49 St Giles*

CELEBRATIONS
OXFORD LITERARY FESTIVAL
Taking place over nine days at the end of March, the Oxford Literary Festival has a superb line-up of speakers, from distinguished writers and academics to first-time authors. Workshops, debates and discussions take place in beautiful college halls, chapels and gardens. *(www.oxfordliterary festival.org)*

OXFORD FESTIVAL OF THE ARTS
A two-week celebration of culture in late June/early July, the Oxford Festival of the Arts features music, literature and theatre events across the city. *(www.artsfestivaloxford.org)*

Ethiopia

ANCIENT RELIGION OF ETHIOPIA

Land of rock-hewn churches, sacred tombs and possible final resting place of the Ark of the Covenant, Ethiopia's north is a realm where Christianity mixes with powerful legends.

Ethiopia's north is a world apart, the kind of place where ancient legends mingle with the country's powerful brand of Orthodox Christianity. It is a world of white-robed pilgrims and stories that resonate down through the ages — it was here that the Queen of Sheba ruled and it is here that, Ethiopians believe, the true Ark of the Covenant resides. That such legends and powerful touchstones of the faith survive here owes much to Ethiopia's fiercely independent spirit — it is, for example, one of very few African countries never to have been colonised — and to the largely impenetrable topography of this jagged mountain realm.

Ancient Aksum is the epicentre of Ethiopian Christianity. Built upon the foundations of one of Africa's most significant ancient civilisations — the soaring monuments to this time watch over countless Christian churches — Aksum is a heady mix of swirling incense and ritual chants, of ornate silver crosses and

NEED TO KNOW
Fly into Aksum and then travel by road (preferably by 4WD), before flying out of Lalibela at the end of this four-day trail.

finely rendered religious paintings, of sound and movement as the devout come to pay homage to the Ark. In Debre Damo and the rock churches of Tigray, which were mostly built between the 10th and 15th centuries but have been much modified in the centuries since, there is little of the power and the passion of Aksum — faith here is a quieter affair of watchful priests and hard-won pilgrimages to reach barely accessible cave churches high upon the sheer cliffs of this forbidding terrain. And in Lalibela, the churches are architectural wonders of rare beauty, hewn from the rock as if by powerful kings aided by angels (as locals believe) and surely among the greatest wonders of the ancient world.

The international gateway to Ethiopia's northern historical circuit is the country's capital of Addis Ababa, which is connected to both Aksum and Lalibela by domestic flights operated by Ethiopian Airlines.

01 © Jon Arnold Images Ltd – Alamy

02 © Jon Bratt / Getty Images

① ANCIENT AKSUM

It is difficult to overstate Aksum's historical and sacred significance. In the Northern Stelae Field, towering obelisks and deep underground tombs tell stories of a sophisticated world and powerful empire that extended far beyond the borders of what is now modern Ethiopia.

But it is the whiff of legend and myth that surrounds these sites, as much as the documented history itself, that gives Aksum its magic. Did the Queen of Sheba really rule over the city from the palace on the western outskirts of the city? Was it from here that she would

journey to Ancient Israel, fall in love with King Solomon and change the course of Ethiopian history forever? And was King Bazen, whose tomb burrows underground in the town centre, really Balthazar, one of the Three Wise Men who attended the birth of Christ? In ancient, mysterious Aksum, anything seems possible.
Sites open 8am-5.30pm

'Ethiopia's Christians believe Menelik I and the Queen of Sheba brought the Ark of the Covenant to Aksum in the 10th century BC'

② AKSUM CHURCHES

If Aksum's history as the capital of a great empire was the reason for its endurance, the city's religious story elevates it into the realm of the sacred. Ethiopia's Christians believe that Menelik I, the son of King Solomon and the Queen of Sheba, brought the true Ark of the Covenant to Aksum in the 10th century BC.

01 The striking facade
of Enda Iyesus Church
in Aksum

03 Ceiling frescoes
adorn a rock church
of Lalibela

02 Pilgrims gather at
striking Bet Giyorgis

04 Religious
procession at Aksum

A modest (and off-limits) chapel is said to be the resting place of the Ark, but it is surrounded by fascinating churches — a vast new church built by the Emperor Haile Selassie, a far superior 17th-century church adorned with glorious iconographic paintings that are an Ethiopian hallmark, and a museum with a gilded collection of priceless crosses, kings' crowns and royal vestments.

Outside the old church is the throne stone upon which were crowned 261 Ethiopian kings. *Churches open 8am-12.30pm & 2.30-5.30pm Mon-Fri, 9am-noon & 2.30-5.30pm Sat & Sun*

03 DEBRE DAMO

Leaving Aksum behind, the road arches up across the mountains with fabulous views en route — you reach Debre Damo 2½ hours after leaving Aksum. Here is surely one of the most stunningly sited churches anywhere in Christendom. To reach it requires a steep 30-minute uphill hike, then a dizzying rope climb up a sheer 15m-high rock wall; local legend has it that God sent down a giant snake to lift the church's founding saint up onto the heavenly perch. Only men are permitted to enter the church.

Your prize for such high-altitude bravery is a sixth-century monastery with beautiful paintings, illuminated manuscripts and views that seem to stretch for eternity, not to mention some serious credits when it comes to fulfilling one of Christianity's more unusual rites of passage. *6am-6pm*

04 ROCK-HEWN CHURCHES OF TIGRAY

There's nowhere to sleep in Debre Damo, so continue on along a well-maintained gravel road to Adigrat and then across into the Tigray Highlands town of Hawzien. Here you'll find yourself surrounded by possibilities. The more energetic among you can scale the extraordinary heights of Abuna Yemata Guh, another clifftop

03 © Philip Lee Harvey / Lonely Planet Images; 04 © JTB MEDIA CREATION, Inc. / Alamy

church of extraordinary power — the last few metres involve a death-defying walk along a narrow ledge hundreds of metres above a vertiginous chasm. If mobility is an issue, the church of Maryam Papaseit is utterly beautiful, has exquisite 17th-century paintings, and is far easier to reach.

And if you've had your fill of ancient churches, spend an hour or two instead at Cheila, an unusually well-preserved village of Tigrayan rural architecture and a fine chance to meet and mingle with the locals. *Churches open 8am-5.30pm*

05 MEKELE

The road from Hawzen ambles across the Tigrayan countryside, passing numerous rock-cut churches en route to Wukro, where you rejoin the main

sealed road. Wukro has churches of its own, an excellent new museum, and main-street restaurants serving what could be the best roasted goat you'll find in sub-Saharan Africa.

Plan to stay overnight in Tigray's capital, Mekele. This modern and confident city represents an excellent complement to the preponderance of churches and ancient sites in this region. Mekele's calling card is instead its excellent restaurants and comfortable hotels. *Wukro Museum; tel + 251 91 029 2927; 9am-12.30pm & 2-4.30pm Mon-Sat*

06 LALIBELA CHURCHES

Leaving Mekele, the paved road runs south to Woldia, from where gravel roads buck and weave across the mountains all the way to Lalibela.

There's nowhere on earth quite like Lalibela. In the heart of town, carved from rock and mountain, the city's 12th- to 13th-century churches are simply extraordinary.

From the monumental grandeur of Bet Medhane Alem, the largest rock-hewn church in the world, to the astonishing perfection of Bet Giyorgis, Ethiopia's most photographed church, Lalibela's 13 churches are otherworldly and possessed of rare and singular beauty.

You can see the best of them in a morning, but take a day to savour this very special place. To truly understand that these are no architectural relics, come just after dawn when the white-robed faithful come to pray. *8am-5.30pm*

06 © Philip Lee Harvey / Lonely Planet Images

07 LALIBELA MOUNTAINS

Perched atop the mountain high above Lalibela and accessible via a sinuous mountain road, Ashetan Maryam is an attractive church but it's the views from here on the roof of Ethiopia that really make the climb worthwhile.

Alternatively, if you hear the call of one last church and make a very early start, Yemrehanna Kristos, a 1½-hour drive from Lalibela, dates from the 11th or 12th century. Sitting under an overhanging cliff, it is an extraordinary mix of ancient design splendour and mysterious spiritual power. If you come here on 10 October when the place throngs with pilgrims, it's plain to see that Christianity Ethiopian-style is very much alive.

BY ANTHONY HAM

05 Northern Stelae Field, ancient Aksum

06 Monk climbing up to the hilltop monastery at Debre Damo

WHERE TO STAY
GHERALTA LODGE
One of the loveliest lodges to stay in Ethiopia, Italian-run Gheralta Lodge in Hawzen has stone-built accommodation, fine food and is the ideal base for exploring Tigray's churches. www.gheraltalodgetigrai.com; tel +251 96 325 485

OLD ABYSSINIA LODGE
This new place in Lalibela has traditionally styled, beautifully decorated circular stone bungalows with jaw-dropping views from each private terrace. There's also a fine restaurant and onsite cooking school. www.oldabyssinia.com; tel +251 33 836 2758

WHERE TO EAT & DRINK
BEN ABEBA
Like a Salvador Dalí creation grafted onto an Ethiopian hilltop perch, Ben Abeba in Lalibela is one of the best eating stops in Ethiopia. The goat burger, made with homemade bread, is one highlight among many, but it's the views that may live longest in the memory. www.benabeba.com; tel +251 92 234 5144; 6am-10pm

GEZA GERLASE
Traditional Ethiopian cuisine has no finer home than this cavernous, wildly popular place in Mekele's centre. It's all about the finest cuts of meat, served on *injera* (Ethiopian sour crepe-like pancakes) and a nightly floor show of local folk music, song and dance. 7am-11pm

CELEBRATIONS
FESTIVAL OF MARYAM ZION
One of Ethiopia's most powerful events, this stirring annual celebration by the faithful, held on 30 November, sees Aksum overwhelmed by a sea of white-robed pilgrims. Come after midnight on the night before for the unforgettable sight of sleeping pilgrims in their thousands, watched over by priests reading sacred texts by candlelight.

TIMKAT
The Epiphany, or Christ's baptism, is marked with special fervour in Ethiopia each January — nowhere more so than in Lalibela, with its massed ranks of devotees and solemn processions through city streets and churches.

Map labels:
YLLÄSJÄRVI
08
07
ROVANIEMI
RUKA
OULU
SWEDEN
FINLAND
VAASA
06 KUOPIO
Gulf of Bothnia
05
TAMPERE
Lake Ladoga
TURKU
01
04
HELSINKI
03
ST PETERSBURG
STOCKHOLM
02
Gulf of Finland
RUSSIA
Baltic Sea
ESTONIA

Finland

FINNISH SAUNA CULTURE

The ritual of sauna-going — complete with its own elf lore — is an age-old Finnish tradition that remains wildly popular today, both in Helsinki design temples and rural backwaters.

A dusting of snow lies thick and luminous-white on the birch and fir trees, like frosting on a Christmas cake. The temperature is -10°C, the lake is frozen and day is swiftly fading into blackest night. It's 3pm. Far from letting the darkness and cold get the better of them, the Finns are embracing midwinter by hanging out in the sauna: a millennia-old tradition that began when the first settlers dug holes in the ground and filled them with hot stones.

Inside the sauna, it's a toasty 80°C and silent but for the crackle of burning wood and the hiss of water being ladled on stones, emitting waves of the fragrant vapour known as *löyly*. Sweat-drenched and naked, the sauna-goers step outside and plunge joyously into a hole in the ice. The water is a shade over zero: so mind-numbingly cold it stings the skin and jump-starts the nervous system. After a beer and a vigorous whipping with a bundle of birch branches (to improve circulation and

NEED TO KNOW
This trail takes you the length of Finland — from the Baltic coast to Lapland. If you can, allow a week to do it justice.

relax and detoxify the body), it's time to pad back through the snow to the sauna to do the whole ritual again. And do it properly they should, else the *saunatonttu*, or sauna elf, will punish them by burning the sauna down.

Fondly dubbed the 'poor man's pharmacy', the sauna is at the very heart of Finnish culture. In this sparsely populated, densely forested country of 5.4 million people, there are three million saunas and counting. Finns go to the sauna to cleanse mind and body, to socialise and do business, to prepare for births, deaths and marriages. Name any important life event and you can bet your bottom dollar a sauna will be involved.

In midsummer, when the sun never sets, many Finns are at their back-of-beyond lakeside cottages, alone with contemplative thoughts, wilderness and a zillion bloodthirsty mosquitos. A sauna is fired up. A swim, forest walk and an open fire await after a good sweating. Life is sweet; to a Finn it literally doesn't get any better.

01 © Ryhor Bruyeu / Getty Images

01 KULTTUURISAUNA

Sleek and functionalist, Helsinki's Kulttuurisauna, or 'Culture Sauna', is the combined vision of architect and designer duo Nene Tsuboi and Tuomas Toivonen. Sitting right on the seafront in the capital's high-rise Merihaka district, it's ecologically heated using wooden pellets. The concept deviates from tradition, bringing in Japanese and Roman bathing influences.

The understated design allows you to concentrate on the big views of the bay through the picture windows and soak up the Zen-like vibe. Post-steam you can swim in the Baltic or rest on the deck overlooking the harbour. *kulttuurisauna.fi; tel +358 40 516 969; Hakaniemenranta 17; 4-8pm Wed-Sun*

'Saunas are a living institution and as old as the pyramids. Most Finns go to the sauna twice weekly, and the country has more saunas than cars'

02 LÖYLY

Emblematic of Helsinki's recent desire for urban regeneration, design-minded Löyly hit the ground running when it opened in 2016. At the capital's newest and coolest 'boutique sauna', you'll steam in style. Designed by Avanto Architects, the pyramidal building, clad in 4000 waste wood planks, can be climbed like a mountain.

Rimmed by parkland, the architecturally innovative, sustainably powered building combines saunas, a restaurant and terrace with spirit-lifting views out to sea. The light inside is exceptional, with the slatted façade allowing the sun to slant in. When the Baltic freezes over in winter, there's an *avanto* (ice hole) for heart-stopping, post-sauna swims. *www.loylyhelsinki.fi; tel +358 96 128 6550; Hernesaarenranta 4; 4-10pm Mon-Wed, 1-10pm Thu-Fri, 7.30-9.30 & 1-10pm Sat, 1-9pm Sun*

01 There are thousands of private lakeside saunas in Finland

02 Design-minde Löyly sauna, Helsinki

03 Traditional birch branches — for circulatory whipping!

04 Gondolas above Ylläs ski resort

03 ULLI'S EXPERIENCE

Helsinki sauna expert and guide Ulla Maija has penned a book on the art of bathing culture. On bespoke guided tours she gives the inside scoop on saunas: from how they evolved more than 2000 years ago to the illnesses and ailments they are said to cure, from rheumatoid arthritis to poor circulation, diabetes, high blood pressure, cardiovascular disease and chronic fatigue.

Ulla says the sauna forms an integral part of Finnish hospitality. 'Saunas are a living institution and as old as the pyramids,' says Ulla. 'Most Finns go to the sauna twice weekly, and the country has more saunas than cars — every family has one or two. The importance of the sauna is revealed in the Finnish proverb "cleanliness is half the meal".'
ullisexperience.fi; tel +358 40 587 9869; Kaivonkatsojantie 5; times on request

04 HERRANKUKKARO'S SMOKE SAUNA

At Finland's southwestern tip, the quaint fishing village of Herrankukkaro (Mama's Pocket) sits serenely on an archipelago just south of Turku. It might easily be overlooked, were it not for its holy grail of a sauna — the world's largest underground smoke sauna, with space for 124 sweat-drenched folk.

It's right on a glorious stretch of coast, a 2½-hour drive west of Helsinki, with hot tubs and pools gazing out over the Baltic, where you can take a skin-tingling dip if you can summon the nerve.
www.herrankukkaro.fi; tel +358 2 515 3300; Herrankukkaro, Luotojentie 245, Naantali; by appointment

05 RAJAPORTTI

Little has changed since 1906 at Finland's oldest sauna. A 15-minute drive west of the lakeside city of Tampere, Rajaportti is Finland's oldest working sauna. True, there are more glamorous saunas, but few are imbued with such a sense of history as this one, which witnessed the Finnish Civil War in 1918.

According to the owners, the resident *saunatonttu* (sauna elf) keeps watch over the wood stove sauna. The *saunatonttu* is the spiritual guardian

of the sauna. Elves regularly pop up in Finnish folklore; lore has it that the sauna elf, the sauna's spiritual guardian, punishes those who behave improperly there — for instance sleeping, eating or talking loudly.

It doesn't get more Finnish than this place, with separate areas for men and women and an appealing coffee house for a *kahvi* (coffee). It's a good place to observe traditional sauna etiquette. According to custom, saunas are nude, hence the separate areas for men and women — unless the sauna is at home, in which case it's often mixed-sex. Bring your own towel — or borrow one at the sauna for a nominal fee — as well as a bathing suit for communal areas. *www.rajaportti.fi; tel +358 50 310 2611; Pispalan Valtatie 9, Tampere; 6-10pm Mon-Wed, 3-9pm Fri, 2-10pm Sat*

06 JÄTKÄNKÄMPPÄ SMOKE SAUNA

A 3½-hour drive northeast brings you to the heart of Finland's lake district in the Northern Savonia region. Sizzling away nicely here in laid-back Kuopio, ringed by lakes and forests, is one of the country's finest smoke saunas — a rustic log cabin with blackened walls and clouds of soft, fragrant *löyly*. It's beautifully positioned on the lake for swims in summer (for the brave) and winter (for the hardy locals and foolhardy all-comers).

It's mixed-sex, so bring a towel. In the adjacent restaurant, accordion music plays and lumberjack demos are held as hungry sauna-goers tuck into good old-fashioned Finnish grub.

Rimmed by lakes and forests, it's

a laid-back town that plays host to many lively summer festivals. *www.rauhalahti.fi; tel +358 306 0830; Kastiskaniementie 8, Kuopio; 4-10pm Tue & Thu Jun-Aug, 4-10pm Tue Sep-May*

07 RUKAN SALONKI

Out on its lonesome in Rukatunturi near the Lappish border in eastern Finland, Rukan Salonki blows hot and cold. Made from huge blocks of ice carved from Lake Salonkijärvi, this visually stunning igloo sauna took many years to perfect. Contrary to all logic, you won't freeze, with temps reaching a moderately warm 60°C.

It opens for the winter months, when the surrounding forests and fells receive a heavy dump of snow. The brave can jump into an ice hole

to cool off. Post-sauna, join fellow Finns for a meal of locally sourced reindeer or salmon and some grog in the barbecue hut.

In order to visit this sauna, base yourself in a peaceful log cottage in Rukatunturi, or it's a 20-minute drive from Kuusamo, where all manner of outdoor activities are on offer. *www.rukansalonki.fi; tel +358 40 564 093; Salongintie 2, Rukatunturi, December-April; by appointment*

08 GONDOLA SAUNA

Ah, what could be cosier than a sauna among friends after a day pounding the slopes? So thought some crazy entrepreneurs who envisaged this gondola sauna in Ylläs, Finland's biggest ski resort. At the top, 718m above sea level, you can soak in an open-air Jacuzzi and grab a drink before disrobing for the gondola sauna.

Here in Lapland, 150km north of the Arctic Circle, the scenery is straight out of a snowglobe, with endless views of snow-covered fells and frozen lakes glistening in the twilight, as you drift silently in a gondola lift over the landscape. *www.yllas.fi/en/services/sauna-gondola.html; tel +358 40 544 7743; Iso-Ylläksentie 44; by appointment*
BY KERRY CHRISTIANI

05 Laid-back Kuopio in Finland's lake district

06 A traditional sauna, Helsinki

WHERE TO STAY
HOTEL INDIGO
In the heart of Helsinki's hip design district, Bulevardi, Hotel Indigo has a sharp Nordic aesthetic, its own sauna and locally sourced Scandi cuisine. *www.hotelindigo.com; tel +358 200 48105; Bulevardi 26*

ARCTIC SNOW HOTEL
Hotels don't come any cooler than this one in Rovaniemi, Lapland. Stay in a glass igloo to watch the Northern Lights play from the comfort of your bed, and sweat it out in a sauna made entirely from ice. *arcticsnowhotel.fi; tel +358 40 845 3774; Lehtoahontie 27*

WHERE TO EAT & DRINK
JUURI
Juuri focused on 'local' and 'seasonal' way before they became buzzwords. This intimate Helsinki bistro puts a distinctively Finnish spin on tapas, such as whitefish with elderflower and horseradish. *juuri.fi; tel +358 9 635 732; Korkeavuorenkatu 27; 11.30am-11pm Mon-Fri, noon-11pm Sat, 4-11pm Sun*

HELLA & HUONE
A slick, monochrome backdrop sets the scene for inventive Nordic molecular cooking at this restaurant in Tampere. Much-lauded chef Arto Rastas heads up the kitchen, concocting dishes with names such as 'beets in a snowy forest' in his palate-awakening tasting menu. *hellajahuone.fi; tel +358 10 322 3898; Salhojankatu 48; 6pm-midnight Thu-Sat*

CELEBRATIONS
MOBILE SAUNA FESTIVAL
Finns are always first in line for a bonkers event and this one in Teuva, western Finland, each August is no exception. Phone boxes, combine harvesters, amphibious tanks, wagons – anything goes as long as it's a mobile sauna.

JUHANNUS
Summer solstice (June) is Finland's biggest party. North of the Arctic Circle, the sun never sets, while across the country Finns embrace summer with a biological urgency. How? With barbecues, fishing, bonfires, bathing — and saunas, naturally.

06 © FORRAY Didier/SAGAPHOTO.COM / Alamy

01

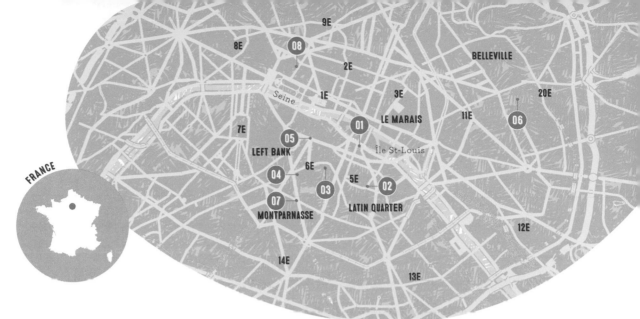

The following places are marked on the map: 01, 02 (LATIN QUARTER), 03, 04, 05 (LEFT BANK), 06, 07 (MONTPARNASSE), 08. Districts labelled: 8E, 9E, 2E, 1E, 3E, BELLEVILLE, 20E, LE MARAIS, 11E, 7E, Seine, Île St-Louis, 6E, 5E, 12E, 14E, 13E. FRANCE (inset map).

France

LITERARY PARIS THROUGH THE EYES OF HEMINGWAY

The French capital has long been home to brilliant writers, and the post-war 1920s years of cabarets and cafe life heralded a special, anything-goes era for the city's literati.

La Ville Lumière (The City of Light) is seriously storied. Over the centuries numerous brilliant writers, French and foreign, have used Paris as their setting or spent time here seeking inspiration. Just one look at the Notre Dame Cathedral and majestic Arc de Triomphe, fabled Champs-Elysées and dazzling white dome of Montmartre's Sacré-Coeur, and it's plain to see this is a world city built on grandiose ideas and big art.

During the 18th century Age of Enlightenment, Voltaire and Rousseau exchanged racy new philosophies over too much coffee at Café Procope, while intellectuals conversed at literary salons hosted by smart Parisian women. In the Roaring Twenties, with the austerity of WWI put firmly to bed, party-mad Paris sparkled as a centre of avant-garde and after WWII, foreign writers again gravitated towards the cafe terraces and bars of the romantic, shamelessly decadent French capital.

NEED TO KNOW
Navigate this two-day trail by using your two feet wherever possible; take the metro for longer distances.

American writer Ernest Hemingway (1899-1961) arrived in Paris with his first wife Hadley in early 1922 and headed straight for the bohemian Latin Quarter; it wasn't until 1927, with his second wife, that Florida beckoned and he decamped back to the US. In the seedy drinking holes of the Latin Quarter, art deco brasseries of Montparnasse and sophisticated cafe pavement terraces of fashionable St-Germain des Prés, Hemingway hobnobbed with expatriate writers, artists and political exiles of the day: WWI was well over, Europe was booming both culturally and economically, and it was an era when Ezra Pound, James Joyce, F Scott Fitzgerald, Picasso, Cole Porter *et al* let their hair down in the anything-goes Paris of cabarets, jazz clubs and dance halls.

This urban itinerary explores the literary trail these luminaries blazed during these *années folles* (crazy years) — the inspiration for Hemingway's own poignant Paris memoir *A Moveable Feast* (1964).

02 © kavalenkava / Shutterstock

01 SHAKESPEARE AND COMPANY

Open the day with *un café*, croissant and inspirational browse in the world's most famous independent bookshop. Buttresses fly and gargoyles grimace atop the Gothic cathedral across the water that inspired Victor Hugo to write *The Hunchback of Notre Dame* in 1831. *Bouquinistes* (second-hand booksellers) huddle in front of weathered stalls on river quays once frequented by a book-hungry Hemingway hunting for a cheap second-hand read.

Inside Shakespeare and Company, a beat-poet clientele mingles over labyrinthine shelves of books – uncannily mimicking Hemingway and

'At the end of WWII Hemingway famously returned to Paris with one single intention — to liberate his favourite bar'

other expat writers who hung out at Sylvia Beach's original Shakespeare and Company shop, at 12 Rue de l'Odéon. The shop was closed during the Nazi occupation when Beach refused to sell her last copy of Joyce's *Finnegans Wake* to a Nazi officer, and it never reopened. In 1951 fellow American and book lover George Whitman rekindled her literary flame with the opening of today's iconic Shakespeare and

Company by the River Seine.

Catch a weekly reading and plot your return to Paris as a legendary 'Tumbleweed'. This is the name given to lucky volunteers who get the chance to sleep in the bookshop for a night. In exchange, Tumbleweeds have to help for a few hours in the shop, read a book and scribe their life story on a single page. Not sure if it's for you? Head up the rickety staircase to check out the single beds

01 The Paris skyline from the top of Tour Montparnasse

02 Bars on Blvd Montparnasse thrived in the Roaring Twenties

03 Cimetière du Père Lachaise: final resting place of literary greats such as Oscar Wilde

04 Sculpture in Jardin du Luxembourg

wedged between bookshelves. *shakespeareandcompany.com; 37 Rue de la Bûcherie. 5e; tel +33 1 43 25 40 93; 10am-11pm*

02 HEMINGWAY'S APARTMENT

It's a 10-minute walk to 74 Rue du Cardinal Lemoine in the fifth arrondissement, where Hemingway and Hadley lived from 1922 to 1923. Below their fourth-floor apartment was Bal au Printemps, a seedy accordion- and whore-fuelled *bal musette* (dancing hall) that served as a model for the one where Jake Barnes meets Brett Ashley in Hemingway's *The Sun Also Rises* (1926).

Across the road at No 71, Irish writer James Joyce (1882–1941) was finishing off *Ulysees* around the time

that Hemingway was living here. Hemingway laboured over his own prose in a rented room at 39 Rue Descartes and got tight on Pernod at Café des Amateurs (today Café Delmas) on Place de la Contrescarpe.

Walk 10 minutes west, past the Sorbonne and neoclassical Pantheon where Voltaire, Victor Hugo and Émile Zola among other literary greats lie, into the Luxembourg Gardens.

03 JARDIN DU LUXEMBOURG

Join Parisians in the timeless French art of *flânerie* (strolling at leisure) in this graceful city park, a romantic patchwork of chestnut groves, rose gardens, apple orchards and vintage statues from the 17th century.

Victor Hugo's lovers Cosette and

Marius met here in *Les Misérables* (1862) and a half-starved Hemingway feasted on Cézanne and Monet masterpieces in its Musée du Luxembourg — that is, when he wasn't hunting pigeons in the park with a pocketful of corn, to take home and eat. *museeduluxembourg.fr; 19 Rue de Vaugiraud, 6e; tel +33 1 40 13 62 00; 10.30am-7pm Sat-Thu, to 10pm Fri*

04 SALON OF GERTRUDE STEIN

Soon enough Hemingway and Hadley were invited to afternoon tea by Gertrude Stein (1874-1946), an eccentric American writer who lived nearby with her partner Alice B Toklas at 27 Rue de Fleurus – a plaque marks the spot.

It was here, at one of Stein's infamous literary salons (1903-38), that Hemingway met other 'lost generation' writers: a term coined by Stein to describe American writers such as Hemingway soul-searching in inter-war Paris, and famously used by Hemingway in his novel *The Sun Also Rises*.

Toklas took a backseat in literary proceedings until 1954, when she published a cookbook containing her scandalous musings on these heady salon days and a recipe for hashish fudge — a sweet made with fruit, nuts, spices and cannabis.

Walk two minutes north along Rue Guynemer, cross Rue Vaugiraud and continue north to Blvd St-Germain. *27 Rue de Fleurus, 6e*

05 BOULEVARD ST-GERMAIN

Despite its gentrification, there remains a cinematic quality to this soulful boulevard where Childebert I built Paris's oldest church in the 6th century and post-war writers mingled over coffee and cocktails. Take breakfast at Hemingway's favourite cafes: Café de Flore at No 172 or Les Deux Magots at 6 Place St-Germain des Prés. The latter is a drapery shop-turned-cafe where Jean-Paul Sartre, Simone de Beauvoir and Albert Camus drank in the 1940s and 1950s.

06 CIMETIÈRE DU PÈRE LACHAISE

The world's most visited cemetery is a short metro ride away. It opened in 1804 as a response to local graveyards being full and was initially avoided like the plague: Parisians did not want to be buried outside the quartier in which they lived.

To help persuade the masses, the city authorities moved popular playwright Molière (1622-73) and poet Jean de la Fontaine (1621-95) here in 1817. The marketing strategy worked and all too soon the cemetery's celebrity roll call took off. French poet Apollinaire and Gertrude Stein – firmly Hemingway's set – are buried here with writers Balzac, Proust, Colette and Oscar Wilde. *www.pere-lachaise.com; 16 Rue du Repos & Blvd de Ménilmontant, 20e; metro Père Lachaise or Gambetta; tel +1 43 70 70 33; 8am-6pm Mon-Fri, 8.30am-6pm Sat, 9am-6pm Sun*

07 BOULEVARD DU MONTPARNASSE

A metro ride south to the sixth arrondissement, zip up to the 59th floor of the 1970s eyesore Tour Montparnasse for a spectacular view of Paris, then dive into the mythical brasseries on Blvd du Montparnasse.

Tiny brass plaques on the tables at La Closerie des Lilas (The Lilac Enclosure) at No 171 tell you precisely where Hemingway, Picasso, Apollinaire, Man Ray, Jean-Paul Sartre and Samuel Beckett stood, sat and keeled over when drunk. Hemingway sat on a stool at the bar, famously reading Scott Fitzgerald's *The Great Gatsby* manuscript here and penning parts of his own *The Sun Also Rises*.

Consider lunch at art deco seafood temple Le Dôme at No 108, perhaps ordering freshly shucked oysters and white wine – a Hemingway staple. Red-canopied La Rotonde at No 105 and American bar Le Select (No 99), with its quintessential racing green-trimmed bistro chairs, are other 1920s brasseries Hemingway frequented.

08 THE RITZ

End with drinks amid Hemingway memorabilia at Bar Hemingway, inside the luxury Ritz hotel (1898). Hemingway drank here in the 1920s and at the end of WWII famously returned to Paris with one single intention — to liberate his favourite bar. He rocked up at the Ritz on 25 August 1944, armed and waging war, only to be told that the Nazis had long left and be turned away for carrying a weapon. Hemingway dumped his gun and downed 51 dry martinis at the bar. Order the same – in moderation. *www.ritzparis-com; 15 Place Vendôme; metro Concorde, 1e; tel +33 1 43 16 33 74; 6pm-2am*
BY NICOLA WILLIAMS

05 Hemingway and other expat writers hung out at the original Shakespeare and Company bookshop in the 1920s

WHERE TO STAY

HÔTEL D'ANGLETERRE
Upon arriving from Chicago in 1921, newlyweds Hemingway and Hadley stayed at this small St-Germain-des-Prés hotel in room 14. Period furnishings, original Louis Philippe fireplaces and the odd four-poster bed dress 26 boutique rooms. *www.hotel-dangleterre. com; 44 Rue Jacob, 6e; tel +33 1 42 60 34 72*

L'APOSTROPHE HÔTEL
This literary hotel between Jardin du Luxembourg and Montparnasse pays homage to the written word. Sixteen rooms are uber-contemporary in design. Room U (for urbain) has spray-painted graffiti tags and a skateboard ramp-shaped ceiling. *www.apostrophe-hotel. com; 3 Rue de Chevreuse, 6e; tel +33 1 56 54 31 31.*

WHERE TO EAT & DRINK

POLIDOR
Feast on Hemingway's Paris at this St-Germain crèmerie with 1845 decor, traditional French cuisine and famous tarte tatin (upside-down apple pie). *Midnight in Paris* fans will recognise it as the place Owen Wilson's character meets Hemingway who dined here in his day. *www.polidor.com; 41 Rue Monsieur le Prince, 6e; tel +33 1 43 26 95 34; noon-2.30pm & 7pm-12.30am Mon-Sat, to 11pm Sun*

HARRY'S NEW YORK BAR
Inventor of the Bloody Mary and Sidecar, this old-world cocktail bar from 1911 is a Parisian landmark. Hemingway drank here, often sparring at a nearby gym before indulging in alcoholic refreshment at the mahogany bar, tended by white-blazered bar staff. *www.harrysbar.fr; 5 Rue Daunou, 2e; tel +33 1 42 61 71 14; noon-2am Mon-Sat, 4pm-2am Sun*

CELEBRATIONS

PARIS EN TOUTES LETTRES
Get acquainted with the city's contemporary literati at this annual literary festival, organised in November by La Maison de la Poesie. The 10-day fest includes readings and lectures, poetry concerts, live rap, guided literature-themed walks and so on at various artsy venues. *(www.maisondelapoesie paris.com)*

France
PREHISTORIC ART OF THE DORDOGNE

Surrounded by medieval fortified villages, 14 caves strung across one valley shelter possibly the world's finest collection of prehistoric art from the end of the last ice age.

It seems apt that some of the world's most ancient, spectacular and strangely compelling art galleries are squirrelled away in dark, dank caves in an end-of-the-earth valley in the deeply rural Dordogne, southwest France.

At the end of the last ice age, between 20,000 BC and 10,000 BC, when much of northern Europe still slumbered beneath vast glaciers and ice sheets, the nomadic Cro-Magnon people roamed the Vallée de la Vézère (Vézère Valley). A far cry from the verdant green valley it is today, this 200km stretch was hostile, dangerous territory. It was bitterly cold. Vegetation was scant. Ferocious cave lions, woolly rhinoceros and tusked mammoths kept intruders at bay.

Tracking the migration routes of their prey, it was here that Cro-Magnons hunted and foraged for food — reindeer, bison, berries and birds. Being skilled

NEED TO KNOW
We recommend two or three days for this scenic countryside trail; a car is essential for getting around the rural areas.

craftsmen, they constructed temporary tipi-like shelters on the banks of the Vézère River and upcycled their hunted or salvaged spoils.

Then there was art. Using primitive oil lamps fuelled with reindeer fat and a juniper branch for light, Cro-Magnon artists created a bewitching menagerie of horses and mammoths, ibex, aurochs, bulls and stags deep inside limestone caves pocketing the valley. These undeniably complex, sophisticated and at times sinister works are among the world's finest prehistoric art — yet to this day no one knows what they mean or why they were created.

Today, 14 decorated caves in the valley are Unesco sites, an easy road trip from Bordeaux, Bergerac or Brive Vallée de la Dordogne airports. And then, of course, there are the Dordogne's medieval villages and gourmet food markets to visit, and the prestigious vineyards and age-old wine cellars of Bordeaux and Bergerac to explore...

01 © Trave Pictures / Alamy & © ADAGP Paris and DACS, London

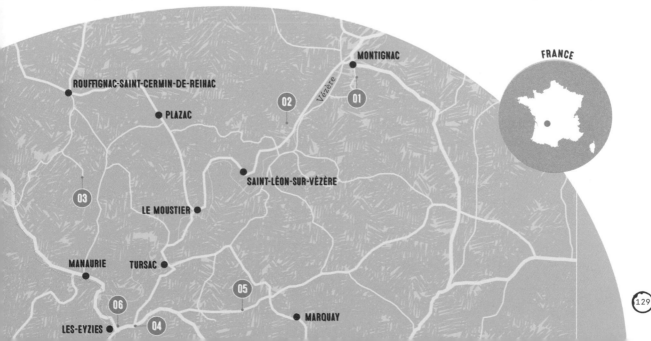

FRANCE

MONTIGNAC

ROUFFIGNAC-SAINT-CERNIN-DE-REILHAC

PLAZAC

Vézère

02

01

SAINT-LÉON-SUR-VÉZÈRE

03

LE MOUSTIER

MANAURIE   TURSAC

05

06

MARQUAY

LES-EYZIES

04

‘Descend into the chilly depths of the cave where colourful herds gallop across dazzling-white, calcite walls’

01 LASCAUX CENTRE INTERNATIONAL DE L'ART PARIÉTAL

Shut your eyes, cross your fingers and hurl yourself off the edge of the soft limestone rock into the dark abyss below — or shift the joystick sideways and skip the terrifying six-metre jump that Cro-Magnon man took to reach the cramped, pitch-black cavern hidden deep down below.

Otherwise known as the Shaft, it was here, in the most secret and inaccessible part of the world-famous Grotte de Lascaux (Lascaux Cave) that early artists created one of their most baffling paintings: a human figure with what appears to be a bird's head and an erection, standing between a bison and a bird. Thanks to virtual-reality stations and other fantastic, interactive digital technology at Montignac's stunning Centre International de l'Art Pariétal, it is at last possible to explore the Grotte de Lascaux — the Sistine Chapel of prehistoric art — in its entirety.

The original cave, discovered 100m further up the same hill by four teenage boys and their dog in 1940, was shut to visitors in 1963. A replica of a small section of the cave (Lascaux II) opened in 1983, but it is the titanic Centre International de l'Art Pariétal – a sensational piece of contemporary architecture chiselled into the hillside, unveiled in December 2016 — that reproduces the entire cave to scale. Galleries too hazardous to reach on foot can be experienced virtually.

Guided tours open on the rooftop with panoramic views of the Vézère Valley. Then descend into the chilly depths of the labyrinthine cave where colourful herds of horses, stags, aurochs and clashing bulls — many larger than life-size — gallop across dazzling-white, calcite walls. With

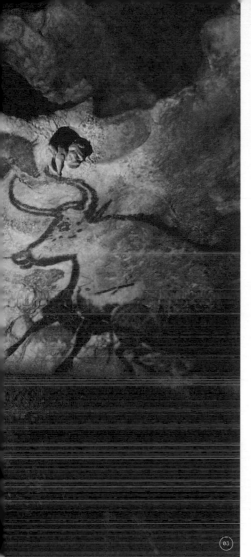

01 The caves at Les Eyzies, where Cro-Magnon specimens were discovered in 1868

02 Les Eyzies-de-Tayac-Sireuil's prehistory museum

03 Cave replica at Lascaux II

04 & 05 The new Centre International de l'Art Pariétal, showcasing Grotte Lascaux

the aid of a touchscreen tablet, key paintings are analysed in greater depth in the subsequent Atelier de Lascaux, a light and airy space with interactive painting stations.

Continue to the Théâtre de l'Art Pariétal and 3D cinema to watch films on cave research, and end in the Galerie de l'Imaginiare where you can create your own electronic gallery of cave-inspired art. Allow a good two to three hours in all for your visit. *www.lascaux.fr; tel +33 5 53 50 99 10; Ave de Lascaux, 24290 Montignac; 8.30am-8pm Jul & Aug, shorter hrs rest of yr*

02 LE PARC DU THOT

After lunch, mingle with extinct prehistoric species — the formidable cave bear that towered 2.5m tall and the mammoth with its spiral ivory tusks included — at the Thot animal park, a 15-minute drive south of Montignac. With its vast outdoor spaces populated with Tarpan horses, deer, ibex, European bison and other real-life descendants of the prehistoric animals depicted by the Cro-Magnons, Le Thot is the perfect partner to Lascaux.

End the day with a hands-on *atelier* (workshop): forge an engraving blade from a stone flint or learn to paint using ancient ice-age techniques. Cro-Magnons made the colour black from manganese dioxide and mixed vivid yellows, reds, oranges and browns from natural ochres. Pigments were applied to the rough rock using handmade brushes, fingers or wads of animal fur. They cut stencils in animal hide and tree bark to create sharp outlines, then coloured the empty space by blowing paint through the hollowed-out bone of a bird: spray-painting! *www.semitour.com; tel +33 5 53 50 70 40; 24290 Thonac; 10am-7pm daily Jul & Aug, to 6pm May, Jun, Sep & Oct, shorter hrs Tue-Sun rest of yr*

03 GROTTE DE ROUFFIGNAC

Day two, the mystery deepens 21km west along the Vézère Valley in Thonac. Here, plunging 8km into the limestone earth, is the huge tri-level cave of Rouffignac — discovered in 1956 and decorated with 254 different etchings and black-contour paintings (no colour here) by prehistoric man. These, like Lascaux, point to the cave's use as a sanctuary for religious, spiritual or cultish rituals.

With their crude round-bellied horses, sinister human figures and realistic bisons painted in both summer-red and winter-black coats, just what exactly were the Cro-Magnons trying to say? Why didn't these detail-sharp artists portray the sun and the moon, stars, plants and small animals too?

Board an electric train to explore a 1km maze of richly decorated galleries. Highlights include the frieze of 10 mammoths in procession, one of the largest cave paintings ever discovered, and the awe-inspiring Great Ceiling, with more than 65 animal figures. Nests of long-extinct cave bears inject bags of creepy, prehistoric atmosphere. *www.grottederouffignac.fr; tel +33 5 53 05 41 71; 24580 Rouffignac-St-Cernin-de-Reilhac; 9-11.30am & 2-6pm Jul & Aug, 10-11.30am & 2-5pm Apr-Jun, Sep & Oct, closed Nov-Mar*

04 GROTTE DE FONT-DE-GAUME

Reserve your 45-minute guided tour well in advance at this rare and valuable site, 20 minutes south of Rouffignac along the quiet D31 and D47. This is the only cave in the valley to showcase original two-tone or polychrome paintings that is still open to the public.

Visits climax in the Chapelle des Bisons, a mesmerising montage of courting reindeer and cantering horses captured in motion. *www.sites-les-eyzies.fr; tel +33 5 53 06 86 00; 4 Ave des Grottes, 24620 Les Eyzies-de-Tayac-Sireuil; guided tours 9.30am-5.30pm Sun-Fri mid-May-mid-Sep, 9.30am-12.30pm & 2-5.30pm Sun-Fri mid-Sep-mid-May*

05 ABRI DU CAP BLANC

While most of the Vézère Valley's caves contain engravings and paintings, unusually, this rock shelter — 7km east of Font-de-Gaume —

07 © imageBROKER / Alamy

only contains evocatively carved sculptures, shaped using simple flint tools some 14,000 years ago. Enjoy horses and bison galloping across the rock as the guide plays the flashlight across the contours of the 40m rock frieze.

Purchase tickets well in advance online or try your luck on the day back at the Grotte de Font-de-Gaume ticket office. *www.eyzies.monuments-nationaux. fr; tel +33 5 53 06 86 00; 24620 Marquay; guided tours 10am-6pm Sun-Fri mid-May–mid-Sep, 10am-12.30pm & 2-5.30pm Sun-Fri mid-Sep–mid-May*

06 MUSÉE NATIONAL DE PRÉHISTOIRE

Completely and utterly puzzled? Backtrack 9km west to the small riverside town of Les Eyzies-de-Tayac-Sireuil to hunt for answers at this fantastic, state-of-the-art prehistory museum inside a striking concrete edifice wedged dramatically in ancient limestone cliffs. *www.musee-prehistoire-eyzies.fr; tel +33 5 53 06 45 65; 1 Rue du Musée, Les Eyzies-de-Tayac-Sireuil; 9.30am-6.30pm daily Jul & Aug, shorter hrs Wed-Mon only rest of yr*
BY NICOLA WILLIAMS

07 A medieval street in Montignac

08 Thonac castle, near the Grotte de Rouffignac

WHERE TO STAY
LE LASCAUX
Ten contemporary rooms are bang on the money at this two-star, quintessentially French village inn with candy-striped awning and skittles, croquet and other traditional wooden games to play in the pretty back garden. There's a restaurant, too. *hotel-lascaux.jimdo.com; tel +33 5 53 51 82 81; 109 Ave Jean Jaurès, 24290 Montignac*

LA LICORNE
Guests are warmly welcome by hosts Isabelle and Hervé Tourneur at this enchanting five-room maison d'hôtes, 6km from Montignac. The traditional gold-stone property has a heated pool and serves scrumptious homemade evening meals around a shared table. *licorne-lascaux.com; tel +33 5 53 50 77 77; Le Bourg, 24290 Valojoulx*

WHERE TO EAT & DRINK
HOSTELLERIE LA ROSERAIE
Dining on the summer terrace of this bourgeois 19th-century mansion, framed by rose gardens and palm-fringed pool, is idyllic. Feast on local seasonal produce and pat yourself on the back for bagging a spot at Montignac's finest table. *www.laroseraie-hotel.com; tel +33 5 53 50 53 92; 11 Place des Armes; 7.30-9pm Fri-Wed, noon-2.30pm Sun Apr-Oct*

LE BISTRO DES GLYCINES
Foie gras, *confit de canard* (preserved duck), snails and guinea fowl find their way into the open-plan kitchen of this stylish lunchtime bistro, inside Les Eyzies' top posh pad. *www.les-glycines-dordogne.com; tel +33 5 53 06 97 07; 4 Ave de Laugerie, 24620 Les Eyzies-de-Tayac-Sireuil; noon-2pm Wed-Sat Jan-mid-Nov*

CELEBRATIONS
FESTIVAL CULTURES AUX COEURS
World music takes to the stage and streets in Montignac during this annual, a six-day festival that transforms the otherwise rural, slow-paced village into a vibrant melting pot of art, dance and music from every corner of the globe. *(www.festivalde montignac.fr)*

01

France

PICASSO ON THE RIVIERA

The Spanish artist didn't move to France's Riviera until he was in his 60s, but its influence on him was immense and Picasso's presence can still be felt in the chic villages and ports.

With a luminosity and intensity of light unknown elsewhere, the Impressionists and 20th-century artists were naturally drawn to the French Riviera (Côte d'Azur), a region of dazzling azure-blue skies and seductive seaside landscapes on the Mediterranean coast in France's hot south.

Paul Cézanne (1839-1906) was bewitched by the extraordinary radiance and chameleon nature of Montagne Sainte Victoire, immortalising the mountain near his native Aix-en-Provence time and again on canvas. An ageing Pierre-Auguste Renoir (1841-1919) was lured to the Riviera by its warm sunny climate, considered the cure of all ills, including his own arthritis. Pointillist Paul Signac (1863-1935) sailed into the quaint fishing port of Saint Tropez in 1892 and never looked back. And fauvist Henri Matisse (1869-1954) spent his most creative years lapping up the brilliant sunlight and vivacity of palm-fringed shores around Nice. It was no coincidence that Queen Victoria wintered in this same elegant seaside resort. English nobility adored the Riviera in the 1890s, but only in winter darling – the crazy notion of a summer season would not take off for another 30 years.

It was against the backdrop of this phenomenal artistic and cultural heritage that Pablo Picasso (1881-1973) moved permanently to the Riviera in 1946 – fresh from Paris and hand-in-hand with new lover and muse Françoise Gilot, 40 years his junior. The unorthodox Spanish artist was already in his mid-60s but the influence this sun-drenched part of France had on him was immense.

Picasso masterpieces pepper the Riviera's flagship art museums – MAMAC in Nice, Saint Tropez's Musée de l'Annonciade, Fondation Maeght in St-Paul-de-Vence. But it is this coastal trail of dedicated collections, all within easy reach of Nice, that enables art lovers to experience first-hand that same intoxicating Riviera charm that inspired one of the 20th century's greatest artists.

NEED TO KNOW
Two or three days cover this trip, which is easiest by car but feasible using a pre-planned combo of bus and train.

Musée Picasso, Antibes

① MUSÉE PICASSO

No single address screams Picasso quite like this spectacular chateau looking out to sea in Antibes, a fashionable port with sculpture-studded ramparts and uber-chic beach life, 30km south of Nice.

Monaco's Grimaldi family lived here in the 14th century and in 1925 the chateau became the town museum, albeit a museum sufficiently vast and void of exhibits in August 1946 for Picasso to be offered studio space in it. Picasso leapt at the chance. He sent for art materials from Paris, salvaged wood and boat paint from fishermen on the quays in Antibes, and swiftly moved into the medieval guards hall, where he worked with ferocious new zeal for two months.

'A collection of black-and-white snapshots in the history museum in the priory show a bare-chested Picasso at work in his studio'

The 23 paintings and 44 drawings he produced — all of which he gave to Antibes on the proviso they remain forever in the town — form the backbone of today's riveting Picasso Museum. Mythical beasts prance across centrepiece *Joie de Vivre* (1946), evoking the mythology of the ancient Greek city of Antipolis (Antibes). Sea urchins in *Ulysses and the Sirens* (1946) were inspired by the spiny, green-violet sea creatures

Picasso feasted on with wife Françoise at a simple cafe in Golfe-Juan. *Château Grimaldi, Place Mariejol, Antibes; tel +33 4 92 90 54 20; 10am-6pm Tue-Sun mid-Jun-mid-Sep, 10am-1pm & 2-6pm rest of yr*

② PLAGE DE LA GAROUPE

Picasso's love affair with the Riviera took off during *les années folles* (the 1920s 'crazy years') on Plage de la Garoupe, 4km down the coast from

01 A sea of umbrellas on fashionable Plage de la Garoupe

02 Outside the Musée Picasso, Antibes

03 Picasso's one-time Cannes home, La Californie

04 Cycling the chic village of Mougins

03

Antibes, many years before he moved there. The plage is a relentlessly popular sandy beach, but it wouldn't be what it is today if it hadn't been famously raked of seaweed by American musician Cole Porter and artist Gerald Murphy in 1922 to host a revolutionary beach party.

Murphy persuaded local hotelier Antoine Sella at Hôtel du Cap to open for summer 1923 and invited Picasso to the party. Picasso travelled down by train from Paris with his first wife, Russian ballerina Olga, and their two-year-old son Paolo. They had a ball and life on the Riviera was never the same again: the summer season was born.

Follow the rocky coastal path for 3km along Cap d'Antibes' southern tip. Riddled with steep steps and

the occasional scary drop, there is no finer lookout on the rugged coastline here — a Picasso-admired masterpiece of nature.

⓸ MUSÉE DE LA CÉRAMIQUE

On day two, motor 10km inland to Vallauris, the small potters' town where Picasso met ceramicists Suzanne and Georges Ramié from the Madoura pottery and subsequently dabbled in ceramics. Picasso threw pots, plates and vases emblazoned with goats, owls and nymphs while Françoise cared for their two young children at the family villa in Vallauris — home from 1948 until 1955.

On main street Ave Georges Clemenceau, push part the tourist galleries and rainbow of shiny glazed

wares, displayed on pavement terraces like spilled candy, to reach the town's Renaissance chateau. Inside, the Musée de la Céramique showcases several of the 4000 ceramics Picasso produced during this period.
Place de la Libération, Vallauris; tel +33 4 93 64 71 83; 10am-12.15pm & 2-6pm Wed-Mon, to 5pm mid-Sep—mid-Jun

⓸ WAR & PEACE

War — a haunting figure brandishing blood-smeared sword and sack of skulls — looms large in *La Guerre et La Paix* (1952), Picasso's most monumental work, plastering the barrel-vaulted stone walls of the former chapel in Château de Vallauris.

Dramatic and disturbing in equal measure, this political composition

was painted on plywood panels in the secrecy of Picasso's Vallauris studio on Rue des Grands Augustins. Identify the subliminal visage of muse Françoise, looming large above frolicking children, a white-winged horse and joyous dancing nymphs. Less than a decade on, Picasso had a new muse: Jacqueline Roque, whom he quietly wed in Vallauris town hall in 1961. *Place de la Libération, Vallauris; tel +33 4 93 64 71 83; 10am-12.15pm & 2-6pm Wed-Mon, to 5pm mid-Sep-mid-Jun*

05 LE SUQUET, CANNES

Follow Picasso 6km south along the D803 to showbiz Cannes. Strut the length of glitzy boardwalk La Croisette, and head uphill into the historic quarter of Le Suquet, home to Picasso from 1955 until 1961. The coastal panorama — captured in the appropriately all-blue *Le Baie de Cannes* (1958) — from his hilltop villa was sensational. When a new-build blocked his view at La Californie (22 Ave Coste Belle), he moved.

06 MUSÉE DE LA PHOTOGRAPHIE ANDRÉ VILLERS

Motor 7.5km north inland to Mougins, an utterly chic medieval village that Picasso first discovered in 1935 with lover Dora Marr and where he lived with final love Jacqueline Roque from 1961 until his death in 1973. Candid black-and-white photographs of the charismatic artist — shirtless in his studio, at play with his children, sitting at the kitchen table — hang on whitewashed walls inside the small Photography Museum. Most are the work of French photographer André Villers, who met Picasso in 1953. *Rue de l'Église, Mougins; tel +33 4 93 75 85 67; 10am-12.30pm & 2-7pm Tue-Sun, to 6pm mid-Sep-mid-Jun*

07 CHAPELLE NOTRE DAME DE VIE

From the photography museum it is a mellow 1.8km walk (or 4km drive) to this 17th-century chapel and priory with centurion cypress alley. Stillborn babies were traditionally brought here to be baptised. Picasso was captivated by the place and in 1961 he bought the neighbouring villa. A collection of black-and-white snapshots in the history

museum inside the priory show a bare-chested Picasso at work in his studio inside the villa (today privately owned).

Burials were forbidden in private gardens in Mougins so upon the death of 92-year-old Picasso in 1973, his body was laid to rest in the grounds of 17th-century Château de Vauvenargues (nearby, but closed to the public). Picasso bought the chateau in 1958 primarily for its much-cherished location – in the foothills of Montagne Sainte Victoire, the mountain immortalised by his lifelong master and artistic father, Cézanne. *Chemin de la Chapelle, Mougins; tel +33 4 92 92 50 08; 10am-12.30pm & 2-7pm daily Jul & Aug, Sat & Sun May, Jun & Sep, 10am-4pm Sun Oct-Apr* **BY NICOLA WILLIAMS**

05 Looking out to sea towards Antibes' historic port

06 Musée de la Céramique entrance, Vallauris

WHERE TO STAY

HÔTEL DU CAP-EDEN ROC
Picasso summered here in 1923 and the guest book is hardcore A-list. Mythical and magical in equal measure, this luxurious Cap d'Antibes hotel is the ultimate in French Riviera pampering and celebrity hobnobbing. Dress to kill. *www.hotel-du-cap-eden-roc.com; tel +33 4 93 61 39 01; Blvd JF Kennedy, Antibes*

LA MAISON DU FRÊNE
For artistic inspiration with an affordable price tag, check into this boutique maison d'hôtes in artsy Vence. The 18th-century house with four whimsical suites is sprinkled with modern art collected by owner Thierry, Picasso pastiches included. *www.lamaisondufrene. com; tel +33 4 93 24 37 83; 1 Place du Frêne, Vence*

WHERE TO EAT & DRINK

LA COLOMBE D'OR
The Golden Dove, 5km south of Vence, opened in 1920 as a simple cafe where owner Paul Roux fed struggling artists in exchange for a painting. A priceless art collection that includes originals by Matisse, Renoir, Chagall and Picasso decorates the legendary hotel-restaurant today. *www.la-colombe-dor. com; tel +33 4 9332 80 02; St-Paul de Vence*

PLAGE DE LA GAROUPE
Pop yourself into Picasso's *Baigneurs à la Garoupe* (1957) tableau with a bathe and lunch on the artist's favourite sandy beach. Pick from excellent-value Le Rocher, with swooning sea view, or Le César on private Plage Keller with white-tablecloth dining, valet service and pontoon with chaises longues. *Chemin de la Garoupe, Antibes*

CELEBRATIONS

VALLAURIS
In mid-July proud locals in Vallauris celebrate their favourite artist with fireworks, street parties and inevitable art exhibitions during the Vallauris Fête Picasso. In even-numbered years, the town marks the opening of the Biennale Internationale de Céramique de Vallauris — an international ceramic fair attracting competing artists from all over the globe.

Greece

ARTISTIC ATHENS OVER A MILLENNIUM

Antiquities and emerging art collide in the Greek capital, where temples symbolising ancient artistic perfection are enthroned above graffiti-splashed city streets.

Ancient and modern, with equal measures of grit and grace, busy Athens is a heady mix of iconic art history and contemporary cultural edginess. Throughout the city, iconic Greek monuments mingle with first-rate museums jammed with priceless art. Meanwhile, modern-day Athens serves as the focal point for the current Greek art scene, with myriad contemporary art galleries and performance spaces showcasing emerging and established local artists.

Inhabited since Neolithic times (4000–3000 BC), the historic centre of Athens is a veritable open-air museum, and the city's present-day cultural and social life takes place amid these ancient landmarks, merging past and present. The magnificent Acropolis rises above the sprawling metropolis and has stood witness to the city's many transformations. Pericles, ruler from 461 BC to 429 BC, transformed the city during the period known as Athens' golden age — the pinnacle of the

NEED TO KNOW
This three-day trail is easiest by foot and metro in central Athens; you'll need the ferry to get out to Hydra Island.

classical era. Most of the monuments on the Acropolis today date from this period. Drama and literature flourished then due to such luminaries as Aeschylus, Sophocles and Euripides. The sculptors Pheidias and Myron and the historians Herodotus, Thucydides and Xenophon also lived during this time.

Today, you'll wander spectacularly graffiti adorned streets combining pointed messages with brilliant flights of artistic fancy, and stop in at spaces dedicated to showing top visual and creative art. While you're perusing the city's rich artistic offerings, you'll also be able to partake in Athens' stylish restaurants, sophisticated shops and hip hotels.

The surrounding region holds excellent art and antiquities as well, and a day trip across the sparkling Saronic Gulf to the island of Hydra combines an historic car-free stone village with summertime exhibitions by both local artists and international art superstars.

01 © Adrienne Pitts / Lonely Planet

'It's said that 1000 wild animals were sacrificed in the magnificent arena at Hadrian's inauguration in AD 120'

01 ACROPOLIS

Perhaps the most important ancient site in the Western world, the Acropolis is crowned by the Parthenon and stands sentinel over Athens, visible from almost everywhere in the city. Its monuments and sanctuaries of Pentelic marble gleam white in the midday light and gradually take on a honey hue as the sun sinks, while at night they stand brilliantly illuminated above Athens.

This temple complex, dedicated to the cult of Athena, once combined lavishly coloured colossal buildings and gargantuan statues, some of bronze, others of marble plated with gold and encrusted with precious stones. Major restoration programmes are continuing.

Many of the original sculptures have been moved to the Acropolis Museum. To reach it, stroll down the south slope of the Acropolis, past the enormous Odeon of Herodes Atticus, still in use as a theatre today, and the Theatre of Dionysos – the birthplace of drama. *odysseus.culture.gr; tel +30 210 321 0219; 8am-8pm Apr-Oct, to 5pm Nov-Mar, last entry 30 minutes before closing*

02 ACROPOLIS MUSEUM

This dazzling €130-million modernist museum showcases the Acropolis's surviving artistic treasures still in Greece. The museum cleverly reveals layers of history, floating over ruins of an ancient Athenian neighbourhood with the Acropolis resplendent above.

Among its beautifully presented artworks you'll find the five famous Caryatids, the maiden columns that held up the Erechtheion, the temple dedicated to Athena and Posedion (the sixth is in the British Museum). The top-floor Parthenon Gallery is the museum's crowning glory: a

01 & 03 Views
from the Acropolis,
and looking
towards the
Acropolis

02 Ancient
maidens propping
up the Parthenon

04 Graffiti on the
streets of urban
Athens

05 Plaka cafe life,
at the foot of the
Acropolis

glass atrium built in alignment with the temple — visible across the way — displaying its metopes (a series of marble panels that once adorned the façade of the temple) and the 160m-long frieze of the Panathenaic Procession.

Other exhibits include a forest of statues and bronze artefacts from temples predating the Parthenon (destroyed by the Persians). *www.theacropolismuseum.gr; tel +30 210 900 0901; Dionysiou Areopagitou 15; 8am-4pm Mon, to 8pm Tue-Sun, to 10pm Fri Apr-Oct, reduced hours Nov-Mar*

03 NATIONAL MUSEUM OF CONTEMPORARY ART

Stroll down Leoforos Andrea Syngrou to reach this temple to cutting-edge art, which inaugurated its spectacularly renovated new quarters at the former Fix Brewery in 2015.

The museum shows top-notch rotating exhibitions of Greek and international contemporary art, and its permanent exhibitions include paintings, installations and new media, as well as experimental architecture. *www.emst.gr; tel +30 211 101 9000; Kallirrois & Frantzi; 11am-7pm Tue, Wed & Fri-Sun, to 10pm Thu*

04 PANATHENAIC STADIUM

The grand Panathenaic Stadium lies between two pine-covered hills, 1.6km northeast of the National Museum, and is the embodiment of architecture as art, with its sweeping arc of harmoniously proportioned seats and perfectly oval field.

Originally built in the 4th century BC as a venue for the Panathenaic athletic contests, it's said that 1000 wild animals were sacrificed in the magnificent arena during Hadrian's inauguration in AD 120. Later, the 70,000 seats were rebuilt in Pentelic marble by Herodes Atticus.

The stadium made a stunning backdrop to the archery competition and the marathon finish during the 2004 Olympics. It's still used for concerts, public events and the annual Athens marathon. If you don't fancy hiking out here on foot, take bus 10 or 550 from the Olympiaki stop on Syngrou.
www.panathenaicstadium.gr; tel +30 210 752 2984; Leoforos Vasileos Konstantinou; 8am-7pm Mar-Oct, to 5pm Nov-Feb

05 TAF

Two kilometres northwest, in the bustling Monastiraki neighbourhood past the verdant National Gardens, lies Taf (The Art Foundation). The warren of spaces in a series of crumbling 1870s brick buildings function as art, music and theatre venues. Athens' emerging artists show their work here, and many performances and screenings are free. The central courtyard cafe fills with an eclectic young crowd. The Monastiraki quarter is also worth a wander, with its magnificent classical sites (the Ancient and Roman Agoras, Hadrian's Library) and its chintzy antique and flea market.
www.theartfoundation.gr; tel +30 210 323 8757; Normanou 5, Monastiraki metro station; noon-9pm Mon-Sat, to 7pm Sun

06 NATIONAL ARCHAEOLOGICAL MUSEUM

One of the world's most important museums, Greece's National Archaeological Museum is just a hop away on the metro and houses the finest collection of Greek antiquities: more than 11,000 items in an 8000-sq-metre, 19th-century neoclassical building.

Treasures offer a comprehensive view of Greek art from the neolithic to classical periods. The fabulous collection of Mycenaean antiquities, dating from the late Bronze Age and made from elaborately crafted gold and precious stones, are the museum's tour de force, especially the gold Mask of Agamemnon.

The Cycladic collection displays superb figurines from the 3rd and 2nd millennia BC, which inspired modern artists such as Picasso. Don't miss the Minoan frescoes from Santorini (Thira).
www.namuseum.gr; tel +30 213 214 4800; 28 Oktovriou-Patision 44, Viktoria metro station; 8am-8pm Apr-Oct, reduced hours Nov-Mar

07 GRAFFITI IN EXARHIA

The bohemian Exarhia district (abutting the Archaeological Museum to the southeast) has an alternative culture and history that sets it apart from Athens' other neighbourhoods. A hotbed of students and anarchists, its homegrown graffiti is a bold treat, mixing excellent painterly technique with sharp messaging.

Start at the Strefi Hill end of Themistokleous and simply wander the neighbourhood, looking for the latest expressions of both fancy and ire.

08 HYDRA ISLAND

Nearby Hydra is the gem of the Saronic Gulf and stands alone among Greek islands as the one free of wheeled vehicles. No cars. No scooters. Just tiny marble-cobbled lanes, exquisitely preserved stone architecture, donkeys, and clear sea.

Artists (Brice Marden, Nikos Chatzikyriakos-Ghikas, Panayiotis Tetsis), musicians (Leonard Cohen), actors and celebrities (Melina Mercouri, Sophia Loren) have all been drawn to Hydra through the years, and it remains an art powerhouse.

Every June to August, collector Dakis Joannou's Deste Foundation (www.deste.gr) hosts an exhibit at the island's former slaughterhouse, featuring one international contemporary art superstar. Both he and fellow collector Pauline Karpidas are part-time Hydra residents. Pauline similarly fills a gallery on the port with a major artist's work each summer, and the Melina Mercouri Gallery and the Historical Archives Museum host ever-changing exhibitions. The ferry journey over to Hydra takes about 1¾ hours from Piraeus port.
www.hsw.gr
BY ALEXIS AVERBUCK

06 The perfectly proportioned Panathenaic Stadium

07 Ancient art is the backbone of the ultra-contemporary Acropolis Museum

08 Hydra Island is something of a timewarp: new construction on the island is banned

WHERE TO STAY

ELECTRA PALACE
In the charming, historic quarter of Plaka, this smart hotel is one for romantics — have breakfast under the Acropolis on your balcony (in higher-end rooms) and dinner in the chic rooftop restaurant. Rooms are buffered from the sounds of the city streets. *www.electrahotels.gr; tel +30 210 337 0000; Navarhou Nikodimou 18*

HERA HOTEL
This elegant boutique hotel, a short walk from the Acropolis, has been totally rebuilt – but the formal interior design is in keeping with the lovely neoclassical facade. The rooftop restaurant and bar have spectacular views. *www.herahotel.gr; tel +30 210 923 6682; Falirou 9*

WHERE TO EAT & DRINK

CAFÉ AVYSSINIA
Hidden away in the middle of Monastiraki's flea market, this bohemian restaurant specialising in mezedhes gets top marks for atmosphere, food and friendly service. There's live Greek music on weekends and Acropolis views upstairs. *Tel +30 210 321 7047; Kynetou 7*

FUNKY GOURMET
Nouveau gastronomy meets fresh Mediterranean ingredients at this two-Michelin-star restaurant. Elegant lighting, refinement and sheer joy in food make this a top stop. *www.funkygourmet.com; tel +30 210 524 2727; Paramithias 3, cnr Salaminas*

CELEBRATIONS

HELLENIC FESTIVAL
The ancient theatre at Epidavros and Athens' Odeon of Herodes Atticus are the headline venues of Greece's annual cultural festival held June to August, featuring a top line-up of local and international music, dance and theatre. *(www.greekfestival.gr)*

ART-ATHINA
Athens' annual three-day contemporary-art fair (usually in May) showcases a broad spectrum of art from Greek and international galleries, with satellite exhibitions held around town. *(www.art-athina.gr)*

01

Hungary
ART NOUVEAU BUDAPEST

Visionary designers and craftsmen once transformed the Hungarian capital into one of Europe's most fashionable artistic centres. Now, many landmarks have been restored.

Budapest is a city that takes the breath away, divided and defined by the mighty Danube river. On one side lies stately Buda, marked by monumental royal castles, museums and medieval churches. On the other bank is Pest, the downtown life and soul of this lively metropolis, and a paradise of sumptuous art nouveau architecture.

From the 1890s till the beginning of WWI, this cosmopolitan, flamboyant city was one of the most fashionable destinations in Europe. In 1896, the nation celebrated the Magyar Millennium — a thousand years of proud history — that sparked a building spree, transforming Budapest into the capital of art nouveau architecture, a 'New Art' also known as Jugendstil, Liberty style and Secession across other parts of Europe. Inspired by nature, art nouveau was typified by organic design using flowing curves — it was an art form for a confident new world bravely approaching the 20th

NEED TO KNOW
Budapest is great for walking and biking, but also has excellent tram and metro networks. Book a four-day stay.

century, encompassing not just architecture but all aspects of decorative arts in daily life.

As well as visionary designers such as Ödön Lechner, Hungary was blessed with a goldmine of highly skilled artisans who could produce all the decorative arts and crafts that make art nouveau so unique: Zsolnay tiles and ceramics, Miksa Róth stained glass, and Ödön Faragó's furniture, plus metal workers, sculptors and painters. At the 1900 Paris World Fair, more than 1500 Hungarian craftsmen presented their art nouveau creations.

Today, Budapest is booming again, with brilliant craft beer bars, inventive food and a nightlife scene that includes the unique Ruin Pubs — anarchic venues that transform abandoned factories and crumbling mansions. What's more, the city's landmark art nouveau buildings have come to life again after decades of neglect under the Communist regime, and a tour of the city reveals them restored to their former glory.

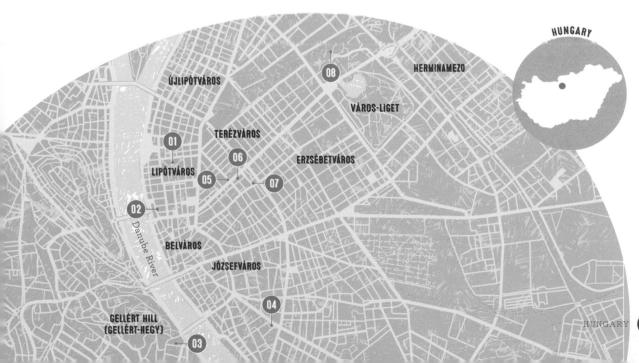

HUNGARY

ÚJLIPÓTVÁROS

08

HERMINAMEZŐ

VÁROS-LIGET

TERÉZVÁROS

01

06

LIPÓTVÁROS

05

ERZSÉBETVÁROS

07

02

Danube River

BELVÁROS

JÓZSEFVÁROS

04

GELLÉRT HILL
(GELLÉRT-HEGY)

03

01 BEDŐ HOUSE

Bedő House sits on an elegant street by the Hungarian Parliament, a neighbourhood filled with landmark secessionist buildings. Designed by Emil Vidor in 1903 for the wealthy Bedő family, this is the perfect setting for a museum dedicated to Hungary's unique contribution to art nouveau.

The building's form is influenced by the great Belgian architect Victor Horta and would not look out of place in Gaudí's Barcelona. But the interiors are pure Budapest art nouveau, and there's a goldmine collection of furniture cabinets decorated with swirling floral motifs; sculptures and paintings of women with flowing

locks dramatically symbolising the seasons; and porcelain and glassworks inspired both by the exotic graphism of Japanese design and traditional Hungarian folk patterns.
www.magyarszecessziohaza.hu; tel +36 1 2694622; 3 Honvéd Utca; 10am-5pm Mon-Sat

02 GRESHAM PALACE

There are half a dozen extravagant art nouveau hotels dotted around Budapest, but nothing compares to the magnificent Gresham Palace, looking out across the Danube, just 10 minutes' walk from Bedő House.

One of the world's finest examples of art nouveau, the Gresham was

built in 1906 by English assurance company Gresham Life. It hired local architect Zsigmond Quittner, who called upon the finest Hungarian decorative artists, painters and craftsmen to create the interiors.

Today the Gresham has been totally restored to its old opulence as a luxury hotel, and the restaurants, bar and spectacular glass-domed entrance hall are accessible to the public.
www.fourseasons.com/budapest; tel +36 1 2686000; 5 Széchenyi István Tér

03 GELLÉRT BATHS AND SPA

Cross the Danube by the mighty Chain Bridge to the medieval Buda side and take tram 19 to Gellért Hill.

'Bedő House is influenced by Belgian architect Victor Horta and would not look out of place in Gaudí's Barcelona'

01 Budapest's Museum of Applied Arts, clad in brilliant Zsolnay tiles

02 Buda castle, at the heart of the city's medieval Castle District

03 Photographer Mai Manó's art nouveau house, now a museum

04 The sweeping organic staircase at Gerlóczy Rooms De Lux

The ancient spa here dates back to the 13th century, but today's hotel — and what was Europe's first modern thermal baths — was built in 1918 in a riot of late art nouveau style. It's as popular today as ever.

The main hall is adorned by 10 meticulously designed stained-glass windows, the steam-filled baths and fountains are decorated with turquoise tiles, swirling mosaics, and angelic statues, and the glass-roofed pool is lined with elaborately sculpted marble pillars. A visit to the baths is unforgettable. *www.gellertbath.com; tel +36 1 4666166; 4 Kelenhegyi Utca; 6am-8pm*

MUSEUM OF APPLIED ARTS

Tram 47 crosses back over the Danube to Kálvin Sq, a few minutes' walk from the unmistakable green- and yellow-tiled domes of the Museum of Applied Arts, the creation of Budapest's founding father of art nouveau, Ödön Lechner.

The palatial museum was built in 1896 for the millennium celebrations to showcase Hungary's acclaimed art objects, design and furnishings. Its stunning façade, covered in bewitching patterns of golden-green Zsolnay tiles, contrasts with the stark white interiors. But it is exactly these subdued interiors that allow the incredible collection of everything from furniture to metalwork, ceramics to glassware, textiles, jewellery and garments to stand out for themselves.

Zsolnay tiles, an art form in themselves, are a hallmark of Hungarian art nouveau. Zsolnay was a local ceramics manufacturer that treated its tiles with revolutionary eosin, firstly making them frost-resistant and perfect to decorate art nouveau buildings, but also adding a unique luminosity to the glaze of its colours — look out for them around the city. *www.imm.hu, tel +36 1 4565107; 33 Üllői Utca; 10am-6pm Tue-Sun*

03-04 © John Brunton

(05)

(06)

05 © Sarah Coghill / Lonely Planet; 06 © Will Sanders / Lonely Planet

05 MAI MANÓ HOUSE

Three metro stops away near Oktogon station, the ornate tiled facade of Mai Manó House stands out on a side street off Andrássy Av. Mai Manó commissioned the building of this splendid eight-storey studio-house in 1893, just before being appointed Imperial and Royal Photographer. He used the greatest art nouveau designers and craftsmen, who painted frescoes, carved staircases, designed maiolica terracotta and stained glass.

Today, Manó's studios — where he did most of his photography work until his death in 1917 — have been perfectly restored, and the house is now a prestigious photography museum, with ground-floor cafe, gallery and bookshop. *www.maimano.hu; tel +36 473 2666; 20 Nagymező Utca; 2pm-7pm Mon-Fri, 11am-7pm Sat & Sun*

06 ALEXANDRA BOOK CAFÉ

Across Andrássy Av stands one of Budapest's most dramatic art nouveau buildings, the Párizsi Nagyáruház — Budapest's first luxury department store, opened in 1910. The opulent Párizsi is now home to a bookshop with a hidden secret on its first floor — a literary cafe that is better known by its original name, the Lotz Hall.

This lustrous salon, once a palatial ballroom, is decorated with glittering chandeliers and flamboyant ceiling frescoes by renowned artist Károly Lotz, after whom the hall takes its name. Today, shoppers come here to take a break with hot chocolate and *sachertorte* (chocolate cake), students use the free wifi, and businessmen read newspapers relaxing in leather armchairs. *www.lotzterem.hu; tel +36 1 4615835; 39 Andrássy Utca; 10am-10pm Mon-Sat*

07 LISZT MUSIC ACADEMY

At the back of the Párizsi store runs Franz Liszt St, lined with funky restaurants and bars. At its end, a dignified statue of Hungary's greatest composer surrounded by cherubic musical angels dominates the lavish façade of the immense 1900s academy that bears his name.

Going to listen to a classical concert inside the spectacular auditorium makes for an unforgettable

experience. But for those without tickets, it is still worth pushing open the main doors to get a glimpse of the ceramics, stylised mosaics, symbolic tableaux and graphic stained-glass windows decorating the entrance. *www.zeneakademia.hu; tel +36 1 4624600; 8 Liszt Ferenc tér; concerts every day, guided tour 1.30pm*

08 BUDAPEST ZOO & BOTANICAL GARDEN

The most surprising art nouveau venue is a short metro hop away, by the landmark Széchenyi Baths. By Városliget, two elephant statues and an elaborate azure arch and dome mark the entrance to one of the world's oldest zoos.

Founded in 1866, it is the pavilions built in the early 1900s that stand out, especially the glass-and-metal Palm House designed by Károly Kós with Gustave Eiffel's company in Paris, and the infamous Elephant House. The latter's domed roofs and minaret adorned with turquoise tiles were modelled on a Turkish mosque in a not-so-subtle insult to an occupying power resented by native Hungarians. *www.zoobudapest.com; tel +36 1 2734900; 6 Állatkerti Körút; 9pm-4pm, to 6pm in summer*
BY JOHN BRUNTON

05 Opulent Alexandra Book Café in a former ballroom

06 Entrance to the Gellert baths

07 The classic art nouveau façade of Bedő House

WHERE TO STAY
LAVENDER CIRCUS HOSTEL
One of the quirkiest places in town, each of the Lavender's rooms are decorated with flea-market furniture. The walls are covered with bizarre, witty drawings by owner Ádám Szarvas, and you may find yourself with a bathroom that has a goldfish tank embedded in a window. *www.lavendercircus.com; tel +36 70 417 7763; 37 Múzeum Körút*

GERLÓCZY ROOMS DE LUX
In a shady square, a stately 1890s mansion has been transformed into a romantic boutique hotel. The ground floor houses a bustling bistro, while guests enter by a side door where a swirling art nouveau staircase topped by a stained-glass cupola climbs to reception. *www.gerloczy.hu; tel +36 1 5014000; 1 Gerlóczy Utca*

WHERE TO EAT & DRINK
NEW YORK CAFÉ
Budapest's legendary 1891 New York Café has been wonderfully restored. To soak up its rich belle époque history, grab a stool at the splendid bar

and order a chilled martini or a glass of Hungary's luscious Tokaj wine. *www.budapest.boscolo hotels.com; tel +36 1 3223849; 9 Erzsébet Körút*

GREAT MARKET HALL
One of Europe's greatest markets, this colossal red-brick hall has many art nouveau touches. Upstairs are dozens of cheap-and-cheerful buffet bars serving traditional Hungarian home cooking, from goulash soup to *lecsó* — a delicious ratatouille. *www.budapestmarkethall. com; tel +36 1 3663300; 1 Vámház Körút*

CELEBRATIONS
FŐZDEFESZT
Budapest is one of the world's craft beer capitals, epitomised by September's Főzdefeszt, a wild beer and street-food festival. *(www.fozdefeszt.hu)*

ST STEPHEN'S DAY
On 20 August Budapest celebrates St Stephen's Day, the founding of Hungary. Buda Castle and the river bank down below host a huge artisans fair, with wine and food tastings, live concerts and spectacular fireworks over the Danube.

07 © Stefano Politi Markovina / Alamy

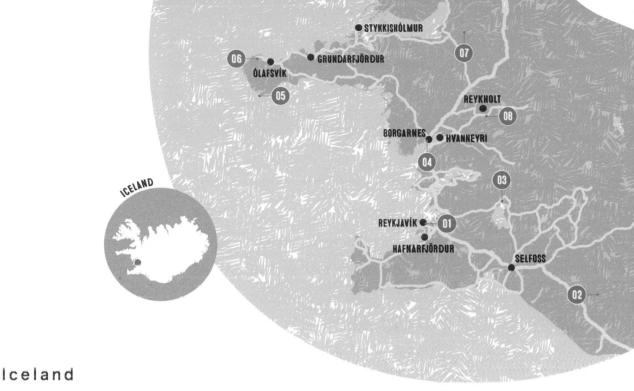

The following places are marked on the map:

STYKKISHÓLMUR
07
06
GRUNDARFJÖRÐUR
ÓLAFSVÍK
05
REYKHOLT
08
BORGARNES
HVANNEYRI
04
03
ICELAND
REYKJAVÍK
01
HAFNARFJÖRÐUR
SELFOSS
02

Iceland

IN VIKING FOOTSTEPS

The legends of Iceland's Viking forefathers are celebrated in epic literary sagas, but the tangible heritage of these infamous explorers lives on in the island's southwest.

Before the modern era, no group of people documented their history so specifically and with such fantastical detail as the original settlers of Iceland. Their tomes of stories — known locally and collectively as the Sagas — recorded elaborate family histories, delineated land claims and recounted the exploits of seafaring Vikings who battled enemies and trolls, and created the world's first parliament.

But the legacy of the great Vikings isn't just one of marauding and malice. The first individuals to arrive in Iceland, in the second half of the 9th century, were Norse men and the Celtic women they picked up in Ireland along the way.

They were highly educated and their geographic isolation spared them from the Dark Ages of the rest of Europe — while their Scandinavian brethren were waging religious battles, Icelanders were fighting the elements (think: bitter cold and boiling volcanoes) and exploring

the Arctic waters all the way to modern-day Canada. Today, a journey through southwestern Iceland reveals that the Viking world of more than a thousand years ago is still very much in tact. It's found almost everywhere you look, from the turf-house ruins on the side of the road to the old patronymic names of the new local friends you'll make along the way.

NEED TO KNOW
Give yourself three days to complete this trip at a leisurely pace. Hire a private vehicle; you'll need it for rural stops.

Celebrations surrounding the winter solstice remain deeply rooted in Norse paganism; household recipes too, like the ones for hearty rye bread baked beneath the earth by the heat of the volcanic soil, date back to the time of Odin and Thor.

And after winding through hundreds of barren lava fields and forgotten black-sand beaches you too will begin to craft your own legends of ghouls and trolls, inspired by the clefts in the rocks and the haunting splashes of frozen magma along the sea.

'According to legend,
Christopher Columbus spent a
winter on Snæfellsnes learning
from the Viking descendants'

01 REYKAVÍK 871+/-2

Start your Viking adventure in
the heart of Iceland's capital at a
museum curated around a single
10th-century longhouse.

An inspired amalgam of
archaeology and technology tells
the story of Iceland's first citizens
in a refreshingly balanced manner.
Interestingly, the museum reveals
that archaeologists have not found
any evidence of organised religion
among the first settlers.
*www.reykjavik871.is; tel +354 411
6370; Adalstræti 16, Reykjavík;
9am-8pm*

02 KELDUR

Zip along the Ring Road out of the
capital region, heading towards the
town of Vík. About 5km before the
township of Hvolsvöllur, follow the
bumpy Rte 264 inland as it traces
the Rangá river valley. Owned and
operated by the National Museum
Trust, the ruins at Keldur are true
remains from Viking times. The site's
medieval turf-roofed farm once
belonged to Ingjaldur Höskuldsson,
a major character in *Njál's Saga*,
one of Iceland's most nuanced and
brutal Viking stories — it starts as a
petty squabble between wives and
turns into a full-blown battle between
families, leading to the demise of
almost every character.
*www.thjodminjasafn.is; tel +354 530
2200; Keldur; 24hrs*

03 THINGVELLIR

Head for Rte 36 and as you curve
around a quiet glacial lake, the craggy
valley of Thingvellir will reveal itself
along the horizon. Earning a Unesco
World Heritage Site decree in 2004,
this rift-ridden area was the site of the
world's first democratic parliament,
the Althing, established in 930.

The original *lögberg*, or 'law rock'

01 Northern Lights over the Snæfellsnes peninsula

02 Sculpture of Bárður, the half troll of Viking legends, by Ragnar Kjartansson the elder (Murk), in Snæfellsjökull NP

03 The craggy valley of Thingvellir

04 A traditional turf-roof house

05 Wooden carving of *Egil's Saga* character at the Settlement Centre

is located at the bottom of the area's most prominent walk-through gorge. It was here that new laws were recited aloud to the gathering of council members: 48 voters, 96 advisers and two bishops. Very little evidence of the Althing remains, but it's a place of lonely beauty where visitors can witness the tearing apart of the continental plates.
www.thingvellir.is; tel +354 482 2660

04 SETTLEMENT CENTRE

Find the Kaldidalur Road (F550) that will take you along a gravel track beneath a haunting glacier, and when you emerge on the other side you'll pull into the small town of Borgarnes on the edge of a striking fjord.

Housed in a restored warehouse along the harbour is the Settlement Centre, which artfully recounts the details of *Egil's Saga* — Iceland's ultimate antihero story — through interesting wood carvings, dioramas and spooky stage lighting.

A second exhibit further details the history of Iceland's settlement for visitors.
www.english.landnam.is; tel +354 437 1600; Brákarbraut 13-15; 10am-9pm

05 SNÆFELLSJÖKULL NATIONAL PARK

Continue north out of town and follow Rte 54 past the haunting crater at Eldborg, which ushers you into the hallowed realm of the Snæfellsnes peninsula — a rugged arm of land dotted with ancient viking tombs and blanketed in mossy lava stone.

The southern entrance to the national park boundaries is located just beyond Hellnar, the birthplace of Gudridur Thorbjarnardóttir. The original Viking feminist, Gudridur was one of the first Vikings to reach Vinland (present-day Newfoundland

in Canada), bore the first European child in the New World (a son, Snorri), and later converted to Christianity travelling all the way to Rome to meet the Pope.

Today, a beautiful sculpture marks the site of her farm at Laugarbrekka. Follow Rte 572 down to the wild black-sand beach at Djúpalónssandur, where evidence of Gudridur's brood still exists: four 'lifting stones' lie silent on the mist-ridden shores, each one heavier than the next and meant to test the strength of aspiring seafarers. The second-lightest stone, Hálfdrættingur (meaning 'weak'), weighs 54kg — Vikings who couldn't lift the rock were deemed unfit for duty.

The visitors' centre near Hellnar has additional information about the saga history in the park, as well as maps detailing some of the most beautiful short hikes in the country. *www.ust.is/snaefellsjokull-national-park; tel +354 436 6860; Klettsbud 7, Hellisandur; 24hrs*

06 INGJALDSHOLSKIRKJA

Follow the main road, looping around the tip of the peninsula, and as you begin your travels eastward, turn off just before the village of Rif to find the church at Ingjaldshóll. The current structure happens to be the first concrete church in the world (built in 1903), but the real intrigue can be found inside: a large painting depicting Christopher Columbus's apparent visit to the area in 1477.

According to legend he spent an entire winter on the Snæfellsnes peninsula learning from the Viking descendants about safe passage to the New World, and used the information to complete his historic voyage around a decade later. *24hrs*

07 EIRIKSSTADIR

Continue along Rte 54 and as you make your way off the peninsula veer left into the region of Dalir, known as Sagaland to locals for its rich history of explorers. Here you'll find an impressive reconstruction of the farm where Eiríkur Raude (Erik the Red) and Leifur Eiríksson (Leif the Lucky) once lived and planned their expedition and settlement of Greenland.

A faint outline of the original farmstead still stands; the current structure was built using only tools and materials that would have been

available in the Viking Age. Stories of the ancient dwellers are recounted by sword brandishing guides. *www.eiriksstadir.is; tel +354 434 1118; Eiríksstadir Haukadal, 9am-6pm Jun-Aug*

06 SNORRASTOFA

As you trundle back down the Ring Road towards Reykjavik, make one final detour to the town of Reykholt for the medieval study centre, Snorrastofa, devoted to the historian and chieftain Snorri Sturluson.

Snorri is considered one of the most important figures in medieval Norse history, not least because his own historical accounts are considered a cornerstone of this period of Norse history in Iceland. During his time in Reykholt, Snorri penned the *Heimskringla* (a history of Norwegian kings) and the *Prose Edda* (a textbook of medieval Norse poetry), and is thought to have written down *Egil's Saga* too.

In 1241 Snorri's son-in-law Gissur gathered a band of men and stabbed Snorri to death near his soaking pool, Snorralaug, in an attempt to win favour with the Norwegian king. The pool can still be found behind the study centre. *www.snorrastofa.is; tel +354 433 8000; 10am-6pm May-Oct, 10am-5pm Mon-Fri Nov-Apr*
BY BRANDON PRESSER

06 Iceland's annual Viking Festival

07 Statue of Viking explorer Leifur Eiríksson in front of the Hallgrímskirkja church in Reykjavik

08 A traditional wooden church on the Snæfellsnes peninsula

WHERE TO STAY
VOGUR
A constellation of fascinating Viking relics runs right through this modern guest house, including a sacred pool once owned by a two-timing Viking woman famous for turning two brothers against one another. The views from Vogur take in the splendor of one of Iceland's largest and loneliest fjords. *vogur.org; tel +354 894 4396; Fellströnd, Budardalur*

MIDGARD HOSTEL
A new addition to south Iceland's collection of outback stays, Midgard feels like a modern base camp for travellers wanting to really tuck into the Icelandic wilderness. The entire staff is made up of certified mountain guides. *midgardhostel.is; tel +354 578 3180; Dufthaksbraut 14, Hvolsvöllur*

WHERE TO EAT & DRINK
SETTLEMENT CENTRE RESTAURANT
After battling trolls in the museum exhibit, head upstairs to the Settlement Centre's in-house restaurant. Try the fish stew — classic Icelandic comfort food combining whipped fish, potatoes and cream. The lunchtime buffet is a solid deal for road trippers who are short on time. *english.landnam.is; tel +354 437 1600; Brákarbraut 13-15, Borgarnes*

FRIDHEIMAR
Witness the awesome power of Iceland's geothermic water at this working farm and horse ranch close to Thingvellir, where greenhouses — all powered by nature — foster tomatoes and cucumbers that are turned into delicious soups and cocktail garnishes for lunching guests. *fridheimar.is; tel +354-486-8894; Bláskógabyggd, Selfoss*

CELEBRATIONS
VIKING FESTIVAL
Held in Hafnarfjördur, this veritable Comic Con for Viking enthusiasts occurs every June as hundreds of dressed-up wannabes descend upon the Reykjavík suburb to fight with swords, perform pagan rites and scarf down archaic grub. *(fjorukrain.is)*

India

SALMAN'S BOMBAY

The year India gained independence, literary great Salman Rushdie was born in colonial Mumbai, and many of his fantastical tales can be mapped to the city's streets.

Mumbai's — or rather Bombay's — most famous literary son, and certainly its most controversial, Salman Rushdie has lived a life almost as extraordinary as the characters in his magical realist novels. Raised and educated in India, Pakistan and England, he has been feted as a genius, and awarded not just the Whitbread Prize and the Booker Prize but the Booker of Booker Prizes. He has been a fellow of Britain's Royal Society of Literature for more than 30 years, and has been married to four remarkable women (one agent, one novelist, one editor and one movie star). He is author of the world's most controversial novel, and in 1989 was marked for assassination by one of the world's most powerful clerics.

From *Midnight's Children* to *The Satanic Verses*, Rushdie's novels have crisscrossed the subcontinent and the globe, but his most famous works are all, at heart, about Mumbai — its poverty and glamour, its prejudices

NEED TO KNOW
Take two days to explore by taxi, on foot, or using the phenomenally crowded overland rail network.

and inequalities, and, ultimately, about its resilience and humanity. And not just any Mumbai, but Mumbai at a very specific time, in the final days of the Raj and the fevered years after Indian independence, when the city was a haven for tolerance and creativity.

Many locations from Rushdie's novels were plucked from his own life, growing up as the concrete was still drying in the newly built suburb of Breach Candy on Malabar Hill. Since then, Bombay has changed its name and exploded into a global megacity, but the places where Rushdie's characters lived out their hyper-real existences can still be mapped to the streets of India's fastest growing metropolis.

This tour of Mumbai weaves together places from Rushdie's childhood and locations from the magical fantasy world he superimposed over the city streets. Suspend disbelief and step into a Mumbai both real and imagined.

① BREACH CANDY

Sprawling south from the Mahalaxmi Temple — dedicated, appropriately for Mumbai, to the goddess of wealth — the suburb of Breach Candy on Malabar Hill was where Salman Rushdie (b1947) was born, after his family upped sticks from Delhi in the tense run-up to independence.

A well-to-do Muslim family, the Rushdies lived a comfortable existence in a modern home, Windsor Villa, on affluent Warden Rd. You can't see much today beyond the walls, but you can wander through Breach Candy Gardens, under the same palms that shaded the author as a child, before he was plucked out of India and delivered into the British education system.
Warden Rd (Bhulabhai Desai Rd)

'It was here that an 11-year-old Rushdie saw the original *Wizard of Oz*, and was inspired to create one of his first pieces of creative writing'

② SCANDAL POINT

From Breach Candy Gardens, stroll south and duck down to the waterfront at Amarsons Gardens. Named as a homage to the more famous Scandal Point in Shimla, where the bored wives of colonial administrators embarked on impetuous affairs, Mumbai's Scandal Point is a genteel area of parks and palm trees. Viewed through Rushdie's fractured prism, it was also the childhood home of Saladin Chamcha, devil-possessed anti-hero of the oft-misunderstood *Satanic Verses*.

Saladin's narrative partner, Gibreel Farishta, meanwhile, started his rise towards Bollywood superstardom as a lowly dabbawalla — one of the legion of lunch-delivery men who ply their trade around Mumbai's Churchgate Station. At the end of its controversial journey, the novel finishes in tragedy and redemption at Everest Vilas,

02 © sako3p / Shutterstock

01 Echoes of colonial
Bombay, Victoria Station

03 The 1930s Metro
cinema, now a favourite
for Bollywood premieres

02 Apollo Bunder,
dominated by the Taj
and Gateway of India

04 Sunset along
Marine Drive

03 @ Art Directors & TRIP / Alamy; 04 @ Rushabh Sheth / 500px

the home of Farishta's mountaineer lover, uphill from Scandal Point at the highest point on Malabar Hill.
Scandal Point, off Warden Rd

03 GIRGAUM CHOWPATTY

Take a taxi over the ridge of Malabar Hill to Girgaum Chowpatty, used as a setting for Rushdie's most impassioned love-letter to Mumbai.

The Moor's Last Sigh features many of Rushdie's most evocative descriptions of his childhood home, and provides a powerful allegory for Mumbai's contorted religious politics. In one particularly lavish passage, the 'Moor' of the book's title, Moraes Zogoiby, describes his artist mother dancing blasphemously against religious indoctrination from

the walls of her mansion, overlooking the crowds of worshippers below on Girgaum Chowpatty beach.

Aurora Zogoiby was fictional, but Girgaum Chowpatty is the very real centre for the celebrations of Ganesh Chaturthi, when some 50,000 effigies of the elephant-headed Hindu deity are marched into the sea by rapt devotees. Outside of festival season, Chowpatty is one of Mumbai's favourite places to promenade, particularly at sunset, as the sun drops majestically behind Malabar Hill.
Marine Drive

04 METRO CINEMA

For your next stop, take the overland train from Charni Road to Marine Lines, then stroll over to Dhobitalao.

Mumbai is second only to Miami when it comes to art deco architecture, and few buildings from the era evoke such passion as Mumbai's vintage cinemas – the Eros, the Liberty, the Regal, the New Empire and the Metro.

The Metro was built in 1938 by Metro Goldwyn-Mayer, initially to showcase Hollywood movies to a slightly dubious colonial audience, before becoming one of the favourite theatres for red-carpet Bollywood premieres. It was here that an 11-year-old Rushdie saw the original technicolour *Wizard of Oz*, and was inspired to create one of his first pieces of creative writing – a fanciful tale about a boy who finds a rainbow on a Mumbai backstreet that leads to a parallel world.
MG Road, Dhobitalao

05 © CRS PHOTO / Shutterstock

05 THE CATHEDRAL & JOHN CONNON SCHOOL

The next stop lies just across the Azad Maidan, a broad grassy area where locals gather for enthusiastic games of cricket in faded whites. A hodgepodge of Indo-Saracenic and Gothic Revival features, the Cathedral & John Connon School was where Rushdie was educated before his parents traded the chaos of Mumbai for the genteel surroundings of Rugby School in Middle England.

Famously strict, the school had a lasting impact on the young Rushdie — he chose Cathedral and St John Connon for the schooldays of his most famous literary creation, Saleem Sinai, the telepathic child whose life mirrors the trials and tribulations of Indian independence in *Midnight's Children*.

Admire the colonial façade, and stroll east through the streets of Mumbai's Fort Area to Shahid Bhagat Singh Rd.
6 Purushottamdas Thakurdas Marg

06 BALLARD ESTATE

There never really was a Methwold Estate – the colonial housing development where the heroes of *Midnight's Children* are thrown together in the fires of Indian Independence — but there was a William Methwold. Born in Norfolk, England, this colonial wheeler-dealer rose to fame and fortune by persuading the Portuguese to relinquish Mumbai into the hands of British East India Company.

You can, however, glimpse a similarly eccentric colonial world at the Ballard Estate in Fort, created as a tropical facsimile of London by the founder of the Mumbai Port Trust, Colonel JA Ballard. Paying heavy tribute to Edwardian neoclassical architecture, the orderly, planned streets and leafy intersections east of Shahid Bhagat Singh Rd were laid out between 1908 and 1914 as one of Mumbai's last colonial flourishes, before the curtain finally fell on the British Raj.
East of Shahid Bhagat Singh Rd

07 APOLLO BUNDER

Finish south of Fort on the waterfront at Apollo Bunder. Dominated by the towering façade of the Taj Mahal Palace Hotel and the vainglorious

162 MUMBAI

triumphal arch of the Gateway of India, this was where the ships of the British Empire loaded up with riches, and where the colonials departed, tails between legs, after India seized its independence in 1947.

This grand and famous wharfside, perennially popular with tourists, was also the fictional home of Ormus Cama — pop-star protagonist of *The Ground Beneath Her Feet*, Rushdie's rock-opera reworking of the myth of Orpheus. Stand for a moment amid the milling sightseers, street-children, snack vendors, balloon sellers, picnickers and photo-wallahs and you should start to feel the rhythms of Mumbai for yourself.

BY JOE BINDLOSS

05 Ganesh prepares to be dunked during festivities on Girgaum Chowpatty

06 The ritzy neighbourhood of Malabar Hill

WHERE TO STAY

TAJ MAHAL PALACE HOTEL
Mumbai's leading heritage hotel has seen some action in the 100 years since it was founded by billionaire industrialist Jamsetji Tata. With the 2008 siege fading into memory, this is once again Mumbai's most prestigious address. *taj.tajhotels.com; tel +91 22 6665 3366, 1 Apollo Bunder*

RESIDENCY HOTEL
It's hard to improve on this location, in the heart of the British colonial district. From the comfy rooms at this long-established midranger, you're only a short stroll from Marine Drive and the arty enclave of Kala Ghoda. *www.residencyhotel.com; tel +91 22 6667 0555; 26 Rustom Sidhwa Marg, Fort*

WHERE TO EAT & DRINK

MAHESH LUNCH HOME
Ignore the workaday name and concentrate instead on the delectable Mangalorean seafood, said to be the best in town. The catch of the day is delivered fresh from the docks — take your pick from pomfret, ladyfish, squid, lobsters, and sweet mud crabs. *www.maheshlunch home.com; 8B Cawasji Patel Street, Fort; 11.30am-4pm & 7pm-midnight*

BRITANNIA & CO
Tucked into a quiet corner of Ballard Estate, this faded charmer has been around since 1923, serving Iranian-inspired dishes to Mumbai's dwindling Zoroastrian community. *Wakefield House, 16 Sport Road, Ballard Estate; noon-4pm Mon-Sat*

CELEBRATIONS

GANESH CHATURTHI
Mumbai's biggest Hindu celebration creates a riot of noise and colour each August/September, as thousands of luridly painted statues of Ganesh are paraded through the streets and ritually immersed in tanks, ponds, rivers and the sea.

KALA GHODA FESTIVAL
The city's premier festival for visual arts, dance, music, theatre, cinema and literature, held from the first Saturday to the second Sunday of February at venues around Kala Ghoda. *(www.kalaghoda association.com)*

The map shows locations numbered 01–07 across the Shekhawati region, including: JHUNJHUNU, NUA, KER, MANDAWA, FATEHPUR, MUKUNDGARH, NAWALGARH, and LAKSHMANGARH. An inset shows INDIA.

India

RAJASTHAN'S OPEN-AIR ART GALLERIES

In Rajasthan's forgotten corner of Shekhawati, astonishing 200-year-old frescoes adorn the walls of abandoned havelis — lavish mansions built by Marwari merchants of old.

The regal region of Rajasthan — Land of the Kings — is India's big-ticket territory. Tourists the world over come to explore its lakeside palaces, its tiger-filled forests, its whistling sand dunes and, above all, its majestic fortresses, rising imperiously from the desert landscape like fairy-tale mirages from a bygone era. The festivals here — including Pushkar's world-famous camel fair — are a cacophony of commotion, the market bazaars a riot of colour, and yet for all its celebrated ostentation, Rajasthan still manages to keep some of its best cards close to its chest. Lying quietly at one edge of the state's mighty Thar Desert are some of India's most astonishing yet least-known artistic treasures: the incredible frescoes of Shekhawati.

Known affectionately as Rajasthan's 'open-air art gallery' these mesmerising murals bedaub the walls, archways and ceilings of the abandoned *haveli* (courtyard mansions) of 18th- and 19th-century Marwari

NEED TO KNOW
This is a two- to three-day trail, best done with your own transport (though it's possible to village-hop using local buses).

merchants. Many of these grand former homes are in a crumbling state of disrepair, and few are visited by tourists, or indeed anyone, and yet together they act as canvasses for the largest concentration of frescoes found anywhere in the world. Some murals show scenes of traditional Rajasthani life, or retell stories from the Hindu epics. Others, curiously, show glimpses of the West, gleaned it seems from the merchants' dealings in foreign trade.

Part of Shekhawati's appeal is due to these practically palatial *haveli* being found in small, otherwise innocuous towns and villages, connected by single-track roads running through lonely, arid countryside. You might have to endure a long journey from Delhi to get here, but these 200-year-old Marwari masterpieces make it worth going the extra mile. Hire a car and driver either from your hotel in Shekhawati, or from a travel agent in Jaipur (170km away) or Delhi (200km).

01 © FO Travel / Alamy

① DR RAMNATH A PODAR HAVELI MUSEUM

This long-established *haveli* museum, known locally as Podar Haveli, is the perfect introduction to *havelis* and their frescoes.

To get you in the mood before you go, check out the virtual tour on the museum's website. Once here, admire the stunning murals adorning the outside of the fortress-like courtyard structure, built in 1902, before delving into the treasures that lie inside.

You'll find Rajasthani paintings, handicrafts and musical instruments, as well as more than 750 frescoes covering pretty much every inch of

space on the walls and ceilings, both inside and out. Some critics bemoan the restoration techniques employed here (re-painted rather than restored) but this is nevertheless a hugely eye-catching introduction to the art form.
www.podarhavelimuseum.org; tel +91 1594 225446; Rambilas Podar Rd, Nawalgarh; 8am-8pm summer, 8.30am-6.30pm winter

> 'Some frescoes at Morarka Haveli have Western influences too; you'll find depictions of planes and trains, and there's an image of Jesus'

② MORARKA HAVELI MUSEUM

Just down the road from Podar Haveli is this fabulous 117-year-old *haveli*. The majority of frescoes here are religious in nature; of gods and heroes found in ancient texts and mythology. Images of Krishna pop up time and again, particularly Krishna in his amorous aspect as Lord of the *gopis* (milkmaids). But as with most *haveli* art, there seems to be no

01 Decorated doorway in Mandawa

02 Paintings dance floor to ceiling in a Nawalgarh *haveli*

03 A sari-clad woman walks past a painted *haveli* wall

04 Frescoes of Lord Krishna in Nawalgarh

central theme, lending weight to the thought that primarily *haveli* paintings were meant to be decorative rather than ideological or biographic.

Some frescoes here clearly have some Western influence too; you'll find depictions of planes and trains, for instance, and on the top floor there's an image of Jesus.
www.kamalmorarkahavelimuseum. com; tel +91 1594 23907; Naya Bazar, Nawalgarh; 8am-7pm

03 CHHATRI OF THAKUR SHARDUL SINGH

A short 15km drive from Nawalgarh brings you to Parasrampura, a sleepy little village that contains some of the oldest surviving murals in the region, including the unusual ones decorating the domed ceiling of this 18th-century cenotaph — the final resting place of Shardul Singh (1681-1742), who ruled the Jhunjhunu region for 12 years.

Almost reminiscent of Mughal miniature paintings, these exquisitely intricate frescoes do, understandably, have a central theme — the life and times of Shardul Singh — although depictions of him and his family share space with scenes from religious epics such as the Ramayana. Notice the more natural, rusty tones of the pigments here, compared with the brighter colours on the younger

haveli frescoes in Nawalgarh.

This place is so rarely visited that you may have to track down the caretaker to unlock the gate for you; it all adds to the adventure.
Near Gopinath Temple, Parasrampura

04 RANI SATI TEMPLE

For a change of scene, head 50km north to Jhunjhunu. This busy market town also has its fair share of stunning *haveli* frescoes, but first track down this 400-year-old temple dedicated to Rani Sati – a semi-mythical Rajasthani heroine who lived in India some time between the 13th and 17th centuries and

who committed *sati* (self-immolation) on her husband's death. Various temples in Rajasthan are devoted to her worship, but this is the largest and most revered, and the atmosphere here can be intoxicating at times, particularly during morning or evening *arti* (ceremonial prayers) when throngs of devotees gather to sing *bhajan* (spiritual songs), which you can also listen to on the temple's website.

The artistic flavour of the region extends into the main hall, which contains a tile-and-mirror mosaic on the ceiling and a relief frieze on one wall depicting the legendary story of Rani Sati. *www.dadisati.in; tel +91 1592 232755; Chobari Mandi Colony, Jhunjhunu; 5am–1pm & 3–10.30pm*

05 MODI HAVELI

Back on the fresco trail, Modi Haveli is about a 20-minute walk from the temple in the absorbing market streets of Nehru Bazaar. Dating from 1896, it contains some delightfully entertaining murals, including a train running merrily across its front façade. Inside you'll find depictions of British and Indian rulers as well as some carefully protected, glass-covered portrait miniatures, painted on inner archways. *Nehru Bazaar, Jhunjhunu; 9am–4.30pm*

06 MANDAWA FORT

Shekhawati's forts are relatively modest compared with some of the imperious desert citadels found in other parts of Rajasthan, but they do boast some fantastic decorative artwork. Constructed in 1755 by Thakur Nawal Singh, the son of Shardul Singh, whose domed chhatri you visited in Parasrampura, Mandawa Fort was built to protect what was then merely a trading outpost in a remote feudal principality.

The town of Mandawa, now sprinkled liberally with fine examples of *haveli* architecture, soon grew around the base of the fort, which has now been turned into a heritage hotel. Those not staying at the hotel can still appreciate its interior frescoes by paying to tour some of its communal areas. Don't miss climbing up to the roof for great views over the town, which is about 20km southwest of Jhunjhunu. *castlemandawa.com; tel +91 1592 223124; off Mandawa Rd, Mandawa*

07 HAVELI NADINE LE PRINCE

Arguably the best-preserved haveli of the lot (so best saved for last), this French-Indian restoration project has transformed a crumbling 1802 haveli into a fresco-laden arts-centre-cum guesthouse, hosting art exhibitions, artist residencies and a cute little cafe, as well as fabulously inspiring heritage rooms and an outdoor swimming pool.

While you're here, ask about the two-hour self-guided heritage walk of Fatehpur and staff will provide you with a walking map showing the locations of a dozen or so other *havelis* that are dotted around this charmingly undeveloped desert town. www.cultural-centre.com; tel +91 1571 233024; Chauhan Well, Fatehpur; exhibitions usually 10am-6pm
BY DANIEL MCCROHAN

05 On the streets of Fatehpur

06 Peeking through an archway of Modi Haveli in Nehru Bazaar

WHERE TO STAY
APANI DHANI ECO LODGE
A friendly, affordable and award-winning lodge with a good range of organised activities and tours. Rooms are in thatched, mud-hut bungalows that open out onto a bougainvillea-shaded courtyard and there's a genuine home-from-home atmosphere. www.apanidhani.com; tel +91 1594 222239; Old Jhunjhunu Road, Nawalgarh

HAVELI NADINE LE PRINCE
Restored by French artist Nadine Le Prince, this former residence is now one of the best-preserved havelis in Shekhawati. Exquisitely decorated rooms surround a fresco-filled courtyard, while art exhibitions, a garden cafe and a rooftop pool add a dose of vitality. www.leprincehaveli.com; tel +91 1571 233024; near Chauhan Well, Fatehpur

WHERE TO EAT & DRINK

SHEKHAWATI GUESTHOUSE
This simple guesthouse in Nawalgarh offers home-cooked Rajasthani dishes made with vegetables from its organic garden, and you can learn to cook local cuisine here too. www.shekhawatiguesthouse.com; tel +91 1594 224658; Kothi Rd, Nawalgarh

HOTEL MANDAWA HAVELI
Enjoy tasty pan-Indian cuisine in the garden cafe, the dining room, or the rooftop restaurant of this beautifully restored 19th-century haveli hotel in Mandawa. Tel +91 1592 223088; Sonthaliya Gate, Mandawa; 7am-10pm

CELEBRATIONS

SHEKHAWATI FESTIVAL
Held for four days in February at the Surya Mandal Stadium in Nawalgarh, the Shekhawati Festival is a celebration of the region's artistic, cultural and sporting traditions. As well as craft markets and music and dance performances, it showcases traditional Shekhawati games such as *rounder balla*, similar to baseball, and *satoliya*, where one team uses a ball to prevent another team building a tower of stones. (www.shekhawatifestival.in)

Indonesia

THE CULTURE OF BALINESE DAILY LIFE

The unique spirituality of Indonesia's most popular holiday island has helped keep alive traditional arts and religious rituals — nowhere more so than around culture capital Ubud.

Bali is renowned for its unique spiritual culture, which inspires a kaleidoscope of artisans including traditional dancers and musicians, painters and sculptors, mask carvers, and highly skilled silver- and goldsmiths. The secret of how this has survived while the island became one of the world's most popular holiday destinations is that Balinese Hinduism is profoundly ingrained in the rituals of daily life.

Each household is roused early in the morning with prayers, setting down tiny ornate offerings, meticulously prepared by all the family, all over the home; statues of the gods are decorated with fragrant flowers. The year revolves around endless festivities — holy days, temple offerings, death and the cremation process, sacred dances and wedding rites, as well as elaborate and joyous celebrations such as the dramatic Ogoh-ogoh, when each village builds immense statues of

NEED TO KNOW
Bali on foot is hot and hard work, so hire a car, scooter or — if you're brave — a bike. A five-day stay is perfect.

mythical demons that are paraded then burnt. To experience the ultimate expression of Bali's unique spirituality, time your visit with the New Year festival of Nyepi, when every islander downs tools for the day to concentrate on meditation — a very special opportunity for visitors to gain a genuine understanding of locals' extreme devotion.

Bali is blessed with impressive holy temples, but they are busy and often touristy; it can be better to just stop off at a local village temple — respectfully wearing a sarong — and glimpse the activities going on. School kids are taught how to plait palm leaves to make offerings, artists delicately paint grotesque dance masks, and cooks grill chicken and pork over charcoal for the next village feast. It's commonplace to hear the sound of drums, flutes and xylophones from a gamelan orchestra echo out as musicians rehearse for a temple performance.

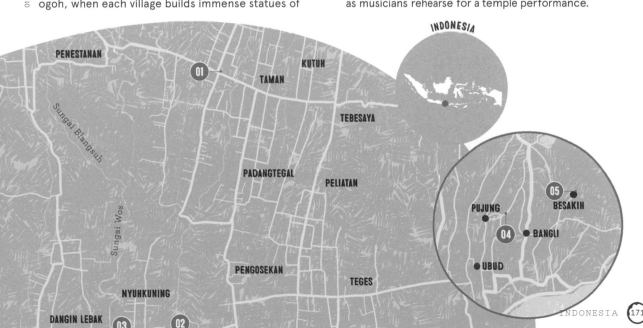

'Artisans survive by producing for tourists, but this allows traditional skills to survive and flourish in a global marketplace'

01 UBUD PALACE

If Ubud is the cultural capital of Bali, its spiritual heart is the exquisite Royal Palace — a labyrinth of red sandstone villas, ornate statues, courtyards, temples and a magical outdoor performance space that comes to life each evening with the mesmerising rhythms of the gamelan orchestra.

As dusk falls different dancers take to the stage: seductive Legong ladies with bewitchingly arching fingers and fleeting eyes, the dashing male Baris, Rangda the evil witch, and the giant Barong, king of the spirits. Dance and music are deeply enshrined in

both religious and artistic life, with performers ranging from tiny children to 80-year-old divas.

While the audience may inevitably be primarily tourists, many locals sneak in, still enthralled by the timeless histories of the Mahabharata and Ramayana recounted in the epic dances. *www.ubudpalace.com; tel +62 361 975057; Jalan Raya Ubud; performances 7.30pm Fri-Wed*

02 BALI CULTURE CENTRE

A 10-minute drive along from Ubud towards Tabanan, a private side-road leads into the lush jungle grounds

housing Bali Culture Centre. While tour groups regularly stop-off and treat the place like a cultural village, a quiet tour of the sprawling, slightly chaotic gardens that lie along a fast-flowing river offers a fascinating slice of Balinese life.

Apart from dazzling dance and gamelan performances, there are demonstrations of *canang* (the intricate constructions of bamboo and coconut leaves made for daily offerings to the gods), traditional methods of pounding rice, and the building of monster effigies that every village contributes for Ogoh-ogoh.

01 Women carry offerings to the village temple

02 A ceremonial funeral pyre

03 Preparing for a Balinese dance performance

04 Women praying

05 Ritual temple offerings are a common sight in Bali

In front of the centre's temple, hundreds of tiny painted stone carvings form a tableau recreating the unique rites of a Balinese cremation ceremony, where villagers carry the corpse in a celebratory cortège that twirls and swirls to throw off evil spirits before arriving at the funeral pyre. www.baliculturecentre.com; tel +62 361 978144; Jalan Raya Nyuh Kuning, Mas; 9am-5pm

03 I NYOMAN JENDRA

Just after the Culture Centre, both sides of the busy road are lined with artisans sitting carving intricate wooden sculptures, painting scenes of rice fields, weaving baskets or decorating the astonishing masks worn in classical Balinese dance. Jendra Nyoman can usually be found in his cluttered studio-cum-gallery, every inch covered with canvases, his son working on abstract compositions while Jendra patiently colours minute details of his latest painting of rural life in the paddy fields.

Visitors are welcome to view, buy, or sign up for his art classes, but Jendra, who has been painting since the age of nine, also exhibits in Bali's major museums. All the tiny rural hamlets surrounding Ubud are populated by thriving communities of artists and artisans, dancers and musicians. They survive by producing for the tourist market, but this allows traditional skills to survive and flourish in a global marketplace. www.balinese-paintings-and-modern-art.blogspot.com; tel +62 81 8565759; Jalan Raya Nyuh Kuning, Pengosekan

04 TAMPAKSIRING

Less than an hour north of Ubud lies upcountry Tampaksiring, home of two of the island's oldest holy sites.

Pura Tirta Empul, better known as Holy Spring Water Temple, includes two open-air stone bathing pools, visited by the Balinese for meditation, purification and healing ceremonies for more than 1000 years. There are always crowds, as old ladies and whole families with tiny children gather beneath bubbling holy water gushing out of sculpted stone spouts. Many tourists cannot resist the temptation to jump in, but it is necessary to stay respectfully clothed in a sarong.

Gunung Kawi is another 11th-century shrine, nearby but much harder to access, at the bottom of more than 200 steps leading down to the lush Pakerisan river valley. Tour groups steer clear, and the 10 enormous *candi* (8m-high monuments) carved into the sheer cliff face are breathtaking. Wandering far from the usual crowds around the meditation caves, cascades and endless rice terraces, there is a genuine sense of Bali's mysticism. *7am–6pm*

05 BESAKIH TEMPLE

It may only be 50km from Ubud, but the journey to Bali's Mother Temple takes a couple of hours. Besakih is the island's most important shrine, an unforgettable sight of more than 20 black temples massed in terraces 1000 metres up the volcanic slope of sacred Mount Agung. It can be an other-worldly vision when covered in a thick mist, as it frequently is, enveloping both the temples and the steady stream of pilgrims making offerings. It is used as a venue for up to 70 festivals a year.

Unfortunately it is also a tourist trap, and perseverance is needed to avoid being cheated by false entry tickets (it's free to enter) and rip-off guides pretending to be compulsory. Don't let that put you off, because the site is unique. Besakih has been a site of worship since prehistoric times, and the present temple complex dates back more than 700 years. Set in the shadow of a potent volcano that erupted barely 50 years ago, the deadly lava stream passed just by the temple yet left it miraculously untouched.

When visiting, be sure to dress appropriately by covering your shoulders, and using a sarong to cover your knees.
Jalan Raya Besakih, Kerangasem; 7am–10pm

09

06 NYEPI

If there is one moment of the year to visit Bali and understand why it is known as the Island of God, it is the festival of Nyepi — a unique 24-hour New Year celebration that focuses on self-reflection. Nyepi is the one moment when everyone steps back and takes the time to meditate without a single distraction, contemplating the past year and year ahead. It is essentially a Hindu celebration, but Nyepi is a purely Balinese interpretation of a religious festival, not practised in this extreme way in other parts of the Hindu world.

There are some simple rules to follow — no fire or light, which means no electricity, no cooking, no working or pleasures, no travelling, no eating or drinking. The whole island effectively shuts down; locals and hotel guests may not go outside, and *pacalangs* (village guards) ensure no one breaks the 24-hour curfew. Even the airport is closed. While luxury hotels still pamper their guests, the best idea is to stay in a simple Ubud homestay and experience Nyepi alongside a Balinese family.

Nyepi lasts from 6am to 6am, falling during the month of March, with the exact date changing each year.
BY JOHN BRUNTON

06 The 11th-century shrine of Gunung Kawi

07 Brilliant effigies paraded during Nyepi

08 Ceremonial bathing pools at Pura Tirta Empul

09 An artist works in a village near Ubud

08 © Hemis / Alamy; 09 © Sioen Gerard / Alamy

WHERE TO STAY
JATI HOMESTAY
Homestays are a unique chance to experience daily Balinese life. In Ubud's back alleyways, well-known painter Dewa Nyoman Jati opened up his chaotic compound of bungalows, temples and studios as a friendly B&B more than 20 years ago. *Tel +62 361 977701; Hanoman St*

BLACK LAVA HOSTEL
For a base in the highlands near Besakih temple, perfect for sunrise treks up Bali's sacred mountains, volcanic Gunung Agung and Mount Batur, book a dorm bed or private room in this helpful hostel overlooking Batur lake. *Tel +62 813 37558998; Jalan Pendakian Gunung Batur, Batur Tengah*

WHERE TO EAT & DRINK
DAYU'S WARUNG
Ubud is a health-food paradise with a host of vegan diners, and Dayu's mainly vegetarian and vegan offering is one of the best. It's a cosy cafe serving detox fruit cocktails and delicious dishes such as creamy mungbean dahl

with tofu and almonds. *www.dayuswarung.weebly. com; tel +62 361 978965; 28 Jalan Sugriwa*

ROOM4DESSERT
At Ubud's favourite evening hangout, American chef Will Goldfarb proposes the perfect mix of innovative cocktails, tempting Balinese-inspired tapas and gourmet desserts, such as Infance: toasted gelato, marshmallow, crispy rice, frangipani and mango. *www.room4dessert.asia; tel +62 361 5532598; Jalan Raya Sanggingan*

CELEBRATIONS
BALI ARTS FESTIVAL
Dance holds centre stage at this month-long festival, but it is also the chance to see Wayang Kulit shadow puppets, art and handicraft exhibitions. www.baliartsfestival.com

GALUNGAN
A three-day festival honoured in every village in Bali at the end of October, Galungan celebrates the victory of good over evil — the perfect moment to respectfully observe temple festivals, costumed processions, dances and village feasts.

Ireland

LITERARY DUBLIN

Inscribed by Unesco as a City of Literature, Dublin's Georgian streets have been pounded by an astounding roll call of storytellers, from James Joyce to Oscar Wilde.

Maybe it's the long history of oral tradition, the penchant for alcohol or simply the legendary Irish gift of the gab, but Dublin has produced, inspired and exported a remarkable number of great writers for its modest size. It's the birthplace of James Joyce, WB Yeats, Oscar Wilde, George Bernard Shaw and Samuel Beckett. It's where Leopold Bloom, the protagonist of Joyce's masterpiece *Ulysses*, wandered on that fateful June day in 1904, the place where WB Yeats started a theatre to encourage avant-garde writing, and the city where Jimmy Rabitte clobbered together a motley soul band in *The Commitments*.

The rich tradition of storytelling here spans centuries, from the professional bards who preserved history and legend in pre-Christian times to the vibrant contemporary writing scene that has nurtured Anne Enright, Joseph O'Connor, Sebastian Barry and Roddy

NEED TO KNOW
Take two to three days for this trail (depending on how long you wish to linger), and make it a leisurely stroll on foot.

Doyle. Quirky bookshops, a host of literary festivals and a glut of pubs where famous writers observed their countrymen conspire to create a city where you're never far from the seed of a story.

This legacy is now acknowledged by Unesco, which has declared Dublin a City of Literature, and as you wander the Georgian squares you'll come across numerous reminders of the city's rich contribution to literature and culture. Unsurprisingly, Joyce and his fictional characters are everywhere, but you'll also find the castle where Bram Stoker worked before penning his famous Dracula, the favourite watering holes of Brendan Behan and Flann O'Brien, and the canal side so loved by Patrick Kavanagh.

Spend any time here and you'll soon realise it's a city of glib bartenders, garrulous taxi drivers and witty pint drinkers where friendly banter, epic conversations and drawn-out debates are the done thing, and a bad day at the office is simply a good story waiting to be told.

① DUBLIN WRITERS MUSEUM

Start your trail and set the scene at the Dublin Writers Museum, which is located in a grand Georgian townhouse in the north inner city. The museum celebrates Irish literary figures from the past 300 years with displays of memorabilia and ephemera such as a first edition of Bram Stoker's *Dracula*, a hand-written edition of Patrick Kavanagh's poem *The Great Hunger*, correspondence from Yeats, Shaw, Swift, Behan and Joyce, and Samuel Beckett's phone.

Perhaps more interesting, though, are the performances and poetry readings at lunch times — check what's on when you arrive. From here, it's a five-minute walk east

to the James Joyce Centre. *www.writersmuseum.com; tel +353 1 872 2077; 18 N Parnell Sq; 9.45am-4.45pm Mon-Sat, 11am-4.30pm Sun*

② JAMES JOYCE CENTRE

Once a fashionable Dublin address just around the corner from where Joyce went to school, a swathe of North Great George's St was facing demolition when this beautiful 18th-century townhouse was saved by a

'Sweny's is kept just as it would have been in 1904. Mahogany counters surround a tiny space, and pride of place goes to the famous lemon soap mentioned in *Ulysses*'

Joycean scholar and turned into a pilgrimage site for Joyce's legions of fans. Along with changing exhibitions and a choice of well-regarded walking tours, the centre offers a unique insight into the life and work of this literary giant.

Interactive installations enable you to explore Joyce's life year by year and examine the making of *Ulysses* in detail, as well as looking at its historical backdrop. A 10-minute

01 Dublin's dusk-lit
Liffey Bridge

02 A reading at the
James Joyce Centre
on Bloomsday

03 North Earl St's
beloved statue of
James Joyce by artist
Marjorie Fitzgibbon

04 Colourful buildings
of Dublin Castle

walk downhill towards the River Liffey brings you to your next stop. *www.jamesjoyce.ie; tel +353 1 878 8547; 35 Nth Great George's St; 10am-5pm Mon-Sat, noon-5pm Sun, Closed Mon Oct-Mar*

03 ABBEY THEATRE

The Abbey Theatre was founded by Irish literary revivalists WB Yeats and Lady Augusta Gregory in 1904 and has been at the heart of Dublin's cultural life since. Today it is renowned for its promotion of new Irish writers but, along with modern-day productions, it regularly features classics by literary greats such as Yeats, JM Synge, Sean O'Casey, Brendan Behan and Samuel Beckett.

You can also join workshops and talks, take a backstage tour or submit work to be commissioned for performance. From the entrance head west to O'Connell St, turn south to cross the river then walk west along Dame St to Dublin Castle. *www.abbeytheatre.ie; tel +353 1 878 7222; 26/27 Lwr Abbey St; box office 10.30am-7pm Mon-Sat*

04 CHESTER BEATTY LIBRARY

A treasure trove of rare manuscripts, unique prints, miniature books and ancient scrolls from all over the world, the Chester Beatty is a remarkable place in the gardens of Dublin Castle.

Here you can find papyrus texts from ancient Egypt, medieval Korans and clay tablets, among other tomes.

Exhibits are expertly displayed and include intriguing explanations on the techniques used to create the original pieces. You can also take part in regular workshops and talks on anything from mapping to origami. *www.cbl.ie; tel +353 1 407 0750; Dublin Castle; 10am-5pm Mon-Fri, 11am-5pm Sat, 1-5pm Sun, Closed Mon Nov-Feb*

05 TRINITY COLLEGE

Suitably imposing and regally grand, Trinity College is Ireland's most prestigious university and an oasis of calm right in the heart of the city, 10 minutes east of the castle. Samuel Beckett, Bram Stoker and Oliver Goldsmith all studied here and Seamus Heaney was an honorary fellow.

03 © Matthiola / Alamy; 04 © Hob Spillane / Shutterstock

Its stately Georgian buildings surround tranquil lawns and quiet playing fields, but its greatest treasures are in the monumental Old Library, home to the glorious *Book of Kells* — an ornate 9th-century illuminated manuscript containing the four gospels of the New Testament.

Alongside it you'll find thousands of rare and very early books in the breathtaking Long Room, the 65m-long main chamber that is lined with towering bookshelves. Take the Lincoln Place gate and head southeast for your next stop.

www.tcd.ie; +353 1896 1000; College Green; Book of Kells 8.30am–5pm Mon–Sat, 9.30am–5pm Sun May–Sept, 9.30am–5pm Mon–Sat, noon–4.30pm Sun Oct–Apr

06 SWENY'S

Described in intricate detail and lambasted as 'the worst pharmacy in Dublin' in Joyce's *Ulysses*, Sweny's is a gem of a place kept just as it would have been in 1904. Mahogany counters surround a tiny central space facing shelves packed with lotions and tonics, bottles and brews.

Pride of place goes to the famous lemon soap mentioned in the book. Volunteers also sell second-hand books and host daily readings from Joyce's work.

It's a great way to gain some insight into those books you always thought you should read but never quite got around to starting.

www.sweny.ie; +353 87 713 2157; 1 Lincoln Pl; 11am–5pm Mon–Sat

07 MERRION SQUARE

Just around the corner, this tranquil square is surrounded by some of Dublin's most exceptional Georgian houses. Oscar Wilde grew up at No 1, while WB Yeats lived at No 82, and AE Russell — an Anglo-Irish nationalist, poet and painter working at the turn of the century — had his office at No 84.

Take a stroll through the square's central park and look for the statue of a reclining Oscar Wilde before popping into No 29 Fitzwilliam St on the southeast corner of the square to get an idea of what living here was like in Georgian Dublin.

www.numbertwentynine.ie; 29 Fitzwilliam St; 10am–5pm Tue–Sat mid-Feb–mid-Dec

06 © ciu / Getty Images

⑧ THE GRAND CANAL

A winding sliver of water running through the south inner city, the Grand Canal was built to connect Dublin to the River Shannon.

It is at its leafy best between Mount St and Baggot St, 10 minutes south of Merrion Sq, and was a favourite haunt of poet Patrick Kavanagh who expressed in verse his desire to be commemorated by 'a canal-bank seat for the passer-by' when he died.

Walking southwest along the canal you'll pass Baggot St bridge before coming to a bench where you can sit and contemplate the passage of time beside a bronze cast of the man himself, perched wistfully forever more with his hat off and arms folded.
BY ETAIN O'CARROLL

05 Oscar Wilde reclining in Merrion Sq by sculptor Danny Osborne

06 The Old Library at Trinity College

WHERE TO STAY
THE SHELBOURNE
This grand dame of Dublin hotels dates from 1824 and has played a significant role in Irish history. It crops up in *Ulysses* on several occasions and is still a popular spot for politicians and journos to meet. *www.theshelbourne.ie; tel +353 1 663 4500; 27 St Stephen' Green*

NUMBER 31
This boutique guesthouse is set in a Georgian townhouse with a sleek modernist muse. Renowned for its unique style and magnificent breakfasts, there are 21 rooms and a gorgeous courtyard garden. *www.number31.ie; tel +353 1 676 5011; 31 Leeson Close*

WHERE TO EAT & DRINK
DAVY BYRNE'S
Leopold Bloom, *Ulysses'* protagonist, enjoyed a glass of Burgundy and a gorgonzola sandwich in this convivial pub where Joyce, Patrick Kavanagh and Brendan Behan were regulars. It serves good pints and excellent seafood. *www.davybyrnes.com; tel +353 1 677 5217; 21 Duke St*

THE BRAZEN HEAD
Reputedly Ireland's oldest pub, the 12th-century Brazen Head was a favourite of Jonathan Swift, author of *Gulliver's Travels* and dean of St Patrick's Cathedral. Come for an evening of traditional storytelling with a candle-lit dinner. *www.brazenhead.com; tel +353 1 677 9549; 20 Bridge St Lwr*

CELEBRATIONS
BLOOMSDAY
Kit yourself out in Edwardian garb on 16 June and enjoy dramatisations and readings from *Ulysses*, a breakfast of liver and kidneys, a pub crawl or a street party. Or you could just eat seedcake from your lover's mouth, as Leopold Bloom does. *(www.bloomsdayfestival.ie)*

INTERNATIONAL LITERATURE FESTIVAL
This week-long celebration is held in late May and features an impressive array of readings, workshops, debates, discussions, performances and screenings of adult and children's fiction, non-fiction, poetry, plays and screen writing. *(www.ilfdublin.com)*

Ireland

TRADITIONAL MUSIC IN THE WILD WEST

Céilís, sing-a-longs and unexpected 'trad' sessions are hallmarks of Irish life passed down through generations — nowhere more so than on the fiercely traditional west coast.

Wild, windswept and starkly beautiful, the west of Ireland is battered by Atlantic rollers, framed by moody mountains and blanketed in sweeping bog. It's a sparsely populated place, home to Ireland's largest Gaeltacht (Irish-speaking area) and a bastion of traditional culture and customs. Music, song and dance are a large part of this and it's hard to travel here without encountering an impromptu pub session, a music festival or a summer school where musicians gather to learn and put the world to rights over a pint or two.

At one time music was played only in private homes but eventually it moved into the pubs, where a *seisiún* (music session) became an impromptu meeting of musicians that starts as soon as a tin whistle, fiddle or flute emerges from a bag and is joined by a button accordion, concertina, banjo or perhaps some *uilleann* (elbow) pipes. Trad music, as it's known locally, comes from a strong oral tradition and wasn't written down, but passed from one musician

NEED TO KNOW
Fly into Ireland West Airport, 55km from Westport, where you can hire a car for this three-day trail.

to another evolving along the way: because of this, it has a strong social aspect.

Renowned for its upbeat tempo, traditional Irish dance music was intended for celebrations and ideal for dancing jigs, reels, hornpipes and polkas. Today you'll see step dancers flicking their ringlets and high kicking across a stage, but as a visitor you really want to look for a *céilí* — a traditional public dance where everyone is expected to join in regardless of experience or desire.

This social enjoyment of music has been very important through history, holding communities together during times of political oppression, famine, mass emigration or unemployment. Songs often made political or social statements and the ballads, laments and drinking songs can inspire intense emotions. If you hear classics such as rebel song *Óró Sé do Bheatha 'Bhaile* and the ubiquitous famine song *The Fields of Athenry* wheeled out at the end of the night, you can be guaranteed a rowdy sing-a-long.

01 © Eamon Ward

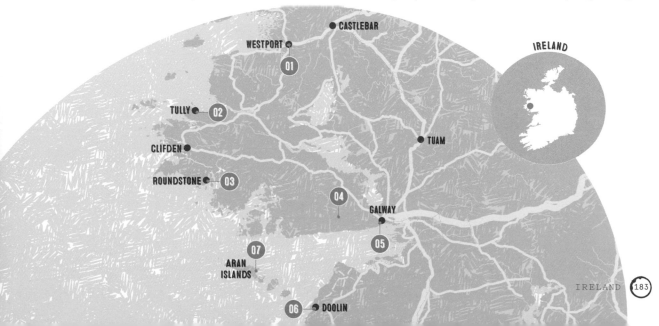

'People would gather in a cottage sharing music, song and stories prior to the arrival of TV and other distractions in the 60s'

01 MATT MOLLOY'S

Start off in stately Westport, a gorgeous Georgian town where handsome streets lead down to a tree-lined riverside mall. You'll find fine restaurants, good accommodation and a host of remarkable pubs here. For music, the finest is Matt Molloy's — known as one of the best music venues in the west, and owned and run by the flautist with legendary trad band The Chieftains.

Matt still plays on occasion and if you can catch him in action you'll be treated to an evening with one of the country's most revered musicians, whose style and interpretation has influenced a whole generation of traditional flautists.
www.mattmolloy.com; tel +353 98 26655; Bridge St; 12.30-11.30pm Mon-Thu, 12.30pm-12.30am Fri & Sat, 12.30pm-11pm Sun

02 TEACH CEOIL

An hour southwest of Westport, the tiny village of Renvyle is set on the Atlantic coast where the ruins of a 13th-century tower house look out over a long white beach. Grace O'Malley, Ireland's legendary pirate queen, lived here and later WB Yeats was a regular visitor. There are beautiful walks along the coast, lots of archaeological sites and on Tuesdays in the summer months a captivating show of traditional music, song, dance and storytelling at the Teach Ceoil (music house).

The show is part of a long-running programme by Comhaltas Ceoltóirí Éireann, the Society of Irish Musicians, and showcases the full spectrum of Irish musical styles. It's a good place to hear harpists and *sean-nós* (unaccompanied solo performances of poetic songs, usually in the Irish language), as

01 An impromptu
music session
draws crowds

02 Locals kick
back at Galway's
Spanish Arches

03 Renvyle beach

04 Roundstone's
petite harbour

05 Master bodhrán
maker Malachy
Kearns

they're not seen very often in the pubs. In the second half spectators are encouraged to play their own instruments if they wish or learn to dance and join in a *céilí*. From Renvyle, take the scenic route south to your next stop, Roundstone — the coastal R341 passes powder-soft sands and turquoise waters. *www.comhaltas.ie/events/seisiun; tel +353 95 41047; Renvyle; Tue Jul-Aug*

03 ROUNDSTONE

A colourful fishing village overlooking a bustling harbour, Roundstone is the picturesque home of master bodhrán maker Malachy Kearns. The bodhrán is a traditional goatskin drum and 'the pulse of Irish music' according to Malachy, whose love for his craft is obvious. He explains that *bodhar* means 'deaf' or 'from deep within' in Irish. 'The bodhrán's racing sounds touch your soul. It's those brilliant, super-dexterous bodhrán players that are the power behind the growth of the bodhrán's popularity – and good makers too, of course!' he says.

You can see Malachy and his team at work in his small factory in Roundstone, where the Riverdance stage drums were made. A presentation explains the history and craft of what they do and you can browse the shop with its numerous instruments, books and crafts. From Roundstone, it's a slow but scenic drive into Galway on winding coastal roads. *www.bodhran.com; tel +353 95 35808; IDA Craft Centre, Roundstone; 9.30am-6pm*

04 CNOC SUAIN

Set well off the beaten track in a restored Connemara hillside village, Cnoc Suain is a cultural retreat and labour of love for husband-and-wife team Charlie Troy and Dearbhaill

Standún. Dearbhaill plays the fiddle with traditional music group Dordán and the retreat offers a fascinating insight into Irish culture and the importance of music, song and dance in rural history.

Dearbhaill explains: 'There was a very strong oral tradition in the country. People would gather in a cottage sharing music, song and stories prior to the arrival of television and other distractions into homes in the '60s. To guarantee the continuation of the oral tradition, organisations such as Gaelacadamh brought children together with a master-musician, ensuring its survival into the future.'

Along with hearing a musician play and learning about Irish music and language, you'll also get an insight into the fragility of the surrounding wild

bogland and the herbs and plants that sustained people during the famine. To visit Cnoc Suain you must join a half-day tour from Galway, which winds through the Connemara Gaeltacht and visits the fishing village of Spiddal en route.
www.cnocsuain.com; info@ cnocsuain.com; near Spiddal, County Galway; Apr-Oct, book in advance

05 THE CRANE BAR

Galway is one of those cities you could instantly fall in love with, even in a torrential downpour. Its brightly coloured streets, compact centre, racing river, boho vibe, glut of buskers and huge number of heavenly pubs make it hard not to like. You'll find live music in almost every city pub,

but serious music lovers head for the Crane Bar, which offers nightly music.

There's a lively mix of established and up-and-coming trad, roots and folk performers in the renowned Listeners' Club upstairs, while in the downstairs bar things are more informal, with musicians dropping in for spontaneous sessions. From Galway head south along the N18 and N67 skirting the rocky, windswept Burren to the coastal village of Doolin. *www.thecranebar.com; tel +353 91 587 419; Sea Rd; 10.30am-11.30pm Mon-Sat, noon-11.30 Sun*

06 GUS O'CONNOR'S

A one-horse town with three great music pubs, Doolin is internationally renowned for its trad sessions. It's often standing room only in

O'Connor's, where all it takes is a nod of the head and a wink of the eye and they're off on another legendary session that sets feet stomping and fiddles hopping.

There's live music here every night, with either planned or spontaneous sessions, friendly banter and back-slapping good cheer, plus two music festivals a year (in February and October). As town local and former O'Connor's owner Séan O'Connor puts it: 'Music really is in all our DNA. Doolin has a long history of music, dancing, singing and conversation that is heavily influenced by the rugged landscape and the weather.'

The town is 1.5 hours down the coast from Galway (two hours if you take the scenic coastal road) *www.gusoconnorspubdoolin.net; tel +353 65 707 4168; Fisher St; 9am-11.30pm Mar-Oct, 10am-11.30pm Nov-Feb*

07 TÍ JOE WATTY'S

Pounded by surf and removed from mainland life, the three Irish-speaking Aran Islands have a beguiling but desolate beauty. It's easy to make a day trip from Galway or Clare, but an overnight stay reveals an entirely more tranquil charm with time to wander between stone walls, ancient forts and spectacular cliffs.

Inishmór, the big island, is the most visited and here you'll find Tí Joe Watty's. It's a raucous place on a summer evening, when music spills out of the doors, punters dance their merry way along the bar and everyone is your new best friend. From Doolin, you can get here by ferry. *www.joewattys.ie; tel +353 86 049 4509; Kilronan; noon-midnight Sun-Thu, 11.30-12.30am Fri & Sat*
BY ETAIN O'CARROLL

08 © Ian Dagnall / Alamy

06-07 A traditional music shop in the heritage village of Doolin, and a session at the village's Gus O'Connor's pub

08 Pub life in the brightly coloured streets of Galway

WHERE TO STAY
THE QUAY HOUSE
Built in 1820 as the Harbour Master's house, this handsome structure went on to become a Franciscan monastery before being restored in contemporary style as a quirky B&B. *www.thequayhouse.com; tel +353 95 21369; Beach Road, Clifden; closed Nov-Mar*

GREGANS CASTLE HOTEL
Set in an elegant Georgian mansion, Grogans Castle overlooks the limestone terraces of the Burren and Galway Bay beyond. It's renowned for its faultless service, superb food and utter tranquillity. *www.gregans.ie; tel +353 65 707 7005; Ballyvaughan, County Clare*

WHERE TO EAT & DRINK
ARD BIA
Effortlessly hip yet totally unpretentious, Ard Bia serves some of Galway's finest food. Its seasonal organic fare is wholesome, heart-warming stuff served by enthusiastic staff in beautiful surroundings. *www.ardbia.com; Spanish Arch, Long Walk, Galway; tel +353 91 561 114*

MORAN'S OYSTER COTTAGE
Run by the same family for more than 250 years, Moran's is set in a traditional thatched cottage and serves oysters straight from the sea as well as lobster, mussels, prawns and crab. *www.moransoystercottage.com; The Weir, Kilcolgan; tel +353 91 796 113*

CELEBRATIONS
CLIFDEN TRADITIONAL MUSIC FESTIVAL
Brush up on your skills, compete in the busking competition, attend lively gigs and rowdy pub sessions or simply dance the night away as Clifden comes alive for four days in late March or early April. *(www.clifdentradfest.com)*

WILLIE CLANCY SUMMER SCHOOL
A gathering of the seriously talented, this week-long summer school takes over Miltown Malbay in County Clare each July. There are formal lectures, recitals and workshops, masterclasses from top musicians, impromptu sessions and nightly *céilí*. *(www.scoilsamhraidh willieclancy.com)*

ITALY

02

01

03

Isola di
San Michele

Canale delle
Fondamente Nuove

CANNAREGIO

Grand Canal

ITALY

SANTA CROCE

SAN POLO

06

CASTELLO

05

07

SAN MARCO

04 DORSODURO

Canale di San Marco

Italy

VENETIAN MASTERPIECES IN UNUSUAL CORNERS

Part of the joy of Venice is getting lost in its maze of canals and backstreets, and there are plenty of art gems waiting to be discovered in lesser-visited pockets of the city.

Visiting Venice can be like trying to solve an enigma. How to avoid the crowds that jam its maze of narrow alleys and bridges crisscrossing slender canals? Whether to follow the distinctive yellow signs to landmark sights such as San Marco and Rialto or turn off into a quiet backstreet with the risk of getting utterly lost? And having to decide between planning a trip that moves from one blockbuster museum to the next, or letting yourself simply go with the flow to find the more authentic Serenissima.

Art and culture are everywhere you turn. Overlooked masterpieces might include a 15th-century painting hidden away in the murky nave of a church, a votive depiction of the Madonna on a street corner, the fading frescoes of an opulent palace where Casanova once planned his adventures, or a hidden 500-year-old synagogue.

Commentators these days often describe Venice as being a museum city, whose ever-shrinking population is dwarfed by the tens of thousands of day-trippers pouring in to visit what has become a cultural theme park. That can certainly be the impression for those that limit themselves to the city's numerous world-class art collections and historic monuments. But there is a lot more to discover in Venice than standing in long queues and crowded salons to view the Renaissance masterpieces hanging in the Accademia, the sumptuous decorations of the Doge's Palace and the Basilica di San Marco, or even the contemporary creations in Peggy Guggenheim's palazzo and the avant-garde Punta della Dogana museum.

For centuries, the world's greatest artists — Canaletto and Titian, Tintoretto and Tiepolo, Carpaccio, Bellini and Guardi, to name a few — have been painting Venice's unique floating world, and the best way to understand the secrets of this unique city is to leave the crowds behind and explore its more hidden secrets.

NEED TO KNOW
Don't rush Venice. Put aside four days and explore on foot as much as possible; enjoy getting lost.

01 MADONNA DELL'ORTO

The massive gothic red-brick façade and soaring bell tower of Madonna dell'Orto loom over a tiny courtyard alongside a narrow canal, hidden away in the quiet backstreets of the residential Cannaregio neighbourhood.

While the church dates back to 1350, its interiors are dominated by a local painter who, two centuries later, lived in an ornate palazzo just across the canal. It happened to be Jacopo Robusti, better known as Tintoretto — one of the greatest Venetian artists.

He painted 10 masterpieces, including a celebrated interpretation of *The Last Judgement*, for his local church, all still displayed here today, alongside his tomb.
www.madonnadellorto.org; tel +39 041 719933; 3512 Fondamenta Madonna dell'Orto, Cannaregio; 10am-5pm

02 SANT'ALVISE CHURCH

A 10-minute walk leads to the unassuming parish church of Sant'Alvise, rarely visited and barely mentioned by most guide books. But like so many of Venice's anonymous churches, visitors are rewarded with a host of little-known treasures.

The 14th-century brick exterior lacks the flamboyance of Madonna dell'Orto, but Sant'Alvise saves its surprises for those who enter. The church underwent major renovations in the 17th century, epitomised by an awesome fresco covering the whole of the ceiling, painted by two obscure artists, Pietro Antonio Torri and Pietro Ricchi.

Among the artworks decorating the walls are three dramatic pieces Giambattista Tiepolo painted just after his more famous frescoes in the Gesuati church over by the Zattere in Dorsoduro.
www.chorusvenezia.org/chiesa-di-sant-alvise; tel +39 041 2750462; Campo Sant'Alvise, Cannaregio; 10.30am-4pm

'Tintoretto painted 10 masterpieces for his local church, all still displayed here today, alongside his tomb'

01 Venice's Rio di San Cassiano Canal

02 Inside the perfectly preserved Casino Venier

03 The exterior of Sant'Alvise belies the treasures within

04 Costumed masquerade

 03 SYNAGOGUES OF THE GHETTO

An arched metal bridge marks the entrance to Venice's historic Jewish quarter, a couple of canals over from Sant'Alvise. *Gheto* is Venetian for iron foundry, but the term has come to mean so much more over the centuries. The world's first ghetto was created here in 1516 and tucked away inside this medieval rabbit-warren are five of Europe's oldest synagogues, founded by German, Italian, Spanish and Levantine communities.

Visits are organised by the educational Jewish Museum, whose top floors are actually where the solemn German and rococo Canton synagogues are hidden away. The most imposing building is the Spanish, built in 1580 in grandiose fashion by the great Venetian architect Longhena, and still in use today. *www.museoebraico.it; tel +39 041 715359; Campo del Ghetto Nuovo, Cannaregio; 10am-7pm Sun-Fri*

04 SAN SEBASTIANO CHURCH

Just outside the entrance to the Ghetto, the 5.1 vaporetto leaves the Guglie stop to chug over to San Basilio in Dorsoduro. San Sebastiano is the most understated of Venice's 'plague churches', built in the 16th century to give thanks for the city's salvation from the plague.

Living in Venice at the time was the great Renaissance artist Paolo Veronese, who transformed this austere church with a dazzling array of paintings, ceiling canvases and frescoes, and chose it as his final resting place. The subtle rendition of San Sebastiano uses sublime pastel colours and hints of his trademark trompe l'oeil technique, echoed in more famous pieces such as the frescoes in the Doge's Palace and *The Wedding at Cana*, which hangs in the Louvre. *www.chorusvenezia.org/en/church-of-san-sebastiano; tel +39 041 2750462; Campo San Sebastiano, Dorsoduro; 10.30am-4pm*

03-04 © John Brunton

05 PALAZZO FORTUNY

Tucked away in the backstreets behind the Grand Canal, Palazzo Fortuny is the heart of the San Marco neighbourhood. This intricate 600-year-old gothic palace takes its name from the flamboyant Mariano Fortuny, an extraordinary Spanish photographer, painter and fashion designer who lived and worked here until his death in 1949.

Today the palazzo can be visited, furnished with his personal collection of artworks, theatre costumes, printed velvet and silk fabrics and signature Fortuny lamps. It also hosts prestigious temporary art exhibitions. But the real pleasure is the chance to get a feel for what it must have been like to live in one of these aristocratic homes, including the vast attic and magnificent views over La Serenissima.
www.fortuny.visitmuve.it; tel +39 041 5200995; 3780 Campo San Beneto, San Marco; 10am-6pm Wed-Mon

06 CASINO VENIER

Following the yellow San Marco signs, Casino Venier is a short stroll away. In the decadent days of Casanova there were more than 100 'casini' in Venice — gilded, private salons where the aristocracy danced, flirted and gambled. The extravagant 1750 Casino Venier is one of the few that has been perfectly preserved, today home to French cultural centre L'Alliance Francaise, which welcomes visitors.

Ring the bell outside this nondescript building, walk up an ancient staircase and push open a heavy door that suddenly opens into a marble-floored salon of swirling stucco, glittering Murano chandeliers and frescoes; a glimpse of what was once a fantasy world of masked libertines, when Venice's sinful carnival lasted for months.
www.afvenezia.it; tel +39 041 5227079; 4939 Ponte dei Baratteri, San Marco; 9am-6pm Mon-Sat

07 SCUOLA DI SAN GIORGIO DEGLI SCHIAVONI

The majestic Doge's Palace sits on Venice's waterfront promenade, Riva degli Schiavoni, leading into the artisans' district of Castello. The Riva was named after the Slavs who traded with the Serene Republic (Serenissima in Latin), and tucked

05 © gab90 / Shutterstock

away in Castello's backstreets lies a tiny *scuola* built by these people from the Dalmatian coast.

The Venetian *scuola* were charitable meeting houses dotted all over the city and some, like the monumental San Rocco, boast prestigious paintings by the likes of Titian and Tintoretto. San Giorgio is far more discreet, but it has an unparalleled collection of early Renaissance religious panels of St George and other Slavic saints by Vittore Carpaccio, painted between 1502 and 1507, which sit in the main hall. *Tel +39 041 5228828; 3259 Calle Furlani, Castello; 9.30am-5.30pm Tue-Sat, to 1.30pm Sun, 1.30pm-5.30pm Mon*
BY JOHN BRUNTON

06 © Piere Bonbon / Alamy

Ø5 Venice's 16th-century Jewish ghetto

Ø6 The Palazzo Fortuny's inner courtyard

WHERE TO STAY
DOMUS ORSONI
The Orsoni glass factory produces exquisite *smalto* (glass mosaics) that decorate the Basilica di San Marco. Its tiny hotel overlooking the furnace workshop and a lush garden has five comfy rooms, and guests can also join a mosaic course. *www.domusorsoni.it; tel +39 041 2759538; 1045 Calle dei Vedei, Cannaregio*

CASA BASEGGIO
In a tiny courtyard adjoining the 14th-century Abbazia della Misericordia, this is a genuine B&B with friendly young owners. In summer, breakfast is served on a sunny terrace overlooking the abbey's gardens. *www.casabaseggio.it; tel +39 041 0994079; 3556 Corte Nova, Cannaregio*

WHERE TO EAT & DRINK
CULTO CAFFE E CIOCCOLATO
Housed in the entrance hall of the Ca' Pesaro palace, the Museum of Modern Art's cafe has a splendid waterside terrace right on the Grand Canal,

perfect for cappuccino and chocolate cake. *Tel +39 041 721127; 2076 Fondamenta de Ca' Pesaro, Santa Croce*

PEGGY GUGGENHEIM CAFÉ
After marvelling at Peggy Guggengeim's remarkable collection of modern art, relax in the palazzo's shady garden cafe for a chilled Prosecco, a smoked beef panino or vegan burger. *www.guggenheim-venice. it; tel +39 041 5228688; 701 Fondamenta Venier dei Leoni, Dorsoduro*

CELEBRATIONS
BIENNALE OF ART
From May to November this prestigious art fest exhibits contemporary artists from around the world. In alternate years, Venice hosts the Biennale of Architecture. *(www.labiennale.org)*

REGATA STORICA
On the first Sunday of September, the Regata Storica holds an unforgettable parade of 16th-century-style boats with extravagantly costumed rowers, gliding by Grand Canal palaces. *(www.regatastorica venezia.it)*

Italy

MEDICI FLORENCE

A powerful family of bankers and art lovers, the Medici dynasty dominated Florentine life for centuries. Today, the city's Renaissance core is the legacy of their patronage.

With its cinematic tangle of medieval streets, Renaissance palazzi and world-class art, urban Florence evokes intriguing tales at every turn. Feel Dante's hellish heartbreak reading dedications of unrequited love on scraps of paper in the candle-lit chapel where the Florentine poet's muse is buried. At the Museo Galileo, learn about the heretical scientist from nearby Pisa, who dared suggest the earth revolved around the sun. Trace the route trodden by 40 men over the course of four days in 1504 as they hauled a gigantic white statue of David weighing 19 tonnes from Michelangelo's workshop to Piazza della Signora. Knock back *un caffè* on the square where wigs, jewels, books, musical instruments, Botticelli paintings and other sinful indulgences went up in flames on Friar Savonarola's chilling Bonfire of the Vanities in 1497.

Stories seep out of every last ancient stone and stucco, but none is more incredible than that of the

NEED TO KNOW
This two-day trail is best experienced on foot; Florence has an international airport and Pisa airport is only an hour away.

Medici dynasty. Powerful, flamboyant, compelling and conceited in equal measure, this influential family of bankers transformed the city of Florence into the romantic, beguiling Renaissance gem it is today. From the 15th to 18th centuries, they dominated Florentine life: the Medici controlled the *signoria* (city government); their bank was Europe's most powerful; and under the enlightened patronage of de facto rulers Cosimo the Elder (1389-1464) and Lorenzo Il Magnifico (1469-92), the arts flourished. Enter Medici Florence, cradle of the Renaissance and cultural capital of 15th-century Italy – until 1492 when the magnificent Lorenzo died, the bank failed and the Medici were driven out of Florence. Of course they returned, first as dukes of Florence and later as grand dukes of the Duchy of Tuscany, which they ruled until 1737 when the last Medici died. This urban trail traces the priceless art and architectural legacy this illustrious family left behind.

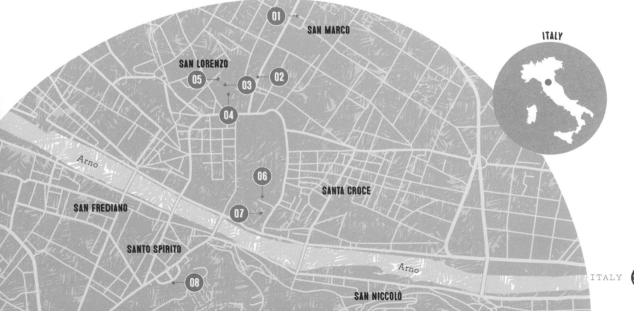

01 MUSEO DI SAN MARCO

Few artists are saints — they're far
more likely to be sinners. Tuscan-
born friar Fra' Angelico (1395-1455)
was a brilliant exception. This did not
go unnoticed by Medici patriarch,
Cosimo the Elder, whose exceptional
eye for artistic talent — and burning
desire to earn a place in heaven —
inspired him to rebuild a 13th-century
Dominican monastery in San Marco
in 1437 and commission the gifted
painter to decorate it with frescoes.

Fra' Angelico's portrayal of religious
figures in all-too-human moments
of uncertainty reflect the humanist
spirit of the Renaissance. Gorge on his
fabulous *Annunciation*, then push onto
Adoration of the Magi in the cell used
by Cosimo as a meditative retreat.

'Fra' Angelico's portrayal of religious figures in all-too-human moments of uncertainty reflect the humanist spirit of the Renaissance'

*www.uffizi.com/san-marco-museum.
asp; tel +39 055 238 86 08; Piazza San
Marco 3; 8.15am-1.50pm Mon-Fri, to
4.50pm Sat & Sun, check website for
regular Sun & Mon closures*

02 PALAZZO MEDICI-RICCARDI

Ogle at hidden portraits of the
conceited Medici clan inside this
beautiful palazzo, a Medici residence
from 1444 to 1540, 400m south of
the Museo di San Marco. The highlight
is the bijou chapel, squirrelled away

upstairs like a precious jewel. Head-
to-toe wall frescoes by Benozzo
Gozzoli, a pupil of Fra' Angelico, are a
supreme achievement of Renaissance
painting — even if the ostensible theme
of *Procession of the Magi to Bethlehem*
is but a slender pretext for portraying
Cosimo the Elder and grandson
Lorenzo il Magnifico in their best light.
Spot the pair hovering in the crowd.
*www.palazzo-medici.it; tel +39 055
276 03 40; Via Cavour 3; 9am-7pm
Thu-Tue*

03 © Conde / Shutterstock; 04 © Pete Seaward / Lonely Planet

03 BASILICA DI SAN LORENZO

Florentine artists flourished under Cosimo the Elder, among them goldsmith Filippo Brunelleschi (1377-1446), who designed the Medici family church in 1425. The resultant Basilica di San Lorenzo, a two-minute walk from the Palazzo Medici-Riccardi, with austere sacristy decorated by Florentine sculptor Donatello (1386-1466), is one of the city's most harmonious examples of Renaissance architecture — observe the characteristic symmetry and geometry of the church interior inspired by classical art, the striking abundance of arches and niches, and the dome.

Michelangelo (1475-1564) was meant to design the façade in the same marble he would later use to bring David to life, but it was never executed — hence the church's jarringly roughshod, unfinished appearance. *www.operamedicealaurenziana.org; Piazza di San Lorenzo; 10am-5pm Mon-Sat year-round, plus 1.30-5.30pm Sun Mar-Oct*

04 BIBLIOTECA MEDICEA LAURENZIANA

Back past the basilica ticket office, look for the peaceful cloister garden with orange trees. Steps lead up into the loggia, from where the Medici library can be accessed — swoon over the world's most beautiful library staircase, designed by Michelangelo in 1524. The curvaceous sweep of stairs, cut in mellow Pietra Serena sandstone, fills the vestibule — a minuscule antechamber designed in Mannerist style as a dark prelude to the light-flooded Reading Room lined with walnut-wood desks. The library was built between 1524 and 1559 in the San Lorenzo cloister for the first duke of Florence, Pope Clement VII (1478-1534), to house the family collection of manuscripts.

Leave the cloister and walk 180m to Piazza di Madonna degli Aldobrandini. *www.bmlonline.it; Piazza di San Lorenzo; 9.30am-1.30pm Mon-Fri*

05 CAPPELLE MEDICEE

Brace yourself. Nowhere is Medici conceit expressed so explicitly as in the breathtaking Medici Chapels, burial place to 49 dynasty members.

A 180m walk from the Medici

library, enter via the newer Chapel of the Princes (1604-40) home to sarcophagi of several Medici grand dukes. The family had been ruling Florence for several centuries when it was built, and it was precisely this domination they wanted to show off so brazenly.

The ostentatious mausoleum drips in granite, marble and dazzling semi-precious stones. Lapis lazuli — the petrol-blue semi-precious stone used by Renaissance painters to make blue pigment — was meant to coat the domed ceiling but was not completed; it was frescoed with scenes from the Old and New Testaments instead, in 1828.

Continue into the older New Sacristy (1520-24) by Michelangelo.

His most haunting sculptures known to mankind are here: *Dawn and Dusk* on the sarcophagus of Lorenzo II de Medici (1492-1519); *Night and Day* on the sarcophagus of Lorenzo il Magnifico's youngest son, Giuliano (1478-1516); and *Madonna and Child* on Lorenzo il Magnifico's own incongruously plain tomb. *www.cappellemedicee.it; tel +39 055 238 86 02; Piazza Madonna degli Aldobrandini; 8.15am-2pm, closed 2nd & 4th Sun, 1st, 3rd & 5th Mon of month*

06 PALAZZO VECCHIO

The next day, weave your way through ancient lanes to Piazza della Signoria, factoring in extra time to linger on Florence's mighty cathedral square

dominated by the Duomo and its separate bell tower and baptistry. Gorge on city views atop crenellated Torre d'Arnolfo before diving into the heavy-handed interior of this 13th-century fortress, ducal palace to Cosimo I (1519-74) from 1540 and an unabashed celebration of Medici power.

Spot Cosimo I portrayed as a god on the bedazzling panelled ceiling in the Salone dei Cinquecento, a gargantuan hall painted with swirling battle scenes glorifying Florentine victories over arch-rivals Pisa and Siena. *www.museifirenze.it; tel +39 055 276 82 24; Piazza della Signoria; 9am-midnight Fri-Wed, to 2pm Thu summer, shorter hours winter*

07 GALLERIA DEGLI UFFIZI

Feast on the world's greatest collection of Italian Renaissance art in the vast U-shaped Palazzo degli Uffizi, commissioned by Cosimo I in 1560 to bring all his government *uffizi* (offices) under one roof. The art collection, bequeathed to the city by the Medici family in 1743 on the condition that it never leave Florence, contains some of Italy's best-known paintings including a room full of Botticelli masterpieces.

With advance planning, one can book a guided tour to cross the river via the Vasarian Corridor, an elevated covered passageway built in 1565 to allow the Medicis to stroll between the Uffizi and Palazzo Pitti in privacy. *www.uffizi.it; tel +39 055 238 85; Piazzale degli Uffizi 6; 8.15am-6.50pm Tue-Sun*

08 PALAZZO PITTI

As the setting sun turns the ginger façade of this Renaissance palazzo (1457) in the Oltrarno quarter a dazzling flamingo pink, bathe in its glorious light. Then head inside to the Brunelleschi-designed pad, home sweet home to the Medici grand dukes from 1549. *www.polomuseale.firenze.it; tel +39 055 294 883; Piazza dei Pitti; 8.15am-6.50pm Tue-Sun Jun-Aug, shorter hrs rest of yr*
BY NICOLA WILLAMS

05 Statue of Cosimo I, still lording it over Florence

06 Harmonious Renaissance style at Basilica di San Lorenzo

WHERE TO STAY

HOTEL ORTO DE' MEDICI
This midrange San Marco hotel is superb for getting under the Medici skin: it's wrapped around the bijou Medici garden where Lorenzo il Magnifico encountered a young Michelangelo for the first time. The 19th-century palazzo has period furnishings, parquet floors and original frescoes. *www.ortodeimedici.it; tel +39 055 483 427; Via San Gallo 13*

ANTICA TORRE DI VIA TORNABUONI 1
Footsteps from the Arno and the designer fashion houses of Florence's smartest shopping street, this four-star boutique palazzo-hotel sports a 13th-century tower and breakfast room with sweeping views. *www.tornabuoni1.com; Via de' Tornabuoni 1*

WHERE TO EAT & DRINK

MERCATO CENTRALE
In the heart of Medici territory, spitting distance from the Basilica di San Lorenzo, is Florence's 19th-century covered food market. Grab a tripe sandwich to go, or head upstairs for pasta, pizza, truffles or a feisty *bistecca alla fiorentina* (T-bone steak) enjoyed with gusto around shared tables. *www.mercatocentrale.it; tel +39 055 239 97 98; Piazza del Mercato Centrale 4*

LA LEGGENDA DEI FRATI
Cross the river to Oltrarno and Michelin-starred Legend of the Friars, romantically set in the Renaissance garden of 17th-century Villa Bardini. Veggies are fresh from the vegetable patch, cuisine is modern Tuscan and the terrace with city view is paradise on Florentine earth. *www.laleggendadeifrati.it; tel +39 055 068 05 45; Costa San Giorgio 6a*

CELEBRATIONS

Florentines have good reason to honour Anna Maria Luisa de' Medici with her own festa each year on 18 February: the last Medici, she bequeathed Florence its vast cultural heritage. Costumed revellers parade from Palazzo Vecchio to her tomb inside the Medici Chapels and state museums are free all day.

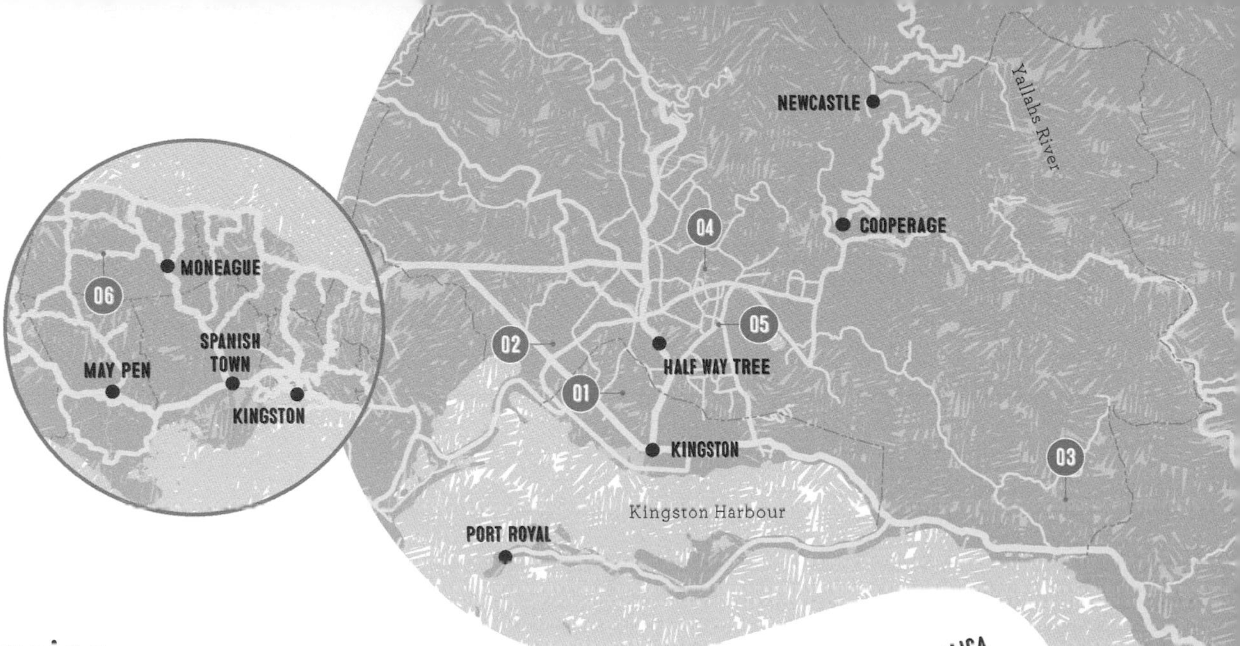

Map labels: NEWCASTLE, Yallahs River, COOPERAGE, 04, MONEAGUE, 06, 02, 05, HALF WAY TREE, SPANISH TOWN, 01, MAY PEN, KINGSTON, 03, KINGSTON, Kingston Harbour, PORT ROYAL, JAMAICA

Jamaica

BOB MARLEY REGGAE TRAIL

Retrace the life and career of the Jamaican reggae legend in the island's gritty capital city of Kingston, where music courses through the streets and Marley's spirit looms large.

At night, Kingston reverberates with slow, ponderous reggae beats. Two massive speakers are set up on opposite ends of a dusty Downtown street. The crowd dances in the space between the two speakers, shuffling, bending their knees, Red Stripe beers in one hand, the air awaft with aromatic ganja smoke. A familiar voice comes from the speakers, singing of life in Kingston's ghettos, of love, peace and salvation, of social justice. Reggae may have been born right here, in Jamaica's crime-ridden yet beguiling capital within its struggling Downtown neighbourhoods, yet its most famous standard-bearer transcended his humble beginnings and his dreadlocked visage, his voice and his message have become familiar worldwide, from America to Ethiopia.

When it comes to music, Jamaica punches way above its weight: along with other music genres, it gave the world reggae. Yet among the reggae legends

NEED TO KNOW
Kingston is one of the Caribbean's biggest air hubs. Take taxis to get around town on this two-day trail; rent a car for Nine Mile.

— Burning Spear, Dennis Brown, Peter Tosh, Gregory Isaacs, Jimmy Cliff — Bob Marley's contributions remain disproportionately large, especially given his early death from cancer at the age of 36. Robert Nesta Marley was born in a tiny village in the north of Jamaica, but his creative awakening and growth took place in Kingston's ghettos, and he is still very much part of Jamaica's landscape; in some parts of the island he has acquired almost prophet-like status.

This tour retraces the course of Marley's life, musical creativity and death, mostly in and near Kingston, though the rest of Jamaica, with its beautiful beaches and waterfalls, delicious spicy food, jungle-covered mountains and rich historical heritage, is a wonder to explore as well. February ('Reggae Month') is the best time to visit, with numerous shows and exhibitions around the city celebrating Marley's birthday and his legacy.

01 © Hemis / Alamy

01 TRENCH TOWN CULTURE YARD

The 'government yard' that Bob Marley sang about in 'No Woman, No Cry' is his simple former home in the impoverished community of Trench Town in the western part of Downtown Kingston.

Trench Town government yards, consisting of blocks of 10 to 20 rooms centred on a common cooking and washing area, were built in the 1940s by the Central Housing Authority to provide affordable accommodation for city residents, and are credited as the birthplace of reggae, ska and rocksteady.

Bob lived in a 'U' block — a spartan two-room dwelling flanked by a long veranda that has been restored and converted into a museum. Some personal effects remain: the infamous single bed, his first guitar, and the burnt-out shell of his Volkswagen camper van.

Vincent 'Tata' Ford, who lived in the same block, taught Marley to play guitar; the Wailers were formed here, and it is here that they composed their first album, *Catch a Fire*. It's safe to walk around Trench Town with neighbourhood guides, but not on your own, due to high rates of gang-related crime.
Tel +876 859 6741; 6-10 Lower First Street; 9am-6pm

02 TUFF GONG INTERNATIONAL RECORDING STUDIOS

Originally based at Orange Street Downtown, Tuff Gong International Recording Studios was founded by Bob Marley in 1965. Bob's nickname was 'the Gong' and you had to be 'tuff' to make it in the Jamaican music business.

The studio moved twice: to Bob Marley's Uptown home, and finally to 220 Marcus Garvey Drive, where it remains one of the largest recording studios in the Caribbean, run by Marley's son, Ziggy. The original mixing board, used in Marley hits such as 'No Woman, No Cry', 'Trenchtown Rock', 'Redemption Song', 'Buffalo Soldier'

'To get fit before going on tour, Marley would take The Wailers jogging to the falls and along nearby Bull Bay Beach'

01-04 Scenes from Nine Mile, where Marley was born and entombed, now a pilgrimage site for fans

and 'Could You Be Loved', has made it to its current location.

Call ahead (there are no set opening hours) for a 45-minute tour of the studio, including the mastering room, stamper room, pressing plant, cassette plant and wholesale record shop. *www.tuffgong.com; tel +876 923 9380; 220 Marcus Garvey Drive*

03 CANE RIVER FALLS

When not composing or recording at Tuff Gong Studios, Marley liked to unwind. He played football, and occasionally he and his bandmates would pile into his camper van and escape the city. About 14km east of

Kingston, there's a tranquil spot with some modest waterfalls that was allegedly Bob's favourite place to wash his dreadlocks. To get fit before going on tour, Marley would take The Wailers jogging to the falls and along the sand at nearby Bull Bay Beach.

Catch bus 97 or 97X to Bull Bay from Kingston and walk to the falls, or hire a taxi to take you there and back.

04 BOB MARLEY MUSEUM

As Bob Marley's fame as an international musician grew, he moved to Uptown Kingston in 1975 and settled at this creaky 19th-century house at 56 Hope Road with his wife Rita. Marley's home until his

death in 1981, it was converted into a museum by his wife six years after his death to preserve his legacy and accomplishments, and remains a shrine to fans. Access to the house itself is by guided tour; displays include a life-size, 3D hologram of Bob from the One Love Peace Concert in 1978, as well as various personal effects, awards such as the Order of Merit presented by the Jamaican government, and his Rastafarian cloaks.

One room is wallpapered with newspaper clippings of his achievements, whereas another replicates Bob's original record shop, Wail'n'Soul'm. Preserved as it had

03-04 © Hemis / Alamy

been when he was alive, Bob's simple bedroom is surprisingly humble, with his favourite star-shaped guitar resting by his bed, while the kitchen where he used to cook vegetarian I-tal food still sports bullet holes from the 1976 assassination attempt.

Unknown gunmen struck two days before Bob was due to perform at a Smile Jamaica concert organised by Prime Minister Michael Manley to ease political tensions; Marley and his wife were both wounded.

The tour closes with a 20-minute film of Bob's life and there are some excellent photos of Bob at the adjoining exhibition hall, which used to be the Tuff Gong recording studios. Marley's sons occasionally come to record at the other

recording studio inside the house. *www.bobmarleymuseum.com; tel +876 927 9152; 56 Hope Rd; 9.30am-4pm Mon-Sat*

05 BOB MARLEY STATUE

Created by Jamaican sculptor Alvin Marriott, who'd previously immortalised Jamaica's other famous sons (Marcus Garvey, Norman Manley, Alexander Bustamante), Marley's life-size likeness in bronze stands in Celebrity Park outside the National Stadium, where Bob came sometimes to support Jamaica's national football team, the Reggae Boyz.

In 1978, during the height of political tensions in Jamaica, Marley and The Wailers played their One Love Peace Concert at this stadium. Marley famously took the opportunity during a

rendition of 'Jammin'' to make Michael Manley and Edward Seaga — the leaders of the two opposing political parties — shake hands onstage.

06 NINE MILE

The tiny village of Nine Mile, about a two-hour drive from Kingston, sits amid the dramatic hilly scenery of Cockpit Country in the St Ann province. In spite of its relatively isolated location, it is regularly visited by fans looking to pay their respects to Bob's place of birth and final entombment.

It's interesting to glimpse the interior of the simple two-room cottage where Bob lived until he was 13 and his mother took him to Kingston following his father's death. Bob is seeing out eternity at

the adjacent marble mausoleum with stained glass windows, alongside his mother Cedella Booker and half-brother Anthony. The compound is easily recognisable by the Rastafarian flags flying from the wall surrounding the mausoleum and cottage.

The relentless commercialisation can be a little off-putting, but for Marley fans it's worth coming to pay your respects and see the humble circumstances from which he came. Entry is by brisk guided tour and zealous guides expect generous tips on top of the entrance fee for pointing out such Marley memorabilia as his 'rock pillow', alluded to in the song 'Talkin' Blues'.
Tel +876 999 7003; 9am-4.30pm
BY ANNA KAMINSKI

05 The Bob Marley Museum, Kingston

06 The Zion Bus Line tour takes in Bob Marley's birth and resting places

WHERE TO STAY

SPANISH COURT HOTEL
Uptown Kingston's best hotel is kitted out with iPod docks and locally designed furniture. The rooftop pool and spa provide the relaxation factor and there's an excellent restaurant onsite. *www.spanishcourt hotel.com; St Lucia Ave, Kingston; tel +876 926 000*

BLUE HOUSE
Comprising luxurious bedrooms on a beautiful property drowning in flowers near Ocho Rios on Jamaica's north coast, this intimate guesthouse is also known for its fusion cuisine. Darryl the Barefoot Cook conjures up three-course feasts incorporating Chinese and Indian influences. *www.thebluehousejamaica .com; tel +876 994 1367*

WHERE TO EAT & DRINK

MOBY DICK
Despite the rough-and-ready surroundings of Downtown Kingston and the plastic tablecloths, this is one of the best places in the capital for classic Jamaican dishes. At lunchtime, lawyers and judges gather here for curried goat and conch. *3 Orange St; 9am-7pm Mon-Sat*

SCOTCHIES TOO
This no-nonsense branch of the famous Montego Bay jerk centre sits next to a gas station in Ocho Rios, tantalising passing motorists with its pork, chicken and sausage, smoked over pimento wood. *Jack's Hall Fair Ground; tel +876 794 9457*

CELEBRATIONS

REGGAE SUMFEST
Taking place near Montego Bay for several days mid-July, this is Jamaica's biggest gig. Numerous reggae legends play until dawn. Bob Marley's youngest son, Damien 'Jr Gong' Marley, and UB40 have both played here. *(www.reggaesumfest.com)*

REBEL SALUTE
Named after reggae legend Tony Rebel, Jamaica's largest Roots Reggae concert takes over Richmond Estate in St Ann's Bay every January. Past performers have included The Abyssinians and Beres Hammond. *(www.rebelsalute jamaica.com)*

Japan
TOKYO POP CULTURE

A topsy-turvy fantasy universe lurks amid the high-rises and neon lights of Japan's capital city, where animated film, TV and comic characters come to life on the streets.

Tokyo is the capital of Japan, but it is also so much more: it is among the world's most populous cities and home to 10% of Japan's population. It is an immense urban conurbation with not one but many city centres. Viewed from atop one of the city's many soaring towers, it appears to be a limitless system of blinking nodes.

In popular culture Tokyo is often depicted as the city of the future; indeed, with its omnipresent neon and video screens, ever-packed, ever-bustling streets and large swathes of concrete, glass and steel, it often appears to be. It is the city that Godzilla destroyed (several times), but it is also the city that created Godzilla: Tokyo is the centre of Japan's pop culture industry. The film studios, the publishing houses, the game companies, the anime (Japanese animation) and manga (Japanese comic book) workshops — they're pretty much all here.

NEED TO KNOW
This two-day feast of pop culture can be completed entirely using Tokyo's excellent public train system.

Japanese pop culture has had a big impact around the globe. Most likely you know at least one of its most famous ambassadors: adorable Hello Kitty; plucky Mario and Luigi from the early Nintendo games; or everyone's favourite Pokémon, Pikachu. Or maybe you've seen one of animator Miyazaki Hayao's masterful, magical films, such as the Academy Award-winning *Spirited Away* (2001).

If you grew up an avid consumer of Japanese anime and manga, Tokyo is likely already on your bucket list. But you don't have to be a fan to get a kick out of the city's pop culture attractions. For starters, they're just plain fun. They're also your entree into the playful side of Japanese culture, a topsy-turvy universe populated by fantastical monsters and giant robots, where fantasy reigns, inanimate objects spring to life and there's never enough colour.

01 © World Discovery / Alamy

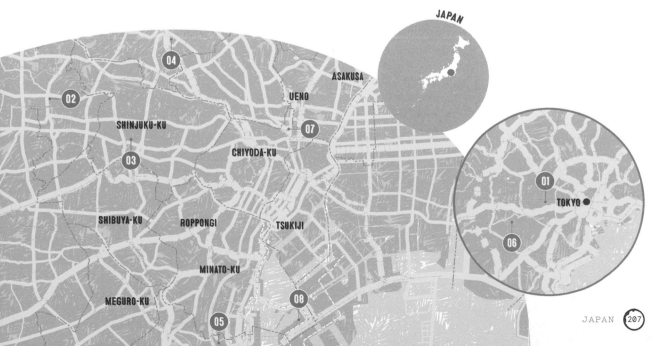

JAPAN

ASAKUSA

UENO

02

SHINJUKU-KU

04

07

CHIYODA-KU

03

SHIBUYA-KU   ROPPONGI   TSUKIJI

01

TOKYO ●

06

MINATO-KU

08

MEGURO-KU

05

02

01 GHIBLI MUSEUM, MITAKA

First stop: the museum that Miyazaki Hayao built to showcase the work of his Studio Ghibli. He designed this museum like he designs the worlds in his beloved animated films: as a place of wonder, discovery and inspiration. There's a theatre that shows original short animations, artwork from his films on the walls, plenty of vintage animation machines to play with and all sorts of nooks and crannies to explore.

Miyazaki's career has spanned half a century (and he has suggested he's not done yet). Even in the digital age much of the work on Studio Ghibli films is done by hand, and often in watercolours, which gives them a dreamy quality. Of Japan's top 10 highest-grossing anime of all time,

Studio Ghibli made six of them. *Spirited Away* is perhaps the most famous, but other must-sees include *Princess Mononoke* (1997), *Castle in the Sky* (1986) and *Nausicaä of the Valley of the Wind* (1984).

The museum allows only a limited number of visitors so it never feels crowded. You must reserve tickets in advance, for the exact day and time of your visit, from a travel agent in your home country; do this as soon as you can, as they sell out fast.

When you're done here, walk through woodsy Inokashira Park — where you can grab lunch or a coffee — to Kichijōji Station. *www.ghibli-museum.jp; 1-1-83 Shimo-Renjaku, Mitaka-shi; 10am-6pm Wed-Mon*

02 NAKANO BROADWAY

When the shopping centre Nakano Broadway was built in the 1960s, it was the height of fashion; now it is a serious time capsule beloved for its vintage vibe. It's also emerged as Tokyo's underground haunt for otaku (fans obsessed with manga and anime). Most of the stores here now specialise in the trappings of fandom: animation cel art, character figures, model kits and vintage toys. Afterwards head for Shinjuku, one train stop away. *www.nbw.jp; tel +81 3 3388 7004; 5-52-15 Nakano, Nakano-ku; noon-8pm*

03 GODZILLA STATUE

Full disclosure: this is a shameless appeal to tourists. All the same, how could you pass up an opportunity to

'Miyazaki Hayao designed this museum like the worlds in his films; as a place of wonder, discovery and inspiration'

01 Parallel universe? Godzilla's head peeping over a hotel

02 Tokyo's Akihabara district is the heartland of anime and manga

03 Cosplay dress-up is commonplace in Tokyo

04 Jicoo floating bar — from the creator of Space Battleship Yamato

see an enormous statue of Godzilla? The installation is part of a hotel and entertainment complex that opened in 2015 (and Godzilla looks like he's ready to devour it). For a closer look, head to the Hotel Gracery Shinjuku's 8th-floor cafe, where you can have tea and sweets (and take even better photos) under the monster's head.

Godzilla — conceived as a cross between a gorilla and a whale ('kujira' in Japanese) — first appeared in Japanese cinemas in 1954, a prehistoric beast animated by nuclear fallout, played by a man in a suit. Over the decades Godzilla has appeared in more than two dozen movies, and the creature has evolved from harbinger of doom to beloved icon. The Shinjuku ward of Tokyo named him an official cultural ambassador in 2015 when this new building complex opened.
Toho Bldg, 1-19-1 Kabukicho, Shinjuku-ku; cafe 10.30am-9pm

04 OTOME ROAD

Cosplay (costume play – ie dressing up as your favourite anime or manga character) is one of the most fascinating elements of Japanese popular culture. Serious fans take it very seriously indeed, pouring their love for the character into picture-perfect ensembles. Otome Road — which means 'Maiden Road' — is a street in Tokyo's northern Ikebukuro neighbourhood with shops that specialise in the goods that girl geeks love, and while female fans are not the only ones who enjoy cosplaying, Otome Road has the best costume shops.

You don't need to have a character in mind to appreciate the shelves of wigs and tights in so many shades as to the make the rainbow seem dull, plus coloured contact lenses, fake lashes and even press-on tears.

Otome Road is on the west side of the massive Sunshine City shopping complex, about a 10-minute walk from Ikebukuro train station.
3 Higashi-Ikebukuro, Toshima-ku; shops noon-8pm

05 MARICAR

Maricar is a dream come true (for a dream you didn't know you had until now): the opportunity to drive around Tokyo in a go-kart while dressed as

your favourite character from the hit 1990s Nintendo video game *Super Mario Kart* (there are other costume options, too — superheroes, Winnie the Pooh, Sesame Street... you name it!).

We recommend a night tour that takes in the famous neon-lit Shibuya Crossing; the crowds that naturally gathered around the intersection will cheer your arrival — and you'll probably wind up the subject of other travellers' photos.

All tours leave from the Shinagawa depot, and reservations are a must. To participate you need to have an international driver's licence issued in your home country. *maricar.com; tel +81 120 819 999; 1-23-15 Kita-Shinagawa, Shinagawa-ku; 10am-10pm*

06 SANRIO PUROLAND

Start your second day at Sanrio Puroland in Tama, a 30-minute train ride west of central Tokyo. Hello Kitty's famous poker face doesn't give away many secrets, but her amusement park does. Here you can peek inside her home; take a boat ride through her enchanting (and very, very pastel) world; and hang out with Kitty and her friends – her friends being the other characters in the Sanrio pantheon.

The current 'it' character is Gudetama, a seriously mopey anthropomorphic egg. Sanrio Puroland has seasonal hours and irregular holidays, so check ahead. *en.puroland.jp; tel +81 42 339 1111; 1-31 Ochiai, Tama-shi; 10am-5pm Mon-Fri, 10am-8pm Sat & Sun*

07 SUPER POTATO RETRO-KAN

While Nakano has more street cred, a pop culture tour of Tokyo couldn't possibly leave out the neighbourhood of Akihabara — the sun of Japan's anime, manga and video game solar system. Among all the shops clamouring for your attention is a tiny video arcade, Super Potato Retro-kan, full of vintage machines playing 1980s classics such as *Pac-Man* and *Street Fighter*. When you've had your fill, take the train to Shimbashi and transfer to the Yurikamome line, a cool above-ground train line that wends through the skyscrapers of downtown towards the man-made island of Odaiba. *www.superpotato.com; tel +81 3 5289 9933; 1-11-2 Soto-Kanda, Chiyoda-ku; 11am-8pm*

ⓞ⑧ JICOO THE FLOATING BAR

Leiji Yamamoto is the creator of the pioneering anime series *Space Battleship Yamato*, which paved the way for more anime with epic story arcs in the 1970s and 80s; he's also the designer of this sleek, futuristic ship that looks, well, like something straight out of an anime film.

During the day it's one of the boats in the Tokyo Cruise tourist boat fleet, but three nights a week it cruises around Tokyo Bay with live music or DJs, offering spectacular views of the Tokyo skyline from the water: a fitting way to end your tour.
www.jicoofloatingbar.com; tel +81 120 049 490; 1-4-1 Daiba, Minato-ku; 8-11pm Thu-Sat
BY REBECCA MILNER

06 © Sean Pavone / Shutterstock / Museo d'Arte Ghibli

05 Sanrio Puroland, the home of Hello Kitty and others

06 Towering robot statue at the Ghibli Museum

WHERE TO STAY
HOTEL GRACERY SHINJUKU
With Godzilla scaling the side, this is the obvious choice for pop-culture fans. You can pay a little extra for a room with a view of the monster. Rooms are crisp and clean, though small. *shinjuku.gracery.com; tel +81 3 6833 1111; Toho Bldg, 1-19-1 Kabukicho, Shinjuku-ku*

KHAOSAN WORLD
To get a glimpse of a different kind of local culture, hang your hat in this hostel (with dorm beds, doubles and family rooms) inside a former love hotel. Much of the kitschy decor is intact (but don't worry, it's clean). *khaosan-tokyo.com; tel +81 3 3843 0153; 3-15-1 Nishi-Asakusa, Taitō-ku*

WHERE TO EAT & DRINK
POPEYE
Dip into Tokyo's craft beer scene at this locally famous bar, which has dozens of brews on tap – the largest selection in town. *Tel +81 3 3633 2120; 2-18-7 Ryogōku, Sumida; 5-11.30pm Mon-Fri, 3-11pm Sat*

KIKANBŌ
A pop culture-themed trip to Tokyo wouldn't be complete without a stop for ramen, the city's favourite food. Kikanbō, not far from Akihabara, has a cult following for its spicy noodles. *Tel +81 3 3256 2960; 2-10-9 Kajichō, Chiyoda-ku; 11am-9.30pm Mon-Sat, to 4pm Sun*

CELEBRATIONS
ANIME JAPAN
Japan's biggest anime trade show, in March, has attractions for industry pros and fans alike. It's particularly famous for drawing large numbers of cosplayers, who gather in the plaza of the venue. *(www.anime-japan.jp)*

SUMIDA RIVER FIREWORKS
Every summer Tokyo puts on several fireworks shows — the largest, Sumida River Fireworks, sends up 20,000 *hanabi* ('fire flowers') over the river on the last Saturday in July. A festival atmosphere prevails, with spectators dressed in colourful *yukata* (lightweight summer kimono) and plenty of street food vendors. *(www.gotokyo.org)*

OKAYAMA

INUJIMA

05

06

JAPAN

07

08

● UNO

TESHIMA

NAOSHIMA

01

04

03

02

Japan

NAOSHIMA'S ART ISLANDS

Forget Tokyo and the other mega cities — Japan's most mind-bending art mecca is a trio of islands hosting outdoor installations and sleepy fishing villages turned into galleries.

Contemporary art doesn't have to be in stuffy sterile spaces. In Japan there are three islands — Naoshima, Teshima and Inujima — so well known for their artistic merits that collectively they are simply referred to as the 'art islands'. This unique culture hub, 200km west of Osaka in the Seto Inland Sea, was proposed in 1985 by the president of a publishing house and the mayor of Naoshima, who both wanted to revive a sleepy fishing village in decline. Their efforts convinced Benesse Corporation to bring over its expanding collection of contemporary art.

A visit here is a unique, refreshing experience. It starts with a sunny ride on a ferry to sleepy fishing towns with an ageing population and a relaxed way of life. The old Japanese houses are still here, but now some of them have been converted into hosts for eye-opening art. The incongruity of stumbling across a transparent hall of colourful, acrylic flowers in rural Japan is like stepping

NEED TO KNOW
Art sites are grouped together on the islands; bus, cycle or walk between areas. You'll need two days to island-hop.

into a dream sequence. On Teshima, walking around the 17m hull-form (used to make Japanese fishing boats) in an abandoned sewing-needle factory as the sun blazes is the stuff of 'only on the art islands'.

Slab-like museums are here too, but they all strive to work with the environment, using eco-heating and cooling. Some play mind games with light, space and surfaces, making them artistic achievements in their own right. Inside, big names include Monet, Warhol, Walter De Maria, James Turrell and, outside, Yayoi Kusama. Lesser-known Japanese artists complete the package.

There is a fun, treasure-hunt element to walking or cycling between sites, with as many stops at cute, arty cafes as you want. It's worth spending the night on either Naoshima, which has plentiful accommodation, or Teshima. The nearest international airport is in Osaka. Trains from Osaka to Hiroshima call in at Okayama, from where the art islands can be easily accessed.

'The red acrylic exterior of Teshima Yokoo is a clue that this entire old house has been turned into a surreal work'

① ART HOUSE PROJECT

Start your weekend on Naoshima, the closest island to mainland Japan, by taking a ferry to the Miyanoura ferry terminal and then a bus to the Honmura area. The scattering of converted traditional Japanese buildings here have interiors converted into art installations. In the dilapidated former Haisha (dentist) office, Tokyo's Ōtake Shinrō (b1955) shows off his trademark collages of 2D pop-culture imagery pressed up against 3D objects — as if the whole building is a neon-lit scrapbook.

Art House Project's other highlight

is by James Turrell (b1943), a contemporary Californian artist known for manipulating perceptions of light and space, who famously spent a year in the most confined space — prison — as a conscientious objector to the Vietnam War. His installations tend to be grand (including a volcanic crater in Arizona) and simple.

It's a pleasant walk between sites with sleepy cafes that open for lunch. When you're finished, take the town bus to Tsutsuji-sō and transfer onto the Chichū Art Museum shuttle bus. *www.benesse-artsite.jp; Honmura area; 10am-4.30pm Tue-Sun*

② CHICHŪ ART MUSEUM

There are only three art installations here, and you may have to queue for them, but each one has been transformed into a monumental experience thanks to the environments in which they sit. The water-lily paintings by Monet (1840-1926) almost glow when arranged in a hall of white pebbles. The other two installations, by Turrell and fellow Californian Walter de Maria (1935-2013) — a 'minimalist' artist known for interactive sculptures that force viewers to think about the scale of the universe — are guaranteed to make

01 Kusama Yayoi's *Pumpkin* sculpture at Benesse House Museum

02 From Shinro Ohtake's 'Shipyard Works' series *Stern with Hole* at Benesse House Museum

03 Richard Long's *Inland Sea Driftwood Circle* and *River Avon Mud Circles by the Inland Sea* at Benesse House Museum

04 Niki de Saint Phalle's *Le Banc* at Benesse House Museum

04 © Osamu Watanabe

viewers feel tiny. It's a 20-minute walk from here to Benesse House Museum. *Benesse House area; 10am-5pm Mar-Oct Tue-Sun 10am-6pm (last admittance 5pm); Oct-Mar 10am-5pm (last admittance 4pm)*

03 BENESSE HOUSE MUSEUM

The themes of space and nature continue at this museum by self-taught Osakan architect Andō Tadao (b1941), who also designed Chichū and other buildings on the art islands. Here, the coast and green hillside come streaming through entire walls of glass and open terraces at bunker-like buildings, which seem to retreat into the hillside.

Andō's Zen notion of beauty through simplicity and emptiness is palpable as you walk through unpainted concrete expanses, taking in works by Andy Warhol, David Hockney, Yves Klein and Japanese artists such as Yanagi Yukinori (b1959 in Fukuoka), whose confronting Forbidden Box (1995) depicts atomic-bomb mushroom clouds escaping from a lead chest.

The real fun is outside though, hunting down the 20 art installations tucked into the cliffs, scattered across the lawn or along the beach itself.

The most famous outdoor installation is the large *Yellow Pumpkin* sculpture by Japanese artist Kusama Yayoi. Pumpkins are revered by Kusama for their quiet exuberance. Its spotty yellow figure stands out, perched on the end of a small jetty. Being the most recognisable icon of contemporary Japanese art, it's a favourite photo-op spot. Once you're finished here, take the town bus back to Miyanoura port, from where it's just a couple of minutes' walk inland to your next stop.
Benesse House area; 8am-9pm

05 © Osamu Watanabe

04 NAOSHIMA BATH - I ♥ 湯

Finish your day on Naoshima at this mixed-up *sento* (traditional Japanese bath house) in the Miyanoura Port area, where the mishmash tiled exterior gives a hint of the visual feast within.

The baths are a picture of gleaming cleanliness, with a paint-splattered skylight, elephant statue, and cacti-garden behind glass, courtesy of Ōtake Shinrō in his scrapbook style. Here he embeds images of vintage erotica under your feet. In this clever deconstruction, the bath's water becomes the lens that warps the image with every movement.

Stay overnight on the island and the next day take the hour-long boat ride to Inujima. The I ♥ 湯 towels for sale make a good keepsake.

2pm-9pm Tue-Fri, from 10am Sat-Sun

05 INUJIMA SEIRENSHO ART MUSEUM

The drawcard on this tiny island is Inujima Seirensho Art Museum, just a few minutes' walk along the coast from the ferry port. It's a copper refinery converted into an eco-building displaying surreal installations by Yukinori that pit nature against politics. Yanagi's works often challenge notions of Japanese identity and modernity. Nature and the 'civilised' world clash in this thought-provoking museum.

The final, moving piece is the deconstructed suicide note by gay Nobel Prize-nominated Tokyo writer and critic of modern Japan, Mishima Yukio (1925-1970); his gold-painted words float in the air, commanding attention across time.

10am-4.30pm Wed-Mon (last admittance 4pm); also closed Wed Dec-Mar

06 INUJIMA ART HOUSE PROJECT

Walk back towards the port and follow the signs for the various Inujima Art House Project sites, cousins to the Art House Project on Naoshima. A stand out is *Ether*, which strings out looms of canary-yellow thread from ceiling beams. The effect looks like light made physical, or stepping into a Windows screensaver. Also check out *Biota*, which evokes the birth of the universe and evolving life forms. Once back at Inujima's port, catch a boat to Teshima, from where it's a five-minute walk to Teshima Yokoo House. *Wed-Mon 10am-4.30pm (last admittance 4pm); also closed Wed Dec–Mar*

07 TESHIMA YOKOO HOUSE

The red acrylic exterior is a clue that this entire old house has been turned into a surreal work by experimental Japanese architect Yuko Nagayama (b1975) and psychedelic artist Tadanori Yokoo (b1936). Note the colourful take on a traditional Japanese rock garden, which locals in this village helped create.

If you suffer vertigo you might feel uneasy stepping into what feels like mid-air within a tower of thousands of postcards of waterfalls, plunging before you. Even the all-chrome bathrooms are wonderfully disturbing.
Mar–Oct 10am–5pm Wed–Mon; Oct–Mar 10am–4pm Wed–Mon, also closed Wed Dec–Mar

08 LES ARCHIVES DU CŒUR

Finish your tour of the art islands at this creation by French conceptual artist Christian Boltanski (b1944), which houses recordings of the heartbeats of people from all over the world. Boltanski's work often reflects on death and the past — he is famous for his work using clothing to recall Nazi concentration camps. There is only one thing to see here — a claustrophobic hall of light globes that throb to the heartbeat being recorded. Yes, you can record your own heartbeat here. You can then search the database by name and country and listen to any heartbeat that has previously been recorded. To get here, take the shuttle bus to Karato-kō bus stop, from where it's a 15-minute walk southeast through a temple gate, following the coast.
Mar–Oct 10am–5pm Wed–Mon; Oct–Mar 10am–4pm Wed–Mon; also closed Wed Dec–Mar
BY PHILLIP TANG

05 An exterior view of Benesse House Park

WHERE TO STAY
BENESSE HOUSE
You don't often get to stay in a museum. Book six months ahead for one of the six rooms in the hilltop Oval wing, where a monorail whisks you to rooms that ring an oval pool of water reflecting the sky. You can clamber up further and stand on a grass roof garden for views across Naoshima.
benesse-artsite.jp/en/stay; tel +81 87-892-3223

TAKAMATSU-YA
A traditional ryokan near Teshima's ferry terminal with English-speaking staff is a real find. This home among the lemon trees was formerly a sanitarium and then ryokan for infants. Not that you would know it now, looking at the seven handsome tatami rooms.
www.takamatsu-ya.jp; tel +81 80-5275-8550

WHERE TO EAT & DRINK
APRON CAFE
Near Naoshima's Art House Project sites is a cafe that you'd swear is a gallery, with polished timber, designer furniture and a faux-grass picnic area. It even makes its own zine and giftware. The artfully arranged lunches include tasting plates of tempura fish, samosas and Okayama black rice.
www.fb.me/aproncafe. naoshima; tel +81 87-892-3048; 777 Honmura

CAFE SALON NAKA-OKU
If you need a homely place to drink on a Naoshima evening, this cafe and bar up on a hill at the rear of a farming plot could be your go-to. It's also easy to sit down at this wood-furnished watering hole for a Japanese set lunch and linger for hours until it's time for a sake.
www.naka-oku.com; tel +087-892-3887; Honmura

CELEBRATIONS
SETOUCHI TRIENNALE
Every three years, the art islands' museums and sights get even more attention with a calendar of art, music, drama and dance that stretches across not just Naoshima, Inujima and Teshima, but also other isles of the Inland Sea. It's worth buying the three-season festival 'passport' ticket, which covers entry to almost all sites.
(setouchi-artfest.jp)

Lebanon
CULTURE & CONFLICT IN BEIRUT

Despite centuries of invasion and occupation, followed by civil war, Lebanon's capital has turned past conflicts into creative drive to carve out a niche in the global art scene.

First impressions of Beirut tend to be chaotic, as the airport taxi plunges into a seething, edgy metropolis of modern high-rise buildings, ramshackle houses, tall minarets and statuesque church towers, fringed on one side by the azure waters of the Mediterranean, on the other by Lebanon's verdant mountain peaks. But this is one of the oldest cities in the world, the eternal survivor, whose rainbow population of some 18 different religions continually reinvents Beirut like a phoenix rising from the ashes.

Exploring different neighbourhoods — the reborn Downtown and legendary seaside Corniche, elegant Hamra and hip Gemmayzeh — there are reminders everywhere of the impact left behind by each invader during the last two millennia; from the Phoenicians and Romans, through Arab, Crusader and Ottoman rule, to

NEED TO KNOW
Beirut is a sprawling metropolis, so take taxis between neighbourhoods, rather than walking, on this four-day trail.

the influential post-WWI French mandate era, followed by Lebanon's Independence in 1943. Since then, Beirut has continued to be a cultural hotbed, refusing to bow to invasions by Israel and Syria, then from 1975, 15 years of horrifying civil war between its Christian and Muslim populations.

Even today, despite — or perhaps because of — being right in the middle of the Middle East conflict zone, Beirut is still an electrifying hub of creativity that runs the gamut from avant-garde artists and film makers to musicians and cult DJs, designers and fashion stylists. This is a city that lives on a precipice, but all around there is an intensity to create because life is so precarious that people simply have to make things happen.

In just a day, a brief snapshot of the city that was once known as the Paris of the Middle East can span archeological ruins and spectacular contemporary art.

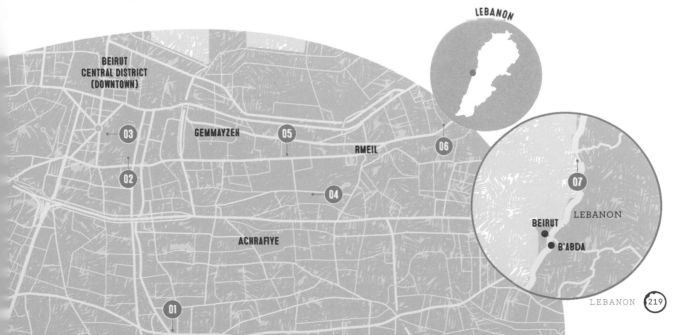

LEBANON

BEIRUT CENTRAL DISTRICT (DOWNTOWN)

03

GEMMAYZEH

05

RMEIL

06

02

04

ACHRAFIYE

07

LEBANON

BEIRUT

B'ABDA

01

01 BEIT BEIRUT

The newcomer on Beirut's cultural scene, this unique project is dedicated to the memory of decades of conflict witnessed here, but also looking to the future with temporary art and photo exhibitions.

What makes the Beit Beirut museum so special is actually the building itself. Situated on the Green Line that divided Muslim and Christian Beirut during the civil war, this 1920s ochre neo-Ottoman villa served as a sniper bunker and has been deliberately preserved in its crumbling half-destroyed state.

The architect, Youssef Haidar, explains how visitors 'begin to experience the museum as soon as they see the building's facade'. He adds: 'Inside, we have preserved the bomb damage, walls riddled with bullets, snipers' graffiti. A visit is intensely emotional both for Lebanese and foreigners.'
www.beitbeirut.org; Independence Street, Sodeco; 10am-7pm Tue-Sun

02 MOHAMMAD AL-AMIN MOSQUE

A 15-minute walk along Damascus St leads to the heart of downtown Beirut and the glittering azure domes and towering, slender minarets of the Mohammad al-Amin Mosque, known as Lebanon's Blue Mosque.

Its architect, local man Azmi Fakhuri, admits he was inspired by Istanbul's renowned Ottoman shrines. This is no ancient monument, as the mosque was only completed in 2008, but it dominates the city skyline both during the day and illuminated at night. Visitors are welcome, outside of prayer times, and the serene interiors are breathtaking, subtly lit by enormous crystal chandeliers, the immense dome covered with intricate Islamic motifs.

To illustrate Beirut's cultural diversity and ancient heritage, a maze of Roman ruins lies right behind the mosque, while next door stands the main cathedral of the Christian Maronites — Levantine Catholics

'We have preserved the bomb damage, walls riddled with bullets, snipers' graffiti. A visit is intensely emotional'

01 Ancient amphitheatre at Byblos, just outside Beirut

02 View of Mohammad al-Amin Mosque from the St George cathedral

03 Outside Sursock Museum, now a modern art museum

04 The journey at Beit Beirut conflict museum starts on the outside

who make up some 40% of the population, with roots in Lebanon that go back to the 4th century. *Martyrs' Square, Central*

03 ST GEORGE GREEK ORTHODOX CATHEDRAL

Beirut's oldest surviving church sits in the shadow of the Blue Mosque, adjacent to the ancient Roman ruins. Dating back 2000 years, this tiny jewel of Romanesque Byzantine architecture has survived earthquakes and wars, been rebuilt a dozen times and, today, is perfectly restored to its original beauty.

Inside the incense-perfumed church, alongside splendid murals and gilded icons of St George, there are pillars and mosaics still marked by civil war bullets and graffiti, left as a powerful reminder of the time when the cathedral was right on the firing line. Down in the crypt, there is a fascinating subterranean archeological museum. *Nijmeh Square, Central; tel +961 1 980920; museum 10am-6pm*

04 SURSOCK MUSEUM

The illustrious Sursock dynasty created an elite millionaires' neighbourhood of opulent mansions and lush gardens, just a five-minute taxi ride above downtown Beirut, that today seems to be preserved in a time bubble. And the jewel in the crown, the sumptuous palace of art patron Nicolas Sursock, built in an extravagant mix of Ottoman and Venetian styles, reopened in 2015 as a stunning modern art museum after a seven-year renovation.

Renowned French architect Jean-Michel Wilmotte has left intact the wedding-cake façade with its swirling balustrades, and created a series of airy salons for contemporary Lebanese art and provocative shows such as *Let's Talk About The Weather*, where artists address the problems of climate change. *www.sursock.museum; tel +961 1 202001; Greek Orthodox Archbishopric St, Sursock; Wed-Mon 10am-7pm; Thu 12pm- 9pm*

03-04 © John Brunton

05 PLAN BEY GALLERY

Right at the bottom of the steep St Nicholas Stairway that links Sursock with bohemian Gemmayzeh, Plan Bey is a hip art gallery with exhibits ranging from vintage photo prints of Lebanon's wars to eye-catching collages of retro glamour posters, provocative graffiti stickers and handmade artist books.

But this is no normal gallery, rather an example of Beirut's dynamic art scene, as the owners are artisan publishers of artists' prints and multi-media creations. So Plan Bey showcases limited-edition prints developed in direct collaboration with numerous Beirut-based artists, and offbeat political comic books such as Barrack Rima's *Beyrouth Bye Bye*, where the city drowns under

mountains of garbage and is attacked by crocodiles and ninjas. Compared with Beirut's many high-priced galleries, Plan Bey makes a principle of promoting affordable art. *www.plan-bey.com; tel +961 70810846; Gouraud Street, Gemmayzeh; 11am-8pm Mon-Sat*

06 ARMENIA STREET

Beirut has made an art of reinventing itself as the party capital of the Arab World – no easy task given the ever-present tensions in this combustible region. The perfect example is Armenia Street, a 10-minute walk from Plan Bey, which a few years ago was nothing more than run-down repair garages in crumbling buildings. Today, every space has been converted into a bar, boutique,

bistro or club, creating an eternal traffic jam after dark.

The retro Internazionale resembles a modish Milan cafe circa 1960, while at Central the pony-tailed mixologist will tell you that he learnt his craft in a fashionable London watering-hole. The romantic Prune looks more authentic than most Parisian bistrots, while the white-jacketed barmen of Anise serve 30 different absinthes and artisan araks from across Lebanon. *Armenia Street, Mar Mikhael*

07 BYBLOS CRUSADER CASTLE

The historic Phoenician port of Byblos lies at the edge of Beirut's teeming suburbs, a swift 30km cab ride from the city centre. On a slight hill above the walled harbour sits a

majestic Crusader castle, built in the 12th century during the religious wars when Christian knights from Europe fought to take control of Jerusalem. Down below, the vista takes in Greek and Roman temples, Ottoman souqs and the beautifully preserved St John the Baptist church.

This part of Lebanon has been inhabited for thousands of years, right back to the Stone Age. Today, Byblos is a hip summer resort – Beirut's St Tropez – its inestimable monuments listed as a Unesco World Heritage Site. The castle has a small museum, but the highlight is to climb its steep steps to the roof of the fortified tower for a panorama that has changed little over the centuries. *Tel +961 9 540001; 8.30am-6pm*
BY JOHN BRUNTON

06 © John Brunton

05 The port harbour at Byblos – now a hip summer resort

06 Lebanese designers and artists are responsible for the decor at Liza restaurant

WHERE TO STAY
VILLA CLARA
French chef Olivier Gougeon and his Lebanese wife Marie-Helene have lovingly restored a grand 1920s villa to create a romantic design hotel and gourmet restaurant, filled with period antiques and paintings by local artists. *www.villaclara.fr, tel +961 1 70995739; Rue Khanchara, Mar Mkhael*

HOTEL GRAND MESHMOSH
Situated half way up the picturesque St Nicolas Stairway – steep steps that climb up to the Sursock Museum – the Meshmosh (apricot in Arabic) is a hip hostel where travellers can choose between simple dorm accommodation or private double rooms. *www.facebook.com/ grandmeshmosh/; tel +961 1 563465; Route Saint-Nicolas, Gemmayzeh*

WHERE TO EAT & DRINK
LIZA
Liza Soughayar's funky restaurant offers a modern interpretation of traditional Lebanese cuisine, with surprising dishes such as *loukoz bel selek* (sea bass with

tahini). The dining rooms are decorated by young Lebanese artists; look out for silhouettes of bombed Beirut on the walls. *www.lizabeirut.com; tel +961 1 71717105; Doumani Street, Achrafeh*

AL FALAMANKI CAFE
This Beirut institution is the place to come to smoke a shisha and nibble on fava beans, carrots with cardamom, raw peas and fresh almonds, while sipping green tea or a cloudy glass of arak. *www.alfalamanki.com; tel +961 1 323456; Damascus Road, Sodeco*

CELEBRATIONS
BEIRUT ART FAIR
Forty galleries from 18 countries around the world arrive each September to exhibit cutting-edge contemporary art. (*www.beirut-art-fair.com*)

BEIRUT DESIGN WEEK
Beirut is a hotbed of young designers and October's design week presents pop-up installations in abandoned buildings, and exhibits such as cutting-edge lamps made from recycled industrial pipes. (*www.beirutdesignweek.org*)

Map labels:
MEXICO CITY
ROMA NORTE
ROMA SUR
04
05
COYOACÀN
ALAMEDA CENTRAL
BARRIO CHINO
CENTRO HISTÓRICO
JUÀREZ
06
03
01
02
07
ROMA
08
MEXICO

Mexico

MEXICO CITY'S COUNTERCULTURE

In the aftermath of revolution, the early 20th century saw Mexico City become a haven for social rebels, and their presence can still be felt in the verve of the modern mega metropolis.

Mexico has had centuries of struggle. Yet after the Mexican Revolution (1910-1920), it's this fighting spirit that nurtured local artists such as Frida Kahlo, and made the country a magnet for foreign exiles such as the Russian communist Leon Trotsky, Spanish film auteur Luis Buñuel, and American Beat poet Jack Kerouac. Hollywood was in depression; Europe was being overrun by fascism. Mexico provided the stage, refuge and hope for a generation of unconventional characters with new visions of art and politics.

Mexico City was always the country's capital — from the centre of the ancient Aztec empire, to the political head of Spain's new world, and then in the 1930s it became the canvas for a new battle. A modern national identity was up for grabs, where social rebels came and realised they were free to be who they wanted. Today it retains this spark and verve, where every street is a

NEED TO KNOW
This trail takes two days. Mexico City's vast metro system is quick and easy to use; if you prefer taxi, it's safer to book ahead.

colourful photo of cultures coming together. The city has a definite rebellious teenager personality, where anything is considered possible and people are willing to give everything a shot. *Defeños* (as those from the capital are known) are keen to embrace modern life and are almost cocky about it, yet you'll find them equally proud of being easy-going and living for the moment.

Artistically, the city is perhaps best known as the home of Frida Kahlo, who turned her physical image and suffering, German-Mexican heritage, marriage to artist Diego Rivera, and uncompromising lifestyle as a woman into intensely personal art — a radical notion at the time, challenging Mexican machismo, national identity and the notion that private female experiences were off-limits. But peel back the layers and there's plenty more to discover: revolutionary echoes reverberate through the Mexican capital, and are easy to tour.

> 'Beat poets such as Allen Ginsberg spent drug-hazed sessions around the plaza's fountain to inspire their works'

01 MUSEO DEL ESTANQUILLO

José Guadalupe Posada (1852-1913) was Mexico's first modern satirical and political artist, and a swag-bag of his engravings are on display here in Mexico City's historic district. These illustrations, which came to be championed by respected local artist Diego Rivera, reduced dictators and political figures to foolish *calaveras* (skeletons), and gave a spotlight to the everyday lives of the people.

The engravings were printed in various newspapers and magazines across the country from the 1870s into the turn of the century, critiquing the government. At a time when many were illiterate, his images revealed to the average person the dictatorship of Porfirio Diaz, whose downfall was brought about by the Mexican Revolution starting in 1910.
www.museodelestanquillo.com; tel +52 5521 3052; Isabel la Católica 26, cnr Madero, Centro Histórico; 10am-6pm Wed-Mon

02 ANTIGUO COLEGIO DE SAN ILDEFONSO

Posada met and inspired a young José Clemente Orozco (1883-1949) to paint political murals in the 1920s. José was part of the Mexican Mural Renaissance and the legacy of this group of Mexican artists can still be seen across Mexico City. A 15-minute walk from the *museo*, Orozco painted murals on the three floors of the main patio at this 16th-century former Jesuit college; look for *La Trinchera* (The Trench; c1926), which depicts a peasant begging for his life before a revolutionary hero.

It was a bold move for Orozco to paint the plight of peasants, which had often been ignored before this art movement. The Mexican Revolution was a tumultuous period

04-05 © David Crossland / Alamy

01 Museo del Estanquillo hosts Posada's satirical illustrations

02 The Palacio de Bellas Artes: belle époque outside, art deco inside

03 The arches and courtyard of Antiguo Colegio de San Ildefonso

04 & 05 Skeletal handicraft displays inside Frida Kahlo's house museum

with no clear winners, but it did give the old elite the boot and gave voice to popular leaders with freedom for radical ideas.
www.sanildefonso.org.mx; tel +52 55 5702 2834; Justo Sierra 16, Centro Histórico; 10am-8pm Tue, to 6pm Wed-Sun

03 PALACIO DE BELLAS ARTES

A 15-minute walk west, the highbrow concertos within the art-deco walls of Mexico City's Palace of Fine Arts contrast with the murals — art made for the masses. Diego Rivera's Man, Controller of the Universe (1934) dominates with a grand snapshot of change in one painting: Mexico's corn crops governed by science and machinery, while white elites are about to be dethroned by multiracial workers uniting with Karl Marx.

It was originally commissioned for the Rockefeller Center in New York City but destroyed when Nelson Rockefeller noticed 'anti-capitalist' figures depicted. So Rivera — who was part of the same controversial mural group as José Clemente Orozco — reconstructed it here in Mexico City as a big two fingers to Rockefeller.

Rivera was eventually overshadowed by his wife, Frida Kahlo (1907-1954), who was 20 years his junior and whom he met during her years as an art student. Her house is a 30-minute taxi ride south, in villagey Coyoacán.
www.palacio.bellasartes.gob.mx; tel +52 8647 6500; Av Juárez, Centro Histórico; 10am-5pm

04 MUSEO FRIDA KAHLO

Frida Kahlo was born, worked and spent her final days in this house, known simply as La Caza Azul (The Blue House) by locals, after its vivid colour; it's now a museum dedicated to her controversial life and art.

Frida was an early feminist and, for the time, extolled shocking ideas about how women should behave. She slept with both men and women, dressed in suits and cultivated distinctive eyebrows, while painting taboo female experiences from abortion to breastfeeding, and turning her car-accident spinal injuries (suffered at the age of 18) into art.

Walk into her studio and you'll find it exactly as she left it, with brushes laid out, a hoard of Mexican *artesanías* (handicrafts), and the two beds she used — after her back injuries she used one for painting on her back, and one for sleeping in. *www.museofridakahlo.org.mx; tel +52 5554 5999; Londres 247, Coyoacán; 10am-5.30pm Tue & Thu- Sun, 11am-5.30pm Wed*

05 MUSEO CASA DE LEÓN TROTSKY

On the run from Stalinist persecution in Moscow, Russian dissident Leon Trotsky accepted asylum in Mexico City in 1937, when, post-revolution, the city had become a liberal haven for political and artistic rebels.

Trotsky and his wife soon met Kahlo through intellectual circles and stayed at *La Casa Azul* for a while (Trotsky sleeping with sexually liberal Kahlo, much to Rivera's displeasure) before shifting to their own home, a 10-minute walk northeast.

Stalin supporters sought to kill Trotsky, and his dark house has bricked-in windows and bullet-holed walls from a failed assassination attempt (by Stalinist David Alfaro Siqueiros, one of the muralists of the Antiguo Colegio de San Ildefonso). In 1940, Trotsky was famously killed with a mountaineering ice axe to the head in his study, by a Stalinist assassin. You can see the study exactly as it had been at that moment, with Trotsky's small round glasses lying undisturbed — a fascinatingly eerie scene. *museocasadeleontrotsky.blogspot. com; tel +52 5658 8732; Avenida Viena, Coyoacán; 10am-5pm Tue-Sun*

06 HOTEL REFORMA AVENUE

Edgar 'Saner' Flores is Mexico's most renowned contemporary graffiti muralist, whose inspiration to paint murals started when he saw Orozco's *La Trinchera*, which was printed on 100-peso notes in the 1970s. The street muralist deals with globalisation, power and identity through imagery from

Mexico's indigenous cultures, and his murals are splashed on buildings across the world. The one on the side of Hotel Reforma Avenue, a 20-minute taxi ride north of Trotsky's house, is a totem of masked figures riding the back of an office worker with a mining pick.
Donato Guerra 24, cnr Paseo de la Reforma

07 LA ROMITA

Spanish filmmaker Luis Buñuel arrived in Mexico in 1947, during a time when Spain was suffering censorship under Franco's fascist regime. Mexico, meanwhile, was in the midst of a cinematic Golden Age. In *Los Olvidados* (The Young and the Damned), Buñuel portrayed the slums of Mexico City in a controversial social realism style and used avant-garde techniques, such as throwing an egg at the camera lens.

Six blocks from Hotel Reforma Avenue, the slums of La Romita where *Los Olvidados* was filmed are now a micro-village with a leafy plaza at its centre. One long-standing *tortilleria* here bears the graffitied words 'los olvidados' on its side.
Plaza de Romita, La Roma

08 PLAZA LUIS CABRERA

In the 1950s, Mexico City was a haven for Beat Generation writers. In Plaza Luis Cabrera, now a tranquil small plaza lined with lovers, upmarket restaurants and boutique hotels, Beat poets such as Allen Ginsberg once spent drug-hazed sessions around the fountain to inspire their works.

To get here, it's a lovely walk southwest of La Romita along Orizaba. Another few blocks away lies the shabby apartment block at José Alvarado 37, where William S Burroughs, his wife Joan Vollmer, Neal Cassady and Jack Kerouac once lived.
BY PHILLIP TANG

06 Leon Trotsky's tomb lies in the garden of his former house

07 Street scene splashed with traditional Mexican tiles

08 Church of Our Lady of Guadalupe

08 © Alberto Loyo / Getty Images

WHERE TO STAY
CASA DE LA CONDESA
This hotel isn't fancy, despite its close proximity to the hip locals that lounge around Plaza Luis Cabrera. It may be nothing like the plaza that the Beat writers witnessed through their drug-sharpened eyes, but there is still sparkle in the light off the fountains at night.
www.casadelacondesa.net; tel +52 55 5584 3089; Luis Cabrera 16, Roma Norte

CHALET DEL CARMEN
Just a short walk west of Frida Kahlo's Blue House, the Mexican and Swiss couple who run the Chalet cultivate an old-world feel with wood panelling and traditional Mexican tiles. The sunny courtyard and use of the kitchen give the sense of a real home.
chaletdelcarmen.com; tel +52 55 5554 9572; Guerrero 94, Coyoacán

WHERE TO EAT & DRINK
COYOACÁN MARKET
Frida Kahlo visited this traditional Mexican market from a young age to buy fresh produce. The colours and scents still pack a punch, and many line up for the *tostadas* (crispy corn shells topped with lime- and cilantro-drenched shrimp and octopus).
Ignacio Allende, cnr Malintzin, Coyoacán

KRIKA'S
William S Burroughs drank at the Bounty Bar with other Beat writers. Now reincarnated as Krika's, it serves simple Mexican lunches such as *enchiladas verdes* (chicken in tortillas, in green-chilli salsa). Grab a tequila and gaze up at the apartment where Burroughs drunkenly shot his wife in 1951.
Tel +52 55 5264 4201; Monterrey 121, cnr Chihuahua, Roma Norte; 9am-8pm Mon-Fri

CELEBRATIONS
DÍA DE LOS MUERTOS
The first few days of November are filled with processions for the Day of the Dead, to communicate with loved ones who have passed away. Museums are decorated with marigolds, *papel picado* (papercuts) and *calaveras* – skeleton figures inspired by José Guadalupe Posada illustrations.

01

Morocco
ARTISAN MARRAKESH

Amid the souqs and funduqs of Marrakesh, the city's creative scene has evolved into a dynamic dance between old and new, where tradition and experimentation collide.

Ducking through the whip-thin lanes of the souqs, as the midday sun rakes through the slatted roof, your eyes suddenly alight on a metalworker hammering a brass lantern into a thousand pinprick stars. Dodging a donkey and the umpteenth offer of mint tea, you're in the dyers' souq, where yarn drip-dries to create rainbow puddles between the old city walls. Another bend and you enter the *funduqs*, the great caravanserais now given over to wood, leather and brass workers, who only pause from their chiselling and tapping when the muezzin's raspy call to prayer drifts over the medina's rooftops.

Marrakesh's artisanal heritage literally confronts you on every street corner. It doesn't all originate here, mind: many potters come from Fez, Berber carpet weavers from the Atlas and carpenters from Essaouira to trade their wares in this great, red-walled crossroads of a city. Neither is it all traditional. For every souk and

NEED TO KNOW
The trail is doable in a day, but allow at least two days if you want to squeeze in a trip to one of Marrakesh's workshops.

Saadian palace there is a cutting-edge gallery and boutique putting a contemporary spin on the Islamic patterns found in *zellij* (mosaic tiling), calligraphy and carved stucco.

Though Fez has traditionally been considered the artisan capital, there has been a recent shift in the artistic winds. Marrakesh's forward-thinking attitude has seen a raft of new wave artisans and artists roost in the city, and the Marrakesh Biennale, founded by Vanessa Branson in 2004, has been the catalyst for the steadily multiplying galleries and museums.

Pretty much anything goes in Marrakesh nowadays — pop art and street art, Berber-inspired jewellery with a nouveau edge and one-of-a-kind crafts made from recycled junk. With artisans exploring pastures new while simultaneously embracing time-honoured techniques, Marrakesh's creative star continues to rise.

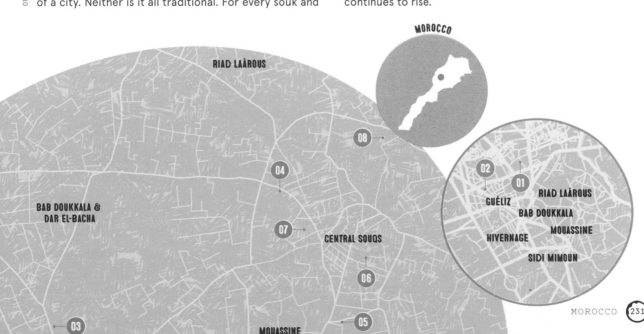

01 MUSÉE BERBÈRE

Electric blue is the colour of the villa harbouring this beautifully curated museum, once the studio of landscape painter Jacques Majorelle. Yves Saint Laurent fell in love with the place and its vibrant gardens, and filled the museum with his extraordinary Berber collection.

Here you can tune into the rich artistry and culture of the country's Amazigh people, eyeing up intricate *choukara* satchels from the Rif Mountains, costumes from the Sahara, Atlas instruments, and wood-, metal- and basket-work. Eclipsing all is the Berber jewellery collection, with elaborate silver headdresses and fibula necklaces of coral, amazonite and amber glittering below a night sky —

'Paintings that might seem wholly abstract at first glance often reveal, on closer inspection, a clever use of Islamic detail'

each one telling the tale of its tribe. *www.jardinmajorelle.com; tel +212 524 31 30 47; cnr Aves Yacoub el-Mansour & Moulay Abdullah; 8am-6pm*

02 DAVID BLOCH GALLERY

Hop in a petit taxi for the five-minute drive west through Ville Nouvelle, Marrakesh's modern French quarter, to this boundary-pushing gallery where the line between crafts and cutting-edge art begins to blur.

The rotating exhibitions focus on some of the most exciting work produced by contemporary Moroccan, North African and international street artists. Paintings that might seem wholly abstract at first glance often reveal, on closer inspection, a clever use of Islamic detail: from the geometric patterns prevalent in *zellij* (mosaic tiles) to the graceful curlicues of calligraphy.

01 The Djemaa El Fna Square comes alive at dusk

02 Piercing blue is a hallmark of YSL's Jardin Majorelle

03 Dyed wool hangs at Souk des Teinturiers

04 Souk Cherifia puts a contemporary spin on craft shopping

www.davidblochgallery.com; tel +212 524 45 75 95; 8 Bis Rue des Vieux Marrakchis; 3.30-7.30pm Mon, 10.30am-1.30pm & 3.30-7.30pm Tue-Sat

03 ATELIERS D'AILLEURS

You can do the souq circuit for crafts, *bien sûr*, but it's eminently more satisfying to learning the tricks of the trade yourself. Cue Ateliers d'ailleurs. Its ethos is to showcase traditional Moroccan crafts in workshops headed by a talented team of *maâlems* (expert artisans).

Whether you want to throw a pot, hone the art of *tadelakt* (polished lime plaster), or try your hand at Berber wood-carving, brass hammering, Islamic calligraphy or *zellij*

mosaics, this is the go-to place. Most workshops are hosted at this medina address, a 10-minute cab ride south of David Bloch Gallery. www.atellersdallleurs.com; tel +212 662 16 60 26; 68 Rue dar el Bacha, Mouassine; half-day workshops 9.30am-12.30pm & 2.30-5.30pm, full-day workshops 9am-2pm & 2.30-6.30pm

04 SOUK CHERIFIA

A 10-minute mosey east through the knotty lanes of the medina brings you to this converted *funduq*. Upstairs, hip young designers (mostly Moroccan and French) put a distinctly Moroccan, contemporary spin on quality, one-of-a-kind crafts.

Alongside funky hand-woven

shopping baskets and straw hats by Original Marrakesh are black-and-white portraits of Berber women reworked into wallets or cushions and minimalist, camel-embellished crockery at Sissi Morocco.

Equally worth a look are Lalla's leather bags and charms, hand-embroidered linens and *babouches* (traditional slippers) at La Maison Bahira, and clutches made from carpets at Khmissa. *souk-cherifia.com; Souk Kchachbia; +212 678 38 22 54; 10am-7pm*

05 RIAD YIMA

Walk a further 10 minutes south through the mazy medina and you'll hit Riad Yima, the studio-cum-tearoom of much-lauded pop

artist Hassan Hajjaj. A leading light in Marrakesh's creative revolution, Hassan is often dubbed 'Morocco's Andy Warhol' by critics. As you might expect if you're familiar with his work, the riad is so insanely colourful it's borderline hallucinogenic.

Alongside eye-popping photographs defined by urban culture are recycled crafts and furniture — tomato-can lanterns, babouches fashioned from old flour sacks, and Coke-crate benches. His work is often copied, but here you can buy the real deal — or simply admire it over a fragrant mint tea.
www.riadyima.com; tel +212 524 39 19 87; 52 Derb Aarjane; 10am-6pm Mon-Sat

06 CHEZ SOUFIANE

Every carpet tells a story, so they say... To find out why, locate this blink-and-you'll-miss-it stall in the nearby Souk des Tapis, run by the highly knowledgeable Soufiane brothers. It's tricky to find, but call and they'll collect you.

The souq stall is just a taster of what is on offer at their main showroom: a staggering array of kilims (flat-woven rugs); rural Berber carpets with abstract motifs telling the unique stories of their weavers; deep-pile *zanafi* from the Middle Atlas, shot with vivid colour; and shaggy, boho-chic Beni Ourain rugs in earthy shades of ivory and brown. There are frothy white, silver-sequined *handiras* (wedding blankets)

too — each of which takes days, if not weeks, to weave.

And the best bit? There's no hard sell here: just genuine enthusiasm from people who really know what they're talking about.
Tel +212 615 28 56 90; 13 Souk des Tapis, Rahba Kedima; 10am-9pm

07 SOUK DES TEINTURIERS

Two minutes' walk west, you'll be singing a rainbow and lunging for your camera in the city's most colour-charged corner: Souk des Teinturiers. The cedar wood you see in Marrakesh hails mostly from Essaouira and the pottery from Fez, but the age-old art of dyeing textiles is still done right here, where skeins of wool in shades of indigo-purple, mint-green, poppy-red and saffron-yellow are hung to dry between the medina's sun-baked walls.

For more insight, check out the cubby-hole workshops where the dyers toil over bubbling vats and can tell you more about the process and natural pigments.
Souk des Teinturiers; 10am-9pm

🄢 ALI BEN YOUSSEF MEDERSA

If the greatest wonders in the Islamic world are wrought for the glory of Allah, the artistry on display at this former *medersa* (Quranic school) beggars belief. Upon entering the courtyard, the gaze is lifted inch by inch to kaleidoscopic patterns of polychrome *zellij*, bands of Kufic calligraphy spun with naturalistic detail, layers of lace-fine stucco and ornately carved Atlas cedar wood, and *mashrabiya* (wooden-lattice screen) balconies.

Though founded in the 14th century under the Merenids, the *medersa* is an A to Z of 16th-century Saadian craftsmanship. Like the pages in the books of the most diligent theology pupils, no surface is left bare. The *medersa* is a five-minute walk north of Souk des Teinturiers.
www.medersa-ben-youssef.com; tel +212 524 44 18 93; Place ben Youssef; 9am-7pm, to 6pm Nov-Mar
BY KERRY CHRISTIANI

05 Intricate *zellij* and calligraphy work at Ali ben Youssef Medersa

06 Modern art by Marrakesh artist Hassan Hajjaj is hung for a show

WHERE TO STAY
DAR CHARKIA
A stylish Asia-meets-Africa riad in a quiet corner of the medina, Dar Charkia has a courtyard plunge pool and roof terrace with Atlas views. Owner Lisa can point you in the direction of local artisans.
www.darcharkia.com; tel +212 524 37 64 77; 49-50 Derb Halfaoui, Bab Doukkala

RIAD ZINOUN
Bang in the heart of the medina, five minutes' walk from Djemaa el-Fna, this riad goes for the rustic-chic look, with *zellij* mosaics, Berber rugs and *tadelakt* walls as smooth as eggshell. It has its own hammam, and the owners can arrange *tadelakt* workshops.
www.riadzinoun.com; tel +212 524 42 67 93; 31, Derb Ben Amrane Riad Zitoune Lakdim

WHERE TO EAT & DRINK
CAFÉ CLOCK
Art-slung Café Clock in the Kasbah is right on the hipster radar, with a menu that spans everything from camel burgers to veggie tagines and date smoothies. The cafe hosts regular jam sessions and cultural workshops.
cafeclock.com; tel +212 5243 78367; Derb Chtouka; 9am-10pm

DAR CHERIFA
This literary cafe lodges in a late 15th-century Saadian riad — an exquisite setting for contemporary art exhibitions, which spotlight Moroccan and foreign artists. Come for a saffron coffee and tagine.
dar-cherifa.com; tel +212 524 42 64 63; 8 Derb Chorfa Lakbir; 10am-8pm

CELEBRATIONS
MARRAKECH BIENNALE
Arts are in the spotlight at this cross-cultural biannual festival, with an emphasis on cutting-edge visual arts, literature and film. Exhibitions, debates, installations and screenings are held across the city.
(www.marrakech biennale.org)

ALWALN'ART
All of Marrakesh is a stage for street performers at this free fest in April. Acrobats, head-spinning Gnawa beats, circus and dance acts draw thronging crowds to city squares.
(www.awalnart.com)

01

01 AUCKLAND
02
03
TAURANGA
HAMILTON
ROTORUA

06
04
ROTORUA 07
05

NEW ZEALAND

New Zealand

THE ESSENCE OF MĀORI SPIRIT

The traditional culture of New Zealand's original Polynesian settlers remains intertwined with present-day island life, particularly in the spiritual landscapes of the North Island.

Since crossing the vast expanses of the South Pacific to reach New Zealand from their Polynesian homelands more than eight centuries ago, Māori culture and spirituality has been tightly entwined with the rugged forests and coastal landscapes of their island home.

According to legend, seven great ocean-going *waka* (canoes) journeyed to the islands known to Māori as Aotearoa (Land of the Long White Cloud); travellers in New Zealand's North Island can journey through the homelands of ancestors from the Tainui and Te Arawa canoes. Constants along the route are superb examples of art, architecture and performance, recognition of the spiritual connection Māori have with the natural world and how this unique culture is held in regard by all New Zealanders.

Beginning with a sunrise welcome and blessing high above Auckland's Waitemata Harbour, this trail explores Māori mythology, history and art. It takes in the city's

NEED TO KNOW
This trail can be completed in three to four days and having your own vehicle is ideal; fly in and out of Auckland.

museum and a stirring performance of the haka — the traditional challenge performed by New Zealand's world champion All Blacks rugby team before every match provides an energetic coda before travelling south to Tainui country around Hamilton.

The forested volcanic lakes around Rotorua are Te Arawa country — according to tradition the canoe made landfall north at Maketu Harbour — and the natural power of the region's geothermal landscapes has been harnessed by local Māori for centuries. Myths and legends are illuminated with energy and grace in waiata (songs) performed by Rotorua's world-renowned *kapa haka* (Māori performing arts) cultural groups, and traditional foods are served steaming from the hangi (earth oven).

Beyond these traditions, Rotorua's art galleries and jade-carving studios feature contemporary updates of traditional motifs, revealing how Māori culture is also a vital part of modern New Zealand.

❶ TĀMAKI HIKOI

Begin your exploration of New Zealand's indigenous Māori culture watching the sun rise in the country's biggest city. Local tour company Tāmaki Hikoi, founded and staffed by members of Auckland's Ngāti Whātua *iwi* (tribe), helps travellers understand the city from a Māori perspective as the region's traditional guardians for three centuries.

Following a welcome to their ancestral *marae* (meeting place) at Orakei above Auckland's Tamaki Drive, an ancient *karakia* (blessing) celebrates the start of a new day. Visitors can plant native tree saplings to forever bond their spirit with that of the

whenua (tribal lands) they are sharing, and planting a tree also acknowledges Papatuanuku — the Mother Earth giving birth and nourishment to all living things. It is a spiritual and emotional way to begin a New Zealand journey. *www.tamakihikoi.co.nz; tel +64 9 336 1670; 59B Kitemoana St, Orakei*

❷ AUCKLAND WAR MEMORIAL MUSEUM

The harbour views along Tamaki Drive back to Orakei, about 6km away, are excellent from the terrace of this grand 1929 neoclassical edifice where two galleries showcase the world's finest Māori collection.

He Tāonga Māori (Māori Treasures)

includes more than 1000 artefacts from around New Zealand. Distinctive Māori wood carvings decorate Hotonui, a *whare whakairo* (meeting house) that was a wedding gift between North Island tribes in 1878.

Te Ao Tūroa (the Māori Natural History Gallery) further reinforces the importance of spirituality and nature for Māori, and brings alive the epic ocean-going journeys the first Māori settlers made to arrive in Aotearoa from Polynesia in the 13th century.

More than 800 years later, vibrant Māori culture still underpins New Zealand society, and performances from the museum's cultural group conclude with an energetic version

'Ohinemutu's residents still use Lake Rotorua's geothermal activity for cooking and bathing'

01 Mt Taranaki, a dormant North Island volcano

02 Whakarewarewa thermal reserve, home to Māori for centuries

03 Traditional wood carvings can be seen all over the North Island

04 St Faith's Anglican Church meshes Māori and European design

of the famed haka — the traditional challenge originally performed before Māori warriors went into battle. *www.aucklandmuseum.com; tel +64 9 309 0443; Auckland Domain, Parnell; 10am-5pm*

03 WAIKATO MUSEUM

Hamilton is a relaxed riverside city a two-hour drive south of Auckland, surrounded by New Zealand's premier dairy farming country. In 1995, the local *iwi* Ngāti Tainui were the first Māori tribe to successfully negotiate compensation from the New Zealand Crown for 19th-century land confiscations — a settlement process ongoing with other Māori tribes in the

21st century — and Tainui's economic base, including property and dairy, now exceeds NZ$1 billion.

In Hamilton's excellent riverside Waikato Museum, exhibits about the earlier history of Tainui include Waka o Te Winika, a 200-year-old war canoe gifted to Hamilton by the late Māori queen, Dame Te Atairangikaahu. *www.waikatomuseum.co.nz; tel +64 7 838 6606; 1 Grantham St; 10am-5pm*

04 OHINEMUTU & ST FAITH'S CHURCH

With your first glimpse of sprawling Lake Rotorua, 90 minutes south of Hamilton, you'll probably also get a whiff of the sulphur-rich aroma

of New Zealand's most dynamic geothermal area, and your first stop should be the lakeside village of Ohinemutu. Local Māori families still live in close proximity to steaming natural vents and pools of boiling hot mud, and Ohinemutu's beautiful St Faith's Anglican Church is a fascinating synthesis of Māori and European design.

Built in 1914, the church's battened exterior is faux Tudor, but inside it is decorated with Māori wood carvings and *tukutuku* reed panels woven in geometric designs. Ohinemutu's residents still use the region's geothermal activity for cooking and bathing, and walking respectfully

through the village is allowed. Just be careful to stay on the marked paths for safety.

Ohinemutu; 8am-4pm, services at 9am Sunday

05 WHAKAREWAREWA

Five kilometres away, Rotorua Māori have lived amid the geysers, silica terraces and mud pools of the Whakarewarewa thermal reserve for centuries, and the *tangata whenua* (people of the land) of this area are generous and welcoming hosts. Accessed by a bridge across a river warmed by hot springs, guided tours incorporate local crafts including flax weaving, wood carving and *ta moko* (traditional Māori tattooing).

It's good to visit 'Whaka', as it is known, with an appetite because eating opportunities include butter-laden sweetcorn cooked in a hot mineral pool, and the fuller meal of a hangi — the traditional Māori feast of vegetables and meat steamed to delicate perfection. Most hangi are cooked underground on hot stones, but Whakarewarewa's offering is lowered carefully into steam vents directly infusing the area's landscape. *www.whakarewarewa.com; tel +64 7 349 3463; 17 Tryon Sy, Whakarewarewa; 8.30am-5pm*

06 MITAI MAORI VILLAGE

Set amid bush dotted with flickering glow worms, 8km from Whakarewarewa, the family-run Mitai Maori Village provides authentic entertainment every evening. The cultural performances, including the verve of the haka and the finesse of the poi dance, are among Rotorua's best; included is a demonstration of how warriors used the *taiaha* (fighting staff) for combat in past centuries.

Modern warriors now steer a waka down Mitai's own freshwater stream, and the evening's hangi is served with quintessential Māori warmth and humour. *www.mitai.co.nz; tel +64 7 343 9132; 196 Fairy Springs Rd; 6.30-10pm*

07 RĀKAI JADE

Jade — known in New Zealand as greenstone or *pounamu* — has been important to Māori for many centuries, and the milky-green rock found in the isolated river valleys of the country's South Island was

06

traditionally used for tools such as chisels and fishing hooks.

In modern times, *pounamu* is now crafted into jewellery and visitors can work with Rākai's experienced carvers to design and craft their own pendant. Popular traditional designs include *hei matau* — fish hooks representing good luck and safe travel across the water — and the gentle and elegant spiral of the *koru*, an unfurling fern frond symbolising new life and growth.

Excellent finished pieces are also for sale, but Rākai's 'Carve Your Own' opportunity enables travellers to create a special personal memento of New Zealand's Māori culture. *www.rakaijade.co.nz; tel +64 27 443 9295; 1234 Fenton St, Rotorua; 9am-5.30pm Mon-Sat*
BY BRETT ATKINSON

Ø5 Ariel view of Mt Eden, Auckland

Ø6 Māori culture show at Mitai Maori Village

06 © frans lemmens / Alamy

WHERE TO STAY
GREAT PONSONBY ARTHOTEL
A short walk from the restaurants of Ponsonby Rd in Auckland, this spacious Victorian villa is colourfully decorated with art inspired by Māori and Pacific culture. Villa rooms include compact decks, while self-contained studio apartments segue to a sunny courtyard. *www.greatpons.co.nz; tel +64 9 376 5989; 30 Ponsonby Tce, Ponsonby*

REGENT OF ROTORUA
This centrally located spot offers a cut-above accommodation experience. Elegant decor, fun mirrors and retro wallpaper combine with sparkling white bathrooms, and it's a short stroll to Eat Street, Rotorua's best dining precinct. *www.regentrotorua.co.nz; tel +64 7 348 4079; 1191 Pukaki St*

WHERE TO EAT & DRINK
GOTHENBURG
Relax for lunch on Gothenburg's riverside deck and enjoy an easy-going ambience and culinary sophistication. Shared plates are inspired by world cuisines and the well-informed drinks list includes an ever-changing selection of craft beers from local Hamilton brewers. *www.gothenburg.co.nz; tel +64 7 834 3562, 17 Grantham St, Hamilton; 9am-11pm Mon-Fri & 11am-late Sat*

EAT STREET
Indian, Thai and Italian cuisines all feature along Rotorua's 'Eat Street', and more eclectic options include the town's very own Croucher beers at Brew, or cosmopolitan Asian and Mediterranean flavours at Atticus Finch. End the night with cocktails inspired by local Māori legends at the Ponsonby Rd bar. *Lake end of Tutanekai St, Rotorua; 11am-late*

CELEBRATIONS
POLYFEST
Secondary schools from around Auckland participate in this energetic festival in mid-March, dedicated to music and dance from the city's Māori and Pacific Island communities. Come to see the next generation of *kapa haka* performers. *(www.asbpolyfest.co.nz)*

New Zealand

OAMARU, THE UNLIKELY CAPITAL OF STEAMPUNK

What was once an unassuming South Island heritage town has become a global centre for the retro-futuristic steampunk movement thanks to an overhaul by local enthusiasts.

Tucked between a rocky outcrop and the vast expanse of the Pacific Ocean on the east coast of New Zealand's South Island, Oamaru is an inauspicious town that was once a busy shipping port but faded into obscurity in the 1970s. Then in 2016, seemingly out of nowhere, it entered the Guinness World Records book for hosting the largest steampunk gathering on the globe.

Steampunk, if you didn't know, is a science-fiction subculture that blends imaginary futuristic machinery with a 19th-century-inspired steam-powered aesthetic. All leather and brass, think of the movie *The Golden Compass*, with its incredible neo-gothic contraptions and architecture. The alternative histories behind steampunk are commonly set in Oxford, Paris and New York. The story of how this remote, antipodean town rose to steampunk prominence is one of necessity and spirit.

First settled by Māori more than a thousand years ago,

the Pākehā (white Europeans) came to Oamaru for whaling. The gold rush of the 1860s created wealth, enabling the port to be constructed in 1875. Unlike more northerly towns that relied on timber for building, this area has plentiful white limestone – Oamaru stone – perfect for carving the ornate Victorian facades that have given the town its distinctive look.

When the port was closed in 1974, Oamaru became one of the first places in New Zealand to realise the value of its heritage, tidying up the charming Victorian buildings and cobbled streets that sit behind the industrial outer suburbs. Against this beautiful backdrop, local steampunk enthusiasts created a haven for the subculture, blending traditional architecture with curious creations that began attracting international attention in 2010. It's an essential stop on any Kiwi road trip itinerary, and is located about a two-hour drive north of Dunedin Airport.

01 © Jonathan Bower New Zealand / Alamy

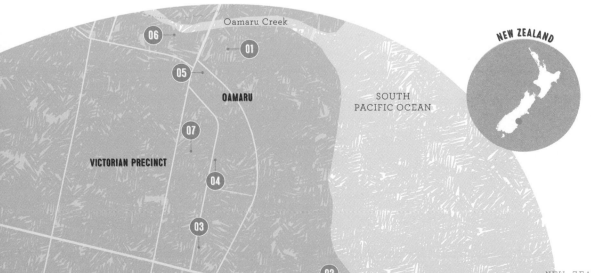

Oamaru Creek

06
01
05

OAMARU

07

VICTORIAN PRECINCT

04

03

02

SOUTH PACIFIC OCEAN

NEW ZEALAND

'What better way to explore an alternative reality than to enjoy a dram in a neo-Victorian drawing room?'

🄀 STEAMPUNK HQ

At the gateway of old Oamaru is Steampunk HQ, a self-styled destination housing curiosities in the former historic Meeks Grain Elevator Building. The location itself has an otherworldly quality, particularly when set against solid blue sky, as it is one of the tallest buildings in the immediate vicinity.

You only have to put a dollar in the steam train out front to realise this is a museum like no other. The 'punked' train begins to whir and hiss, spitting out flames and steam from the funnel and making a noise that could be a

whistle, but could also be a scream...

The HQ's roots go back to 2010, when local man Damien McNamara created a temporary installation called The Libratory to house steampunk-inspired works. Another Oamaruvian and fellow steampunk fanatic Iain Clark — aka Agent Darling, his steampunk alter-ego — thought this was a cracking idea and contacted Weta Workshop, the prop and special effects company based in Wellington famed for its work on major films such as *Avatar*, *Lord of the Rings* and *Planet of the Apes*. It donated half a shipping container

of steampunk-esque creations to display. They found a home in the Meeks building and the HQ was born.

The exhibition has a largely industrial feel with post-apocalyptic undertones. It's all a bit Mad Max, especially in the yard, where you can enjoy large, industrial machines in various stages of being punked. Inside you will find a variety of devices labelled as 'aetheric' – a running theme in steampunk based on the idea that technology can be used to harness a sort of scientific magic that is ever-present in the atmosphere.

Here, many of the devices have

01 A customised
steam train outside
Steampunk HQ

02 Retro-futuristic
dress-up, part of
the steampunk
aesthetic

03 Oamaru's
harbour

04 A Victorian
steam train chugs
down to the water

05 Just your
average Oamaru
street scene

a medical theme, claiming they can augment humans or change the future. Seek out the 'metagalactic pipe organ', which visitors are invited to play, and The Portal, offering a short visit to an alternative dimension. *www.steampunkoamaru.co.nz; tel +64 27 778 6547; Tyne St, South Hill; 10am-5pm*

02 FRIENDLY BAY PLAYGROUND

Outside the HQ you can hire 'pedal punks' — four-wheeled, four-seater bikes — or use the 'wai wai express' (your feet, in Maori) to follow the HQ's outdoor trail through the old Victorian rail yard. Turn left after the train tracks and enjoy a selection of slightly unnerving sculptures before the buildings give way to the harbour vista.

Across the tracks you will see a playground like no other — a giant penny farthing makes up the frame for the swing set, a three-horned elephant in a leather mask holds up a lookout, and public barbecues are dressed like steam generators.

Adjacent is The Galley — a rusted metal-clad cafe Jules Verne would be proud of — for milkshakes and burgers of apocalyptic proportions.

03 THE NEW ZEALAND WHISKY COLLECTION

Steampunk is often described as retro-futuristic, and what better way to explore an alternative reality than to enjoy a dram from what was once the world's most southerly distillery, in a neo-Victorian drawing room? On nearby picturesque Harbour St, your next stop is The New Zealand Whisky Collection.

Enter the cellar door, a wood-panelled parlour in the ground floor of a Victorian warehouse, for respite from the bustle outside and a flight of whisky from the now-defunct

Willowbank distillery. There are just over 400 barrels left of this nectar, and when Willowbank closed in 1997 it marked the end of distilleries in New Zealand.

The passion of the team and the quality of the tipple will help you imagine what might have been. This is a chance for your senses to retreat into history.
www.thenzwhisky.com; tel +64 3 434 8842; 14 Harbour St; 10.30am-4.30pm

04 HARBOUR STREET

Back outside, historic Harbour St is a visual delight in its own right. The old Oamaru stone warehouses you see once housed goods for global shipping, at a time in the late 19th century when Oamaru acted as the Australasian gateway for imports and exports. Now they house a variety of delights, from vintage clothing outlets to Deja Moo handcrafted gelato, gift shops, and a traditional Dutch bakery.

05 REGALIA'S TIME PIECES

Nestled in a heritage building on nearby Tyne Street is this small but enticing store run by local lady Deborah Blackgrove. 'My steampunk name is Madame Regalia, which is where the name of the store came from,' she laughs. 'It's a bit long, but I like it!'

What started as a market stall has become a passionate business: Deborah upcycles clothing in a steampunk style and makes jewellery. 'Age is no barrier — we just have fun with it,' she says. 'And I love how fascinated people are when they come in. We have visitors from all over the world.'
www.facebook.com/ RegaliasTimePieces; tel +64 27 403 6569; 13 Tyne Street

06 THE WOOLSTORE COMPLEX

Just a short stroll away, Oamaru's Wool Store Complex was built in 1881 to store wool and grain but is now home to a varied group of traders, from a cafe to a small artists' collective.

Look out for Stmpnk25 — a gallery specialising in 2D and 3D mechanical and alternative-reality art, whose sculptures grace the Steampunk HQ — and Nellyrose Design for whimsical jewellery creations with a steampunk feel; lots of the maker's pieces are based around analogue watch mechanics.

The second incarnation of The Libratory, the steampunk exhibit that launched it all, can be found on the first floor, along with 14 other local artists and designers. Before leaving, stop by The Photo Shoppe on the ground floor – your chance to dress in the clothes of yesteryear for a steampunk-esque portrait to take home.
www.thewoolstorecomplex.co.nz; tel +64 3 434 1556; 1 Tyne St; hrs vary

07 OAMARU STEAM AND RAIL SOCIETY

Opposite Steampunk HQ is Harbourside Station, where every Sunday you can catch a restored Victorian steam train. The Oamaru Steam and Rail Society was formed in 1985, and now owns four historic engines with several others on loan. Its privately owned section of track runs past Steampunk HQ and the playground, along the harbour front to what is known as The Red Sheds – a small collection of artisans offering traditional handmade goods.

Take a moment to walk down to Oamaru's well-known blue penguin colony before jumping back on your steam-powered steed for the return.
www.oamaru-steam.org.nz; Itchen St; 11am-4pm Sun
BY JAI BREITNAUER

06 & 08 Heritage landmarks in Oamaru

07 A giant penny farthing functions as a playground swing frame

08 © Hardyuno / Alamy

WHERE TO STAY
CRITERION HOTEL
This small, mid-priced heritage hotel in the heart of old Oamaru dates back to 1877. Quirky decor offers a playful nod to the hotel's Victorian past, staff are friendly and there's an exciting food menu plus craft beers.
www.criterionhotel.co.nz; tel +64 3 434 6247; 3 Tyne St, Harbour Side

PEN-Y-BRYN LODGE
Offering 19th-century opulence, this award-winning hotel was built in 1889 for businessman John Bulleid and his Welsh wife. The mansion is a 20-minute walk to the heritage district and offers views of the Kakanui mountains.
www.penybryn.co.nz; tel +64 3 434 7939; 41 Towey St

WHERE TO EAT & DRINK
STEAM CAFÉ
A great place for lunch, Steam offers cafe favourites with a twist. Its BBQ chicken brioche bun with homemade slaw is infamous around Oamaru, and there's always a selection of delicious seasonal salads. The cafe also roasts its own coffee.
Tel +64 3 434 3344; 7 Thames street, Central; daily til 4.30pm

SCOTT'S BREWING CO
Offering a quirky collection of beers brewed on site, enjoy a pizza from the brewery's wood-fired oven and wash it down with a flight of five beers.
www.scottsbrewing.co.nz; tel +64 3 434 2244; 1 Wansbeck Street

CELEBRATIONS
STEAMPUNK NZ FESTIVAL
Now an annual festival held on the first Monday of June (a public holiday), the inaugural event catapulted Oamaru to fame in 2016 as the largest gathering of steampunks globally. Expect vaudeville style entertainment, craft markets and teapot racing.
(www.steampunknz.co.nz)

OAMARU FARMERS' MARKET
You're invited to 'get fresh with the locals' every Sunday between 9.30am and 1pm. Held behind the Scott's brewery, the farmers market offers local produce, live music and steampunk-themed stalls.
(www.oamarufarmers market.co.nz)

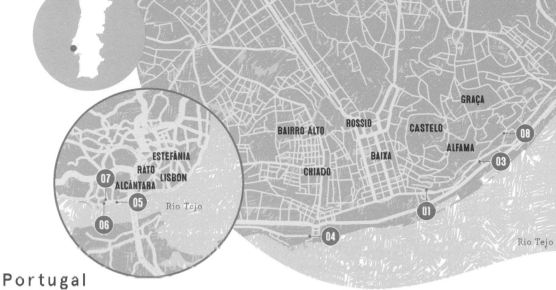

Portugal

ARTISTRY THAT SPEAKS TO THE SOUL IN LISBON

Street scenes and sunset views take on a dreamy quality in the Portuguese capital, captivating artists and musicians, and inspiring a soulfulness that informs daily life.

Day fades into a watercolour sunset by the River Tagus, which shimmers like molten silver as it lopes through Lisbon on its way west to the Atlantic. It's a view that inspires towards the poetic and the profound, whether seen from the hulking hilltop castle or the helter-skelter alleys of the medina-like Alfama.

This same view has undoubtedly inspired Portugal's great artists: Nobel laureate author José Saramago, heart-wrenching *fadista* musician Amália Rodrigues, poet Fernando Pessoa, artist Paula Rego, queen of magic-realism on canvas — and countless more besides.

Indeed, there is almost something artistic about the way Lisbon unfolds like an intricate work of origami — a pop-up *miradouro* (viewpoint) here, a vintage tram and *azulejo*-tiled façade there — all washed in the pure light of an Impressionist painting. The more you wander this city of seven hills, the more little details grab you — be it how the cobbled streets of Alfama look paved with gold in the twilight lamp-light, or the way a hidden arch frames the view like a postcard.

So many artists, musicians and writers have chosen Lisbon as their adopted home recently, and who can blame them? Authentic, unpretentious and open-minded, the Portuguese capital is conducive to creativity. Lisbon sees no need to sacrifice past for present, using its rich history as a gateway to creative pastures new.

Neither are the arts here confined to galleries and concert halls alone — they are deftly interwoven into every aspect of daily life. Take fado, which means 'fate' and harks back to working-class Alfama — to the ditties of homesick sailors and the poetic ballads of the Moors. This plaintive music and its heartache sits side by side with *azulejos* and street murals; art is everywhere and for everyone in this most soulful of cities.

NEED TO KNOW
Though doable in a day (just), devote a couple of days to this itinerary. All stops can be covered on foot or by bus/tram.

01 FUNDAÇÃO JOSÉ SARAMAGO

'Words were not given to man in order to conceal his thoughts,' said late Nobel laureate José Saramago (1922-2010). A literary legend in Portugal, he gave free rein to his thoughts and mined the depth of human experience in his richly imaginative, cynical and darkly humorous novels such as *Blindness, All the Names* and *The Stone Raft*, many of which were set against a uniquely Portuguese backdrop. Behind the pincushion façade of the 16th-century Casa de Bicos, this museum at the foot of Lisbon's historic Alfama district homes in on Saramago's life and soul-stirring writing.

Pick up one of his works in the bookstore to read in a quiet corner

'Fado means 'fate' and harks back to working-class Alfama — to the ditties of homesick sailors and poetic ballads of the Moors'

of the Moorish Alfama, which rises from the river in a higgledy-piggledy maze of laundry-draped alleys. *www.josesaramago.org; tel +351 21 880 2040; Rua dos Bacalhoeiros 8; 10am-6pm Mon-Sat*

02 MUSEU NACIONAL DO AZULEJO

Taking a serendipitous wander through Lisbon's backstreets, every so often your eyes will alight on the glimmer of decorative tiles — in churches and cafes, parks and metro stations. Housed in a beautiful Manueline convent, this museum is a stunning tribute to the art of *azulejos*, introduced to Portugal by the Moors in the 15th century. Treasures include the astonishingly intricate Great View of Lisbon on the 2nd floor, winging you back to the city before the devastating earthquake struck in 1755. Just as evocative is the late 16th-

01 Lisbon's new MAAT has revamped the Belém waterfront

03 Outside the Museu Coleção Berardo, home to surrealist artworks

02 Views across historic Alfama

04 Admiring *azulejos* at their national museum

03 © Sofia PereirasArt / Alamy; 04 © robertharding / Alamy

century altarpiece of Our Lady of Life, one of Portugal's earliest *azulejo* masterpieces. The base is fringed by diamond-tip tiles in Trompe l'oeil design, creating a 3D optical illusion. Ivy-clad columns frame erudite evangelists St John and St Luke, and the centrepiece scene showing the Adoration of the Shepherds.

The museum is a 10-minute bus ride east along the riverfront. *www.museudoazulejo.pt; tel +351 21 810 0340; Rua Madre de Deus 4; 10am-6pm Tue-Sun*

03 MUSEU DO FADO

Heartbreak. Lost love. Remorse. Loneliness. Such are the bluesy, plaintive themes of fado, Lisbon's song of the soul. Central to all fado is *saudade*, the hard-to-translate, distinctly Portuguese concept of nostalgic longing. Fado can be traced back to Alfama, so it makes sense that the museum exploring its history and rise to global fame should be in this historic neighbourhood, a short bus ride and walk from the Azulejo Museum.

The collection takes in recordings, posters, a recreated guitar workshop and fado music store. *www.museudofado.pt; tel +351 21 882 3470; Largo Chafariz de Dentro 1; 10am-6pm Tue-Sun*

04 UNDERDOGS

Lisbon's passion for the arts has always been intertwined with a belief in the underdog. Until a couple of decades ago, some historic quarters of the city were still in tatters. Its recent rags-to-riches transformation has seen many forward-thinking artists roost here — all seeking to eloquently express their love of the city.

Embracing the zeitgeist, Underdogs is part gallery-store, part cafe, part artist residency in the riverside Cais do Sodré district, a 20-minute walk west of the Museu do Fado. Over a caffeine fix, meet the guest artist, see projects in the making or snap up an original: the showcased works are by artists with a background in street, visual and graphic art. This is also the go-to place for fascinating public-art tours. *www.under-dogs.net; tel +351 210 991 678; Rua da Cintura do Porto de Lisboa, Armazém A, Cais do Sodré; 11am-8pm Tue-Sun*

05 © Matt Munro / Lonely Planet

05 ◼ MUSEU DE ARTE, ARQUITETURA E TECNOLOGIA

Rising like a mighty ripple in the river as it flows to the sea, Lisbon's newest icon, the Museum of Art, Architecture and Technology (MAAT), is something else. Bearing the sinuous imprint of much-lauded British architect Amanda Levete, it has totally revamped the Belém waterfront to the tune of €20m.

It's destined to host world-class exhibitions on contemporary art and architecture. The edifice itself is extraordinary: it's clad in a snakelike skin of 15,000 white, 3D tiles, which cleverly reflect the changing light. *www.maat.pt; tel +351 210 028 130; Av Brasília, Central Tejo; noon-8pm Wed-Mon*

06 ◼ MUSEU COLEÇÃO BERARDO

A 15-minute amble west along the river brings you to the avant-garde Centro Cultural de Belém, the crowning glory of which is this museum. It's free to visit the gallery, which harbours billionaire José Berardo's remarkable stash of abstract, surrealist and pop art — Hockney, Magritte, Lichtenstein, Warhol and Pollock originals included.

Among the standouts is Warhol's entrancing portrait of Judy Garland (1979). Back on Portuguese turf, you can't help but be lured into Paula Rego's world of theatrical, nightmarish fantasies in pieces such as *The Barn* (1994) and *Three Blind Mice* (1990). *en.museuberardo.pt; tel +351 21 361 2878; Praça do Império; 10am-7pm*

07 ◼ MOSTEIRO DOS JERÓNIMOS

Just across the way, this Unesco-listed former monastery is Lisbon's most exquisite example of Manueline architecture. Manuel I commissioned it to trumpet Vasco da Gama's discovery of a sea route to India in 1498, back when the world was Portugal's oyster.

Traces of this sea-faring past can be picked out in the cloister, which draws inspiration from the sea with scalloped arches, auger-shell turrets and columns tangled with knots. Draw breath as you enter the church, where tree-trunk-like columns grow into the ceiling — a sight to lift gazes and spirits to the heavens. *www.mosteirojeronimos.pt; tel +351 21 362 0034; Praça do Império; 10am-6.30pm Tue-Sun, to 5.30pm Oct-May*

08 SENHOR FADO

As dusk falls on Lisbon, the lantern-lit alleys of Alfama reverberate to the distant strains of fado, with its heart-breaking trills and poetic soul. Like all the best *fado vadio* (street fado) haunts, Senhor Fado is so tiny and intimate it feels like you're gatecrashing a private family party.

Over hearty country grub and copious amounts of house red, you'll be treated to an emotional double act featuring *fadista* Ana Marina and guitarist Duarte Santos. A word of warning — this place is very popular, so book early or walk away disappointed. *www.sr-fado.com; tel +351 21 887 4298; Rua dos Remédios 176; 7.30pm-midnight Wed-Sun*
BY KERRY CHRISTIANI

05 An intimate Lisbon fado venue

06 Inside the church of Mosteiro Dos Jerónimos

WHERE TO STAY

ALFAMA PATIO HOSTEL
Huddled away in Alfama's mazy, tram-rattled heart, this beautifully run hostel/guesthouse brims with artistic details — custom made bunks, murals and the like. Dorms and doubles are supremely comfy and the views from the sun terrace dreamy. *alfama patio hostel. lisbon-hotel.org; tel +351 21 888 3127; Rua das Escolas Gerais 3*

SANTIAGO DE ALFAMA
A style wand has been waved on this ruined 15th-century palace, transforming it into a boutique hotel that shows off a razor-sharp eye for detail; be it in the glass-encased Roman steps or the luxe rooms. *www.santiagodealfama. com; tel +351 21 394 1616; Rua de Santiago 10-14*

WHERE TO EAT & DRINK

ALMA
The closest you'll get to art on a plate in Lisbon is Alma, the Michelin-starred baby of feted Portuguese chef Henrique Sá Pessoa. The food here speaks to the soul and is delivered with flair. Asian spice ramps up Mediterranean flavours. *www.almalisboa.pt; tel +351 21 3470 650; Rua Anchieta 15; 12.30-3.30 & 7-11pm Tue-Sun*

TI-NATÉRCIA
Aunty by name, aunty by nature... You will indeed feel like you're being treated to some good old-fashioned Portuguese grub by your long-lost aunt at this tiny Alfama restaurant. Go for the *bacalhau* (salt cod) — it's always good. *Tel +351 21 886 2133; Rua Escola Gerais 54; 7pm-midnight Mon-Fri, noon-3pm & 7pm-midnight Sat*

CELEBRATIONS

FADO NO CASTELO
Lisbon's love affair with fado is in the spotlight at this three-day song-fest in June, set against the cinematic backdrop of the Castelo de São Jorge. Admission is free, but tickets are limited. *(www.festasdelisboa.com)*

FESTIVAL AO LARGO
Catch free performing arts — from classical concerts to opera and ballet – in front of Teatro Nacional de São Carlos in July. *(www.festivalaolargo.pt)*

Romania

DRACULA, FROM HISTORY TO LITERARY LEGEND

With a backdrop as gothic as Transylvania's brooding Carpathian Mountains, it's little wonder Romania's most famous son has inspired ghoulish myths, legends and fiction.

The Dracula myth is as eternal as the undead count himself. Dracula endures in music, film and literature — though often in forms far removed from his origins in Transylvania, Romania. By blazing a trail from historic Brașov to the wild Bârgău Valley, you can unlock the mysteries and misunderstandings about the historical Dracula, who was indeed a real person. This journey also weaves in locations linked to the most famous fictional Dracula, Irish novelist Bram Stoker's re-imagining of history.

The black heart of the Dracula myth is Transylvania-born Vlad Țepeș (Vlad III), the famously cruel second son of Wallachian ruler Vlad Dracul 'the Dragon' ('Dracula' means simply 'son of Dracul'). The 15th-century prince of Wallachia went down in history as 'Vlad the Impaler', though many Romanians remember him with reverence. Locals are said to have joked that townships under Vlad's rule were an ideal place to drop one's money: it would lie

NEED TO KNOW
This trail is best undertaken by car over four days, though only far-flung Bârgău Valley is inaccessible by public transport.

untouched, as people were terrified of gleefully inflicted punishments such as amputation or impalement. Most significantly, Vlad fended off Ottoman attacks with military cunning and strategically placed enemies on skewers. On the infamous Târgoviște Night Attack in 1462, Vlad ordered the impalement of tens of thousands of Turks, arranging them in agonised legions to be discovered by Ottoman sultan Mehmed II.

The scale of Vlad's cruelty made him the inspiration for Bram Stoker's *Dracula*. Also set in Transylvania, the Gothic novel re-creates Dracula as a blood-hungry fiend who has outlasted the centuries. Transylvanian folklore has demonic seducers of its own, too; their stories are told and retold on winter nights when winds scream across the Carpathian Mountains. Transylvania's history and folklore were brewed against a backdrop of forbidding valleys and dense forests, cloaked in enough mist to shroud an entire coven of vampires. Grab a crucifix and explore.

01 © Matt Munro / Lonely Planet

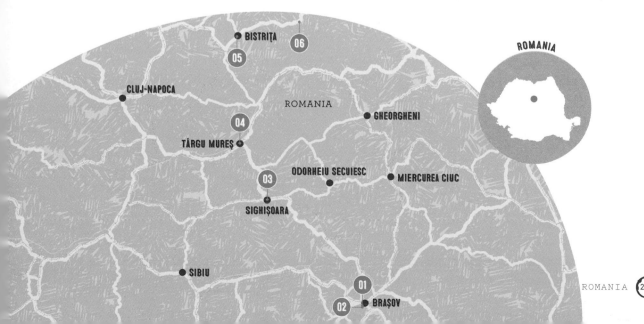

ROMANIA

BISTRIȚA 06
05
CLUJ-NAPOCA
ROMANIA
04
GHEORGHENI
TÂRGU MUREȘ
ODORHEIU SECUIESC 03
MIERCUREA CIUC
SIGHIȘOARA
SIBIU
01
02 BRAȘOV

01 MOUNT TÂMPA

Looming above Brașov's Saxon buildings and watchtowers is forested Mount Tâmpa. Huge, Hollywood-style letters spelling out 'Brașov' cover this 940m hill, but it once sported a much more macabre decoration.

Vlad Țepeș meted out one of his famously gruesome mass punishments here. Brașov's prosperous Saxon merchants refused to pay taxes to Vlad, who was presiding over Wallachia just south. Non-payment reminders weren't Vlad's style; instead he impaled 40 Saxon merchants. Vlad left this forest of staked bodies on Mount Tâmpa as a warning to anyone daring to flout trade rules.

'A myth tells that Vlad himself walked this street, and took advantage of the enclosed space to steal a kiss from his future bride'

A cable car clatters from Aleea Tiberiu Brediceanu to the hilltop, accessing views over Brașov's medieval centre and walking trails to the lofty neighbourhood Poiana Brașov. Take a short hike here, and ponder the grim alternative view you would have encountered in the 15th century. *Cable car tel +40 268 478 657; Aleea Tiberiu Brediceanu, Brașov; Tue-Sun 9.30am-5pm*

02 BRAȘOV'S STRADA SFORII

Five minutes' walk north of the lower cable car station is Brașov's old town. Strolling beneath medieval gateways and peaches-and-cream buildings, it would be easy to miss Strada Sforii, one of Europe's narrowest lanes at 1.2m wide. The street has attracted the reputation of a lovers' lane, thanks to local lore about Vlad Țepeș.

02 © Sami OV / 500px

01 Transylvanian
country graveyard

02 Parts of Sighișoara's
old town are half a
millennium old

03 Sign outside Casa
Vlad Dracul, Brașov

04 Bran Castle's links
to Vlad are tenuous, but
it looks the part

03 © kpzfoto / Alamy; 04 © Prisma by Dukas Presseagentur GmbH / Alamy

A widely disseminated myth tells that Vlad himself walked this street, and took advantage of the enclosed space to steal a kiss from his future bride. In a region speckled with sites of Vlad's merciless deeds, the charming legend of Strada Sforii is a reminder that while 'Vlad the Impaler' seized the imagination of the west, it's the warrior and man Vlad Țepeș who is remembered and romanticised in Romania.

03 CASA VLAD DRACUL

Most vampire-hunters head west from Brașov to Bran Castle – but the castle's links to Vlad Țepeș (and indeed to Bram Stoker's Dracula) are almost entirely disproven. Instead take a lazy drive 115km north of Brașov, past fortified churches and Saxon-style villages, to Sighișoara. Squeezed between medieval towers, Sighișoara's old town has buildings half a millennium old. In the upper room of a mustard-coloured house opposite the clock tower is the place where Vlad Țepeș was born in 1431.

Trading equally on the historic Vlad and the Dracula of fiction, this heroic birthplace is signposted with cut-outs of fanged villains. More surprisingly, Casa Vlad Dracul now houses a restaurant. Throne-like chairs huddle around tables, candelabra hang from the walls, and a carnivorous menu spans goulash and juicy pork chops, ideally washed down with the house's own 'Vin Prince Vlad'. Unsurprisingly, garlic doesn't feature heavily. After a feast fit for a Wallachian prince, it costs an extra 5 lei to climb to the room where Vlad Țepeș was born (brace yourself for a fright).
www.casavladdracul.ro; tel +40 265 771 596; Strada Cositorarilor 5; 11am-11pm

04 CULTURE PALACE

Vlad Țepeș can't claim all the credit for Transylvania's harrowing legends of old: the region's folklore is a dusky tapestry of cautionary tales and

(05)

beguiling beasts. Discover haunting illustrations of these stories at the Culture Palace in the town of Târgu Mureș, less than an hour's drive north of Sighișoara.

This Secessionist-style concert hall and gallery, completed in 1913, is richly decorated with Carrara marble and busts of musical greats. Most striking is the Hall of Mirrors, lined with stained glass depictions of fairy tales from Székely (Transylvania's Hungarian-speaking culture). Seduction and destruction are core themes, so it's easy to see why Bram Stoker pored over Transylvanian folk tales when writing *Dracula*.

Particularly graphic is the ballad of Sára, whose throat and bosom are exposed to a leering fiend; according to the tale, Sára is seduced by the Devil and pays with her life. *palatulculturiimures.ro; tel +40 265 267 629; Strada George Enescu 2, Târgu Mureș; 9am-6pm Tue-Sun Apr-Oct, to 4pm Nov-Mar*

05 BISTRIȚA OLD TOWN

The Vlad Țepeș trail runs cold towards northern Transylvania, but Bram Stoker's *Dracula* was inspired by these yawning valleys. Bistrița, a 90-minute drive from Târgu Mureș, is where the character Jonathan Harker is assailed by superstitious peasants in the novel.

Harker stays overnight at the Golden Crown Inn in Bistritz (the town's former German name). The inn didn't exist prior to Stoker's novel, though a hotel with the same name (Coroana de Aur in Romanian) has since sprung up here.

Stoker knew Bistrița only from descriptions and sketches, but it's clear why he was captivated: from Coroana de Aur, walk down Strada Dornei to Piața Centrală. Renaissance buildings radiate from the Gothic Evangelical Church, with a 76m tower and threatening spires worthy of the Count himself. Fortunately, Bistrița's cobbled streets are lined with cafes, rather than peasants beseeching you not to venture into Bârgău Valley... *Piața Centrală, Bistrița*

06 HOTEL CASTEL DRACULA

The most atmospheric place to conclude this tour lies 45 minutes' drive east of Bistrița. In *Dracula*, hapless protagonist Harker journeys from Bistrița across the Bârgău Valley: a coachman, flogging jet-black horses,

leads him along pathways beset by wolves until the battlements of Dracula's castle come into view.

The journey is still lined with ominous forest, though these days wolf sightings are a rare treat. Exactly where the Count would have lived, Hotel Castel Dracula has been built in homage to Stoker, on a promontory overlooking Bârgău Valley — complete with a statue of the writer. At check-in you'll be greeted by taxidermied animals, then you'll retreat to a white-walled bedroom with crimson drapes. Either you'll doze fitfully, disturbed by winds howling across the valley, or you'll sleep like the undead.
www.hotelcasteldracula.ro; tel +40 263 264 010; DN-17 Piatra Fântânele, Bistrita-Nasaud
BY ANITA ISALSKA

05 Carpathian Mountains

06 Târgu Mureș Culture Palace

WHERE TO STAY

HOTEL COROANA DE AUR
Named after the inn where Jonathan Harker (of Bram Stoker's *Dracula*) stayed before venturing fearfully to the Count's castle, this pleasant hotel has plump-mattressed rooms and sizeable breakfast spreads. It's a five-minute walk to Bistrița's pretty old town. *www.hotelcoroanadeaur ro; tel +40 263 211 872; Piața Petru Rareș 4, Bistrița*

CASA BAROCA
There's stiff competition for the most eerie place to stay in Transylvania, but tiny Casa Baroca in Sighișoara comes closest to a truly vampiric lair. Antique-decorated rooms feature wrought-iron bed frames designed to withstand heavy swoons. *casa-baroca.ro; Strada Cositorarilor 9*

WHERE TO EAT & DRINK

CASA ROMÂNEASCĂ
Crowned with the skull of a stag, this wood-accented tavern near Brașov's old town specialises in Transylvanian country cuisine, from smoked lamb to steaming bean soups. *www.restaurant-casa romaneasca.ro; tel +40 268 513 877; Piața Unirii 15, Brașov; 11am–midnight*

LACI CSARDA
Fill your belly with the best of Transylvanian cuisine at this rustic restaurant in Târgu Mureș: pork stew, gigantic platters of grilled meat and veggies, and *țuică* (fruit brandy) galore. *www.tempo.ro/en/laci-csarda-restaurant; tel +40 265 307 225; Strada Morii 27; 10am–midnight*

CELEBRATIONS

INTERNATIONAL VAMPIRE FILM & ARTS FESTIVAL
Four days of fang-tastic films, exhibitions and Gothic literature readings draw flocks of dark souls to Sighișoara each spring in late May. Book accommodation early. *(ivfaf.com)*

NEDEIA MUNȚILOR
In mid-July tiny Fundata, 45km from Brașov, offers an authentic glimpse of Transylvanian village life. You'll witness line-dancing, tuck into homespun Transylvanian food, and see displays of prized local cheeses, traditionally sealed inside pine bark.

The following labels appear on the map:

SCOTLAND

06
WEST END
River Kelvin
KELVINGROVE PARK
07
01
BLYTHSWOOD SQ
HILLHEAD
GOVAN
GLASGOW
IBROX
02
03
04
KINNING PARK
05
River Clyde

Scotland

MACKINTOSH & THE GLASGOW STYLE

All but forgotten until the 1980s, Scotland's distinctive art nouveau movement deserves a special place in European art history — as does its forefather, Charles Rennie Mackintosh.

He was a true pioneer of his age, worthy of a seat at the table alongside other European architect and design luminaries of his era such as Spain's Antoni Gaudi and Belgium's Victor Horta. So it's a tragedy that Charles Rennie Mackintosh (1868-1928) failed to attract the fame — and financial reward — that he deserved during his lifetime.

Raised in a Glasgow tenement and having attended art school by night, it was while Mackintosh was just a junior at local architect firm Honeyman & Keppie that he won the 1896 competition to design the Glasgow School of Art. The building ignited his career and remains his foremost legacy. Yet it wasn't until the 1980s that Mackintosh gained credit for the movement now known as the Glasgow Style. This distinctive breed of art nouveau rejected the neoclassical overtones of 19th-century architecture in favour of Scottish Baronial (think 'castle') style, inspiration from nature, and nods to Japanese art and architecture.

NEED TO KNOW
Set aside two days for this urban trail, much of which is worth exploring on foot to best appreciate the local architecture.

The Glasgow Style was daring and progressive for its time, and breathed new life into not just Scottish architecture, but also art, crafts and furniture design. Yet Mackintosh was no lone wolf; he was part of a forward-thinking circle of local Scots — including his wife, Margaret Macdonald — whose work all captures an instinctive urge to be different during a time, at the turn of the century, when the world was changing.

To see Mackintosh's achievements, as well as the work of his contemporaries, you must travel to Glasgow. It's a surprising city, cleaved in two by an ugly motorway, but in all other respects a pleasantly intriguing place with architectural splendour around every corner. Glasgow was built on the grit and grime of merchant trade and shipbuilding, but today it is a city of grand shopping boulevards, Norman Foster architecture, artsy enclaves and excellent restaurants, where the genius of Glasgow's most important local is rightfully celebrated.

01 © Eye Ubiquitous / Alamy

'Hopeless at sticking to a budget, Mackintosh decimated the school's modest funds with the first phase of construction'

① GLASGOW SCHOOL OF ART

Many a eulogy has been directed at this historic Glasgow institution since it was partially gutted by a tragic fire in 2014. Before that, it had been fully functional since the east wing's inauguration in 1899. Hopeless at sticking to a budget, Mackintosh had decimated the school's modest funds by the time he finished the first phase of construction and the school had to wait another eight years to raise the money for the west wing. The building wasn't completed until 1909, by which point Mackintosh had spent £42,000 — three times the original budget.

The project took so long that it bookends Mackintosh's short career. Four years after completing the GSA,

having proved he had no head for business, he was let go by architect firm Honeyman & Keppie, of which he was by then a partner. With the onset of WWI shortly after, and without the backing of the firm, Mackintosh struggled to get further work.

Look to the east wing and there are echoes of Scottish castle architecture in the windows, turret and otherwise blank façade. By the time the architect started on the west wing he had altered his designs, looking more towards art deco and even modernism. Notice the stepped architrave above the west wing doorway, very much art deco in style — 20 years before that movement came to the fore.

The wrought-iron work along

the front of the building shows Mackintosh's preoccupation with symbols of nature. Abstracted natural figures such as birds, bees and flowers adorn the ground-level railings.

Since the fire, tours of the GSA focus on the exterior façade and the Mackintosh furniture gallery in the school's ultra-modern Reid Building. The GSA is expected to reopen fully in 2019 after major restorations works. *www.gsa.ac.uk; tel +44 141 353 4526; 164 Renfrew St; 10am-4.30pm*

② DAILY RECORD BUILDING

On a sunny day a noticeable glow illuminates the depths of Renfield Lane, downhill from the art school. Divine inspiration it could be, as Mackintosh

01 Mackintosh
House Museum
— a replica of the
architect's
Glasgow home

02 & 04 The
Lighthouse water
tower, inside
and out

03 Inside the
Kelvingrove Museum

05 A Mackintosh
designed doorway,
Blythswood Sq

intentionally designed the Daily Record
Building (1901) with a façade of glazed
white tiles to help reflect light down
into the narrow alleyway in which the
building sits. At the time, land prices
were sky-high in the thickly populated
east end of the city and this small, dark
plot is all the newspaper could afford.

The building is just one example of
the way Mackintosh sought to harness
natural light in his architectural
spaces. Its design is distinctive,
even by Mackintosh standards. The
blinding white tiling and grid-like
uniformity of the windows strongly
evoke an art deco aesthetic. Bright
green tiles grow up the front of the
building, topped with brown canopies,
depicting tree forms.

⑫ WILLOW TEA ROOMS

Mackintosh's relationship with local
businesswoman Catherine Cranston
was one of the most important of his
career — second only to his relationship
with his wife, Margaret Macdonald.
In the early 1900s Cranston had four
tea rooms in Glasgow, all of which
Mackintosh helped design, and this one
on busy shopping hub Buchanan St was
resurrected in the 1980s in the image
of her original Ingram St tea room.
Book in for brunch or afternoon tea so
you can have a look around.

Ms Cranston was way ahead of her
time. She employed Mackintosh before
he had a reputation, mostly to work on
her ultra-modern tea room interiors.
Mackintosh was not just an architect,

but also a designer who could turn
his hand to everything from furniture
to cutlery and lighting. Her patronage
continued for two decades.

Ms Cranston's family were heavily
involved in the Glasgow temperance
society and her brother Stuart was
a tea merchant; together, they
conspired to draw men out of the pubs
of Glasgow. Each tea room included a
light room for socialising ladies and a
dark room (in this instance, the striking
blue Chinese room) reserved for men.

Mackintosh married Margaret the
same year he began work on the
Ingram St tea room, and it's in the
light-filled interior of the ladies' room,
with curved lines and stained-glass
nature motifs in the light fixtures and

04 © Annelies Leeuw / Alamy; 05 © Lorna Parkes

partition walls, that you begin to see her influence on his designs. She collaborated with him on many of his projects — Mackintosh once told her that she was half, if not three quarters, of the inspiration for all his work. *www.willowtearooms.co.uk; tel + 44 141 204 5242; 97 Buchanan Street; 9am-6pm Mon-Sat, 10.30am-5pm Sun*

04 THE LIGHTHOUSE

Mackintosh had only just finished studying at the GSA when Honeyman & Keppie put him in charge of the commission to build this extension to the Glasgow Herald newspaper offices, his first major project.

Enthusiastic locals sometimes liken the distinctive water tower (now called The Lighthouse) to a Scottish thistle — squint and you might just see it. But what is clear is the first embryonic signs of the Glasgow Style aesthetic, if you look at the abstract imagery of the top of the water tower and the sinuous natural style of the drain pipes running down its sides.

The building now houses Scotland's Design & Architecture Centre, including a Mackintosh museum, cafe and shop. The water tower itself can be climbed for spectacular views of the city. *www.thelighthouse.co.uk; tel +44 141 276 5365; 11 Mitchell Lane; 10am-5pm Mon-Sat, from midday Sun*

05 HOUSE FOR AN ART LOVER

On day two, take a bus or taxi to this modern rendition of a 1901 design by Mackintosh, which was submitted for a competition in a German design magazine. The country house was finally created in 1996 as an homage to the architect, and presents several rooms from his original drawings.

The light, airy spaces of the Oval Room and Music Room would have been ground-breaking at the turn of the century and in stark contrast to the typically dark, cluttered interiors of Victorian buildings of the era.

Many of the decorative features inside the house — willowy female figures, rose buds and heart-headed vines — were heavily influenced (if not designed) by Margaret Macdonald.

House for an Art Lover is situated in Bellahouston Park, about 2.5 miles from the city centre, incorporating a sculpture park and walled garden. *www.houseforanartlover.co.uk; tel +44 141 353 4770; Bellahouston Park, 10 Dumbreck Rd; hrs vary*

06 THE MACKINTOSH HOUSE

A taxi ride away, inside the grounds of the Hunterian Art Gallery in Glasgow's hip West End, lies this reassembled house from 78 Southpark Ave — where Mackintosh and Margaret Macdonald lived from 1906 to 1914. The original house was demolished in the early 1960s but the interiors were saved and eventually installed here. Look out for the decorative panels by Margaret and a rare painting by her sister Frances in the drawing room. *www.glasgow.ac.uk/hunterian; tel +44 141 330 4221; 82 Hillhead Street, University of Glasgow; 10am-5pm Tue-Sat, 11am-4pm Sun*

07 KELVINGROVE ART GALLERY

Finish at the city's poster-boy art museum, housed in a glorious Victorian building near the Hunterian. Its gallery dedicated to Mackintosh and the Glasgow Style includes original interiors from the Willow Tea Rooms, plus jewellery, ceramics, stained glass and other decorative items by fellow Glasgow Style champions such as the Macdonald sisters.

Many of the women represented here were part of a progressive circle of female creatives posthumously known as the Glasgow Girls, who were as instrumental in the Glasgow Style movement as Mackintosh himself. One of Margaret Macdonald's gesso panels (similar to that which can be seen in this gallery) fetched £1.5m at auction in 2008 — the highest price ever paid for a piece of Scottish art at the time of the sale, and a figure that still eclipses any sum paid for Mackintosh's own work. *www.glasgowlife.org.uk/museums/kelvingrove; tel +44 141 276 9500; Argyle St; 10am-5pm Mo-Thu & Sat, from 11am Fri & Sun*
BY LORNA PARKES

06-07 The House for an Art Lover façade and Music Room

08 Glasgow School of Art's west wing before the 2014 fire

08 © John Peter Photography / Alamy

WHERE TO STAY
GRASSHOPPERS
The most convenient base in Glasgow is this penthouse hotel in the walls of the city's Central Station. Double glazing ensures a peaceful night's sleep, and the period rooms are complemented by striking designer wallpaper and modern art. The best bit, though, has to be the free cakes. *www.grasshoppers glasgow.com; +44 141 222 2666; 87 Union St*

DAKOTA DELUXE
This flash modern place around the corner from the Glasgow School of Art is from a Scottish mini-brand that knows how to spoil its guests. Dark, muted interiors give off a classy gentleman's club vibe, and there's an on-site bar and restaurant. *glasgow.dakotahotels. co.uk; tel +44 141 404 3680; 179 West Regent St*

WHERE TO EAT & DRINK
UBIQUITOUS CHIP
Chippy this is not. It's actually one of Glasgow's best restaurants, in the city's trendy West End, with its own farm outside Glasgow and its own grape blends as house wines. The dining space sits within a magical fairy-lit atrium and menus focus on modern Scottish dishes. Try the smooth venison haggis — a house speciality. *www.ubiquitouschip. co.uk; tel +44 141 334 5007; 12 Ashton Lane*

ALCHEMILLA
With an ex-Ottolenghi chef at the helm, you can expect great things from this unassuming restaurant in Finnieston — Glasgow's coolest foodie stomping ground. The menu is small, plates are designed to be shared and staff know their wines. The interior has typical Glaswegian design flair. *Tel +44 141 337 6060; 1126 Argyle St*

CELEBRATIONS
THE MACKINTOSH FESTIVAL
Every October, Glasgow celebrates the life of its premier prodigy with a month of events, exhibitions, workshops, tours and talks, held at Mackintosh venues around town and elsewhere. *(www.glasgowmackintosh .com/festival)*

Spain
CATALONIA'S REBELS

In the late 19th century, Antoni Gaudí and other free-thinkers ushered in an era of creative transformation in Barcelona and its surrounding towns that has to be seen to be believed.

Few places have had the same impact on European architecture and art as Catalonia, and fewer regions have produced such an impressive pantheon of free-thinking architects, artists and sculptors who pushed traditional boundaries. Indeed, Catalonia's rebels transformed the very concept of what a building, a sculpture or a painting can and should be.

The Modernisme cultural movement that sought to break with the ways of the past, to transform Catalan society into a modern one, and to bring new art into being, grew out of the literary movement that followed the 1888 World Exhibition in Barcelona. A new generation of architects, including Antoni Gaudí and Josep Puig i Cadafalch, found themselves abandoning the rigid past styles in favour of organic forms and sinuous curves inspired by nature, blending the two or experimenting entirely with the latter.

NEED TO KNOW
Barcelona is easy to navigate by public transport, but consider hiring a car to efficiently tour sights around the city.

In Spain, Barcelona became the epicentre of this architectural renaissance at the end of the 19th and beginning of the 20th century, and its influence gradually spread to other parts of Catalonia and beyond.

At the same time, Catalonia's art took on a life and direction of its own. One of Spain's most influential artists, Joan Miró, embarked on a lifelong exploration of Surrealism and abstract expression after being exposed to André Breton's Surrealist circle in Paris. He, in turn, influenced the Figuéres-born Salvador Dalí, who drew on other sources of inspiration, from Cubism to the works of Velázquez and Goya to create some of the most remarkable and universally recognised Surrealist dreamscapes in the world.

Starting in Barcelona — with its grand avenues punctuated by striking Modernista landmarks — and venturing further afield, visitors can go right to the source of the inspirations for Catalonia's renegade artists.

01 © age fotostock / Alamy

SPAIN

GRÀCIA
01
SAGRADA FAMÍLIA
02
03
EL FORT PIENC
L'EIXAMPLE
VILA OLÍMPICA
LA RIBERA
BARRI GÒTIC
EL RAVAL
LA BARCELONETA
SANTS
Marina
POBLE SEC
Port Vell
MONTJUÏC
07

FRANCE
PORTLLIGAT
FIGUERES
GIRONA
05
VIC
04
SPAIN
06
TERRASSA
BARCELONA

'Dali's home was a labyrinthine collection of huts linked by secret stairways — like an Escher drawing come to life'

01 SAGRADA FAMILIA

Revere it or revile it, Gaudí's grand masterpiece church is Barcelona's most iconic structure. Its construction began in 1883 and it is due to be completed in 2026 on the centennial of its creator's death. It's a place of worship like no other, with organic style and curved forms mimicking the natural world.

Inside, the roof is held up by a forest of soaring stone pillars, the supporting branches at the top an illusion of a forest canopy. When light hits the stained-glass windows, this creates the effect of sunlight streaming through a dense forest.

It was while working on this church, and close to the building site, that Gaudí was hit by a tram

in 1926. Famously, he was mistaken for a beggar due to his unkempt appearance and did not receive immediate treatment; he died from his injuries a couple of days later. *www.sagradafamilia.org; tel +34 932 08 04 14; Carrer de Mallorca 401; 9am-8pm Apr-Sep, to 6pm Oct-Mar*

02 CASA DE LES PUNXES

Standing at the intersection of three major streets in L'Eixample, this 1905 building bristling with pointed towers is the creation of Josep Puig i Cadafalch, another of the driving forces of Catalan Modernism. He was known for combining structural and architectural elements from the Catalan tradition with northern and central European styles.

Commissioned by Bartomeu Terradas Brutau to design houses for his three sisters, Josep combined three buildings to make them look like a single medieval castle, with distinctive ceramic, wrought-iron, and delicate stained-glass windows – materials and ornamentations that screamed modernism.

As of 2016 the building (also called Casa Terradas) is open to the public for the first time in 100 years. *www.casadelespunxes.com; tel +34 930 185 242; Avinguda Diagonal 420; 9am-8pm*

03 LA PEDRERA

Gaudí is famous for having transformed several of Barcelona's apartment buildings into hallucinatory

02 © pio3 / Shutterstock

01 The modernist
facade of Masía
Freixa in Terrassa

02 Fundació
Joan Miró

03 La Pedrera, the
Gaudí-designed
apartment block

04 Spires of
Sagrada Familia

masterpieces. La Pedrera (the Quarry: officially called Casa Milà). named after its uneven grey stone facade, is one of his best-known works and a Unesco-listed building.

It was constructed between 1906 and 1912, and today can be toured as a museum, complete with a recreation of an original apartment. Its roof terrace, with extraordinary chimney pots and undulating walkway, is the building's most remarkable feature. *www.lapedrera.com; tel +34 902 202138; Passeig de Gracia 92; 9am-8.30pm Mar-Oct, to 6.30pm Nov-Feb*

04 MASÍA FREIXA
A half-hour drive north of Barcelona is Terrassa, a town that played an important role in Spain's industrial revolution and has a clutch of Modernista architecture founded on the wealth of that era. The most spectacular is this 1896 adaptation of an industrial building by local architect Lluís Muncunill i Parellada (1868-1931) into a house for Argemí Josep Freixa.

Freixa was one of a number of wealthy industrialists and other progressives who championed *Modernisme* by commissioning buildings by Gaudí and his contemporaries in an effort to be seen as cutting-edge. Masía Freixa is a stuccoed enigma, covered by a mass of sinuous vaulted Gaudíesque arches. *www.visitaterrassa.cat; tel +34 93 739 74 21; Place Freixa i Argemí 11; 9am-2pm & 5-7pm Mon-Fri, 10am-2pm Sat & Sun*

05 SALVADOR DALÍ HOUSE-MUSEUM
No other place offers such an intimate glimpse into Salvador Dalí's psyche than his home and studio of 40 years in the tiny fishing village of Portlligat, a two-hour drive northeast of Terrassa, where he lived until the death of his beloved wife Gala.

Dalí originally bought one small whitewashed fisherman's cottage here in 1930, but over the subsequent three decades he snapped up surrounding residences to create a labyrinthine collection of huts with whimsically mismatched windows, linked by narrow corridors, mezzanines and secret stairways – like an Escher drawing come to life. Inside, the multitude of objects and decorations

was chosen with infinite care, including the sofa modelled on Mae West's lips.

Dalí was first drawn to Portlligat for its isolation, the light and the landscape, which made a repeat appearance in his work. Just before he moved here, he started living with Gala, a Russian immigrant 10 years his senior who became his lifelong muse and, later, his wife. When they met, she was married to the poet Paul Éluard, and her subsequent cohabitation with Dalí provoked a considerable amount of disapproval in Catholic 1930s Spain.

This disapproval did not abate, since Dalí was known for his bizarre appearance and behaviour, and the Dalí residence continued to attract bohemian guests for decades. Visitors included other surrealists such as

Miro, who introduced Dalí to many of his surrealist friends and who heavily influenced Dalí's work. When Gala passed away in 1972, Salvador became a recluse and abandoned Portlligat in favour of the castle in Púbol that he originally bought for his wife. *www.salvador-dali.org; tel +34 972 251 015; Portlligat; 9.30am-9pm mid-Jun to mid-Aug, shorter hrs rest of yr*

06 TEATRE-MUSEU DALÍ

As befitting the grand master of surrealism, this red building housing the world's largest collection of Dalí's works is a surrealist vision in its own right. The building is Figueres' former theatre, burned during the Spanish Civil War and restored between 1968 and 1974 to create the museum. Golden

Oscar-like statues, plaster croissants and giant eggs adorn its facade.

The town of Figueres is a sleepy spot with little else to recommend it to tourists, but the museum is an absolute must. It houses diverse works from every stage of Dalí's career, including paintings inspired by Gala, such as *Atomic Leda* and *Gala Looking at the Mediterranean Sea*.

A separate entrance leads into the subtly lit Dalí Joies gallery where whimsical, Dalí-designed jewellery is displayed. The man himself is seeing out eternity from the crypt below what used to be the theatre stage. *www.salvador-dali.org; Placa di Gala i Salvador Dalí 5, Figueres; tel +34 972 67750; 9am-8pm Jul & Aug, shorter hrs rest of yr*

⑦ FUNDACIÓ JOAN MIRÓ

The career of Miró (1893–1983), the Barcelona-born painter, sculptor and ceramicist, was one of experimentation and playfulness, combining abstract art with surrealist fantasy. Return to Barcelona for a final stop at his superb museum, the contents of which the artist bequeathed to the city in 1971.

Exhibits chart Miró's artistic development; his trademark style made bold use of primary colours and incorporated imagery of the female form. Highlights include his pieces from the surrealist years (1932–55), plus bronzes and a giant tapestry. *www.fmirobcn.org; Parc de Montjuïc; tel +34 93 443 9470; 10am–8pm Tue–Sat, to 9pm Thu, to 2.30pm Sun* **BY ANNA KAMINSKI**

05 Dalí's former home, in the fishing village of Portlligat

06 The Teatre-Museu Dalí is a surreal vision in its own right

06 © Kiev.Victor / Shutterstock

WHERE TO STAY
HOTEL NERI
In a centuries-old building in Barcelona's Barri Gòtic, this stylish place combines heavy timber furnishings and sandstone walls with state-of-the-art technology. *www.hotelneri.com; Carrer de Sant Sever 5; tel +34 939 040655*

HOTEL CASA FUSTER
This luxurious Modernista mansion is one of Barcelona's plushest hotels. Large windows provide plenty of natural light, bathrooms have hydro-massage tubs and there are great city views from the rooftop pool. *www.hotelcasafuster.com; Passeig de Gràcia 132; tel +34 932 553000*

WHERE TO EAT & DRINK
CINC SENTITS
At the 'Five Senses', four- and six-course tasting menus offer experimental dishes that make the most of seasonal produce. Pair them with wines from small boutique bodegas. *www.cincsentits.com; Carrer d'Aribau 58; tel +34 933 239490; 1.30–3pm & 8.30–10pm Tue–Sat*

CAN CULLERETES
This 18th-century restaurant with old-fashioned, tiled interior is one of Barcelona's oldest. The food is hearty Catalan fare, from roasted suckling pig and wild boar stew to succulent grilled seafood and a superlative version of the seafood paella. *www.culleretes.com; Carrer Quintana 5; tel +34 93 317 3022; 1.30–4pm & 9–11pm Tue–Sat, 1.30–4pm Sun*

CELEBRATIONS
FESTES DE SANTA EULÀLIA
This raucous, week-long celebration in February is held in honour of Barcelona's first patron saint, with various cultural events, open-air art installations, *castells* (human castles), parades featuring *gegants* (giants) and *correfocs* (fire runs). *(lameva.barcelona.cat/santaeulalia)*

MERCAT DE MERCATS
Typically held on the third weekend of October, this week-long Catalan food celebration takes place in front of La Catedral, with locally sourced ingredients, Catalan wines, gourmet food stalls and more.

Map labels:

TRAFALGAR · ALMAGRO · ARGÜELLES · SALAMANCA · SPAIN · 07 · MALASAÑA · JUSTICIA · 06 · CENTRO · CAMPO · 05 · RETIRO · 04 · 01 · ATOCHA · 03 · EL RASTRO · 02

Spain

MADRID THROUGH THE EYES OF AN ARTIST

Visitors wax lyrical about Madrid's tapas and nightlife scene, but world-class art galleries are the city's unsung hero and the works of Goya in particular offer a window into Madrid's soul.

Madrid isn't short of compelling reasons to visit. The Spanish capital is well known for its beautiful plazas, tapas bars and nightlife. But even if Madrid possessed none of these appealing attributes it would still retain one very good reason for spending as much time here as you can — its art.

This relatively young capital (it only became the national seat of government in 1561) may be short on history, but more than makes up for it in the richness of the art its galleries hold. Dozens of collections, large and small, can be found across the city but it's three specific museums — the Museo del Prado, the Museo Thyssen-Bornemisza and the Centro de Arte Reina Sofía — that draw the biggest crowds.

The three points of this Golden Triangle of art sit within a short walk of each other along or just off elegant Paseo de la Castellana, Madrid's main thoroughfare. All have showstopping masterpieces from the greatest artists who ever put paint to canvas, but the highlight for many visitors is the work of home-grown genius, Francisco de Goya (1746–1828). His astute observations, irreverent approach and candid depictions of horrific events he lived through make his work the quintessential window into Madrid life in the late 18th and early 19th centuries.

NEED TO KNOW
To avoid museum fatigue, spend two to three days doing this trail. Madrid's historic centre is compact, so good for walking.

And once you've enjoyed the museums themselves, the city has links to Goya and his fellow artists that help form a greater understanding of the paintings, giving an historical context to both the pieces and the people who produced them.

Hemingway once declared that 'nobody goes to bed in Madrid until they have killed the night'. He might have added that nobody should leave Madrid without experiencing the unrivalled art to be found in this cultural city.

02

❶ MUSEO DEL PRADO

Exploring the Prado, Madrid's premier gallery, could take days, such is the quality and breadth of the collection. The focus is on Spanish painters, and the strongest card in the Prado's artful deck is the work by Goya and artists such as Diego Velázquez who influenced him.

Velázquez's most celebrated painting, *Las Meninas* (The Maids of Honour), was completed in 1656 and depicts not only King Philip IV, his wife and daughter, but also the artist himself. It's an enigmatic portrait thanks to its composition and use of light, which has confounded and delighted admirers over the

centuries. Painted 150 years later, Goya's *La familia de Carlos IV* (The family of Charles IV) is a homage to his artistic predecessor. Like Velázquez, Goya inserted himself into the artwork but, typically for this unorthodox painter, he gave a less-than-flattering portrayal of the monarchy.

His rebellious palette had darker tones too, best seen in the late-career *Pinturas Negras* (Black Paintings) with their terrifying themes of demonic ceremonies and gruesome cannibalism.

The loss of his hearing and the horrors of the French occupation of Spain ultimately led to these

sombre works, and the latter was also the inspiration for two of his most celebrated paintings: *El Dos de Mayo* (The Second of May, aka The Charge of the Mamelukes) and *El Tres de Mayo* (The Third of May) show the people of Madrid rebelling against French forces and the violent retaliation of the invaders.

Just across from the Prado, the Museo Thyssen-Bornemisza gives an excellent overview of Western art with a collection that includes Goya and every other great painter from Rubens to Monet.
www.museodelprado.es; Paseo del Prado; 10am-8pm Mon-Sat, to 7pm Sun

'The loss of his hearing and horrors of the French occupation ultimately led to Goya's later, sombre works'

01 Evening revelry descends on Puerta del Sol

02 Contemplating Goya in the Prado

03 Promenading in front of the Palacio Real

04 Statue of Goya outside the Prado

03 © Matt Munro / Lonely Planet; 04 © Geraint Lewis / Alamy

02 REAL FÁBRICA DE TAPICES

A 20-minute walk south, past the Botanic Garden, leads to the Royal Tapestry Factory. It was here that the young Goya cut his artistic teeth in 1774 after moving to Madrid from his home in Aragón. Asked to help with designs for royal-commissioned tapestries, the patterns he drew, many based on paintings by Velázquez, caught the king's eye and launched the artist's career. Today, tours include rooms filled with tapestries, some for sale, and the chance to see them made.
www.realfabricadetapices.com; Calle Fuenterrabía; 10am-2pm Mon-Fri

03 CENTRO DE ARTE REINA SOFÍA

As Goya recorded the brutalities of 18th-century warfare, so another Spanish artist, Picasso, set down in paint the barbarity of a 20th-century conflict, the Spanish Civil War. *Guernica*, his disturbing, moving piece created in response to the devastating aerial bombardment of the eponymous Basque town in 1937, is the highlight of the Reina Sofía and a worthy successor to Goya's war paintings.

This gallery of modern art, the southern tip of the Golden Triangle, is housed in a former convent and is home to famous works by the likes of Miró and Dalí – but it is Picasso's haunting depiction of suffering that lingers most in the memory after a visit.
www.museoreinasofia.es; Calle de Santa Isabel; 10am-9pm Mon & Wed-Sat, to 7pm Sun

04 PUERTA DEL SOL

A 15-minute walk northwest, through the heart of Madrid, leads to the city's geographical and spiritual home, Puerta del Sol. Today a transport and shopping hub, where people celebrate New Year's Eve and from where all road distances from the capital are measured (look for the 'Kilómetro 0' marker on the square's

south side), this is also where the violent events depicted in Goya's *El Dos de Mayo* took place. It's still possible to imagine the brave local population fighting at extremely close quarters with the French Mameluke troops in the square and narrow surrounding streets.

05 REAL ACADEMIA DE BELLAS ARTES DE SAN FERNANDO

To the northeast is the Royal Academy of Fine Arts, one of Spain's most prestigious art schools and a place with which Picasso, as one of its students, was very familiar. Or at least he would have been had he chosen to spend more time here during the two years he lived in Madrid.

Instead young Pablo preferred learning first-hand from the Old Masters, spending his time in the Prado admiring the likes of Goya – who was one of the early directors of the academy (some of Goya's work is on display inside, including two self-portraits). *www.realacademiabellasartes sanfernando.com; Calle de Alcalá 13; 10am-3pm Tue-Sun*

06 PALACIO REAL

A short stroll west through the streets of Madrid's medieval quarter brings you to the Royal Palace. The modern building was constructed in 1734 after a fire destroyed the earlier Moorish fortress-turned-regal-abode that Velázquez would have visited.

Some 74 years later this was the starting point of the May rebellion, when crowds gathered outside to protest the influence of France over the country.

The opulent palace is no longer home to the Spanish royals, but official functions are still held here. The square in front offers expansive views: look across the Manzanares river and to the left — today you'll see Puerta del Angel neighbourhood, but two centuries ago this is where Goya's house stood.

La Quinta del Sordo (Deaf Man's Villa, named after an earlier deaf owner, not Goya) is where the artist created his *Pinturas Negras*, executed directly onto the walls of his home, where they remained until the villa was demolished in 1909 and the

paintings were moved to the Prado.
*www.patrimonionacional.es; Calle
de Bailén; 10am-8pm Apr-Sep, to
6pm Oct-Mar*

07 ERMITA DE SAN ANTONIO DE LA FLORIDA

Northwest of the Palacio Real (through
Plaza de Oriente with its gravity-
defying, Velázquez-designed statue
of Phillip IV) is this off-the-beaten-
track church. Not only is it home to
jaw-dropping frescoes by Goya, but it's
also the painter's final resting place. His
body lies in front of the altar, placed
here after it was returned from France
where he died in 1828.
*sanantoniodelaflorida.es; Glorieta
de San Antonio de la Florida;
10am-8pm Tue-Sun*
BY CLIFTON WILKINSON

05 Centro de Arte
Reina Sofía: as
outrageous as the
modern art within

06 Pavement bar in
La Latina

WHERE TO STAY
HOSTAL CENTRAL PALACE MADRID
You can't stay in the Palacio
Real itself, but this hotel
is near enough that you
can pretend. Tastefully
decorated rooms have
views across Plaza de
Oriente towards the palace.
*www.centralpalace
madrid.com; tel +34 91 54
82 018; Plaza de Oriente 2*

LAPEPA CHIC B&B
So close to the Thyssen-
Bornemisza that you can
almost see the Cézannes,
Lapepa is perfect for
anyone wanting to save
their feet for walking the
galleries rather than the
streets of Madrid. Some
rooms feature modern art.
*www.lapepa-bnb.com; tel
+34 648 47 47 42; Plaza de
las Cortes 4*

WHERE TO EAT & DRINK
CASA JULIO
Enjoy croquettes so good
they draw celebrities,
while you contemplate the
history of the Malasaña
neighbourhood in which
this bar sits: it's named after
a heroine who fought and
died in the 1808 rebellion.
*Tel +34 915 22 72 74; Calle
de la Madera 37*

RESTAURANTE SOBRINO DE BOTÍN
Travel back to the 18th
century in the world's
oldest restaurant (opened
in 1725). It's not known if
Goya ate in the wonderful
vaulted cellar here, but
he would have gone for
the roast suckling pig or
roast lamb, both house
specialities, if he had.
*www.botin.es; tel +34
913 664 217; Calle de los
Cuchilleros 17*

CELEBRATIONS
FIESTAS DEL 2 DE MAYO
Madrid's inhabitants,
madrileños, take any
opportunity to party,
but in May they really
let their hair down to
commemorate the Second
of May uprising; now a
public holiday, marked by
parades and street parties.

FIESTAS DE SAN ISIDRO
Madrid's patron saint is
celebrated on 15 May,
with festivities that have
been going on since before
Goya's time. The artist
captured the day's events
in two paintings – the jovial,
light *Meadow of San Isidro*,
and the much darker
Pilgrimage to San Isidro,
both now in the Prado.

06 © VICTOR TORRES / Shutterstock

Spain

SEVILLE'S FLAMENCO RENAISSANCE

Spain's most powerful art form originated here in Andalucia's capital, and it's still the best place in the country to feel the emotive force and intangible spirit of live performance.

Coloured by Roma legends, Spanish folklore, word-of-mouth stories and an intriguing air of mystery, flamenco is a culture unto itself; a complicated melange of music, song, dance, art and lifestyle with antecedents going back to the 15th century. Without a doubt, the best place to see it is in Andalucia, the region of its genesis, where three cities — Seville, Cádiz and Jerez de la Frontera — all profess to be the cradle of the art.

If you only have time to visit one of them, proceed directly to Seville, the jovial, passionate, grandiose capital of Andalucia, where not only can you see top-drawer flamenco any night of the week, you can also visit a flamenco museum, attend a festival and partake in an intensive course studying any of the three main disciplines: song, dance and guitar. Seville is a fascinating place to hang out whatever your excuse. Little sullied by modern interferences, here lies the world's finest Gothic

NEED TO KNOW
Set aside three days — more if you sign up to a flamenco course. Seville is mostly walkable, with the occasional taxi.

cathedral, the best spring festival in Spain, and an encyclopedic collection of baroque art.

Flamenco in Seville has deep historical roots. Mixing Jewish, Moorish, Nomadic and folkloric elements, the music originated in the former Roma neighbourhood of Triana before slowly evolving and branching out. In the mid 19th century, the city played a key role in introducing flamenco to the general populace through its *café cantantes* — stylised music halls that sold drinks and organised regular flamenco shows.

Despite the march towards modernity, flamenco remains a largely live phenomenon. Relying heavily on spontaneity and improvisation, the music doesn't transpose well in recordings. Its power lies in the moment, and the unexpected spark of a live recital. The goal for all performers is to inspire *duende* — an intangible spirit felt at the emotional climax of a near-perfect performance. It's a precious and elusive force, but Seville is full of it.

01 © javarman / Shutterstock

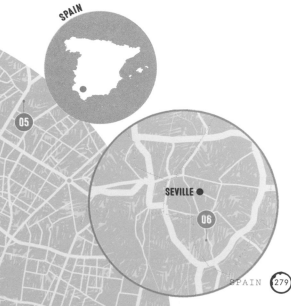

'This is what flamenco is all about: a full-on sensory experience where you are gradually sucked in'

① CASA DE LA GUITARRA

There has been a flamenco renaissance taking place in Seville over the past five years, spearheaded by small, clamorous clubs such as this one where seating room is limited to 60 and the music is close-up and explosive.

Owned by ex-flamenco guitarist José Luis Postigo, who has hung most of his impressive guitar collection on the walls, the club comes with few other embellishments (no food or drink is served), preferring instead to direct the audience's attention 100% towards the stage.

Like a Roma *juerga* (party) of old, the Casa de la Guitarra packs them in so tight that spectators in the front row are likely to feel the swish of the dancer's dress on their faces and the gravel in the singer's voice in their ears. Enjoy the proximity while it lasts. This is what flamenco is all about: a full-on sensory experience where you are gradually sucked in and — if you're lucky — visited by that strange, elusive flamenco spirit known as *duende*.
www.flamencoensevilla.com; tel +34 954 22 40 93; Calle Mesón del Morro 12; 11am-10pm

② MUSEO DEL BAILE FLAMENCO

Spread over three floors of a reconfigured 18th-century palace a five-minute stroll from the Casa de la Guitarra, this important archive of flamenco memorabilia is more than just a museum. It's a de facto cultural centre that also runs flamenco courses and hosts highly lauded evening performances in a specially designed patio.

The project is the brainchild of local flamenco dancer Cristina Hoyos and was set up in 2008. Making full use of modern technology,

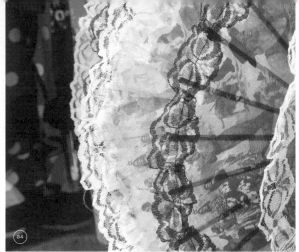

the museum takes visitors on an interactive journey through flamenco's history using film projections, original sketches and paintings, photos of erstwhile (and contemporary) flamenco greats, and an extensive collection of dresses and shawls.

For an all-encompassing flamenco evening, arrive around 6pm, give yourself an hour to look around the museum, and then stay for the electrifying 7pm concert. *www.museoflamenco.com; tel +34 954 34 03 11; Calle de Manuel Rojas Marcos 3; 10am-7pm*

03 CASA DE LA MEMORIA

Neither a manufactured dinner show, nor an intimate *peña* (private club), this attractive cultural institution accommodated in the old stables of the Palacio de la Lebrija is a kind of halfway house between full-on flamenco theatre and the hell-bent Roma get-togethers of yore.

Stylistically, it strikes a good balance between professionalism and passion offering what are, without doubt, some of the most authentic nightly shows in Seville. The centre, a 10-minute walk through central Seville from the Museo del Baile Flamenco,

is perennially popular and space is limited to 100. Reserve tickets at least a day in advance. *www.casadelamemoria.es; tel +34 954 56 06 70; Calle Cuna 6; concerts 7.30pm & 9pm*

04 CASA ANSELMA

The Anselma is an old-school watering hole in Triana decked out like a Roma dive bar, where hordes of locals come to witness (and sometimes partake in) mad jamming sessions enlivened with outbreaks of spontaneous dancing. To call the music here 'pure' flamenco would be

stretching it. Suffice to say, there are guitars, yodeling voices and plenty of pounding on tables.

As far as tourists are concerned, the Anselma is off the radar probably because finding it isn't easy – it's a 20-minute walk from the Casa de la Memoria across the Isabel II Bridge. Make a note: there's no sign outside, it's elbow-in the-face busy, and the place never opens until after midnight. While fluent Spanish is not a prerequisite, a few key phrases such as 'dos cervezas, por favor' ('two beers, please') will smooth the landing.

Shows, once they start, are overseen by a formidable ex-flamenco dancer named Anselma and are loud and boisterous. Unless you're extremely pushy, or a local

flamenco celebrity, it's unlikely you'll get a seat, although you will be expected to buy a drink at the bar (entry is free).

Performances go on for as long as the musicians keep playing. Most of it is pretty improvised, and don't expect choreographed dancing — just members of the audience having a go, drunk or otherwise. The biggest lure: there's nothing remotely like it anywhere else in Seville... nay Spain... nay the world.

Should you wish to explore the neighbourhood further, you'll find Triana awash with old-school tapas bars, musty churches and a museum that investigates the horrors of the Spanish Inquisition.
Tel +34 606 16 25 02; Calle Pages del Corro 49; midnight-late Mon-Sat

05 PALACIO ANDALUZ

Flamenco purists like to quietly dismiss the Palacio Andaluz as a place for tourists. But while the bulk of the audience might be flamenco outsiders keen to log everything on their camera-phones, the criticisms aren't strictly fair. The Palacio's popularity doesn't cheapen the talent of its performers, most of whom are absolute masters of their art.

Occupying the space of an old warehouse on the cusp of the Macarena district, a short taxi ride northeast of Triana, the Palacio is one of Seville's largest flamenco venues — a 500-seat theatre that hosts highly choreographed nightly shows starring up to 20 singers and dancers.

Intimacy isn't the deal here. Think of these skilled if slightly contrived

(09)

performances as more of a spectacle than an interactive experience: a 'greatest hits' of flamenco. You'll hear sad *soleares*, manic *bulerias* and jaunty *alegrias*. What you probably won't hear is seasoned aficionados yelling '*óle!*' from the sidelines.

After the show, head west to the Alameda de Hercules, the hub of Seville's youthful nightlife and gay scene. *www.elflamencoensevilla.com; tel +34 954 53 47 20; Calle de María Auxiliadora 18A; 7-11pm*

06 FUNDACIÓN CRISTINA HEEREN DE ARTE

Flamenco is a complex art. Mastering it is not something that can be ticked off in a weekend — it takes a bit of time and commitment. Aspiring flamencologists in search of some cultural immersion need look no further than the highly respected Cristina Heeren school in the Heliopolis neighbourhood of southern Seville.

Set up by an expat American in 1996, the Heeren has more than 20 years of experience instructing students in all three of the flamenco arts — dance, song and guitar. Its intensive four-week-long summer courses in July are particularly popular. *www.flamencoheeren.com; tel +34 954 21 70 58; Av de Jerez 2* **BY BRENDAN SAINSBURY**

06 Music is close-up and explosive at Casa de la Guitarra

07 & 09 A performance and costume display at Seville's flamenco museum

08 Triana is where flamenco first originated

08 © heybear00 / Budget Travel: 09 © Stillman Rogers / Alamy

WHERE TO STAY
HOTEL ADRIANO
This friendly little nook in the riverside Arenal quarter couldn't be anywhere else but Seville. Economical and understated, none of its rooms are the same; there's an arty cafe out front. *www.adrianohotel.com; tel +34 954 29 38 00; Calle Adriano 12*

HOTEL AMADEUS
Striking a musical note in the higgledy-piggledy, historic Santa Cruz quarter, this hotel is run by an engaging local family. Harps, violins and pianos furnish the common areas (you can play some of them) plus there's a Jacuzzi on a relaxing rooftop sundeck. *www.hotelamadeussevilla. com; +34 954 50 14 43; Calle Farnesio 6*

WHERE TO EAT & DRINK
LA BRUNILDA
A new-school fusion tapas bar in an inconspicuous backstreet in the Arenal quarter where everything — including the food, decor, staff and clientele — is pretty. The menu is full of intriguing experimentation. *Tel +34 954 22 04 81; Calle Galera 5*

CASA CUESTA
Get into Triana's true flamenco spirit in this old-school bar, where ornate mirrors reflect framed bull-fighting posters, gleaming gold beer pumps and wine bottles that look older than most of the clientele. The fish tapas are as good as the atmosphere. *www.casacuesta.net; tel +34 954 33 33 35; Calle de Castilla 1*

CELEBRATIONS
BIENAL DE FLAMENCO SEVILLA
Seville's biannual flamenco festival celebrated in September of even-number years is, not surprisingly, one of the world's most prestigious, attracting the cream of international performers. *(www.labienal.com)*

FERIA DE ABRIL
Seville's spring festival is legendary; a perfect manifestation of what the city is all about, with music and dance playing a big role. Drink tents and a fairground are set up in a special area in the district of Los Remedios where people dance a traditional folkloric form of flamenco called *sevillanas*.

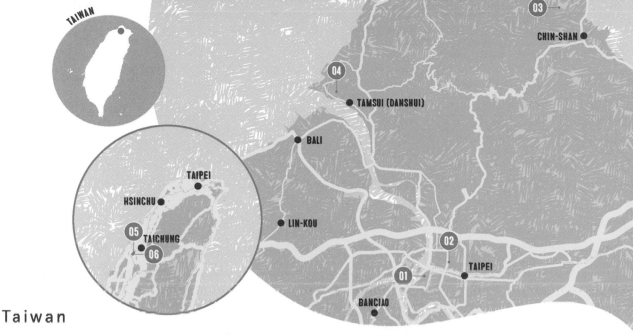

Taiwan

TAIWANESE FOLKLORE REIMAGINED

Indigenous rites and local folklore walk hand in hand with modern culture on Taiwan — an island that is unafraid to rewrite its traditions with an eye to the future.

The nine-day Matsu Pilgrimage, one of the world's most spectacular festivals, sees oceans of pilgrims and spectators escort a statue of the Goddess of the Sea through 50 Taiwan towns. Some jostle each other to touch her sedan chair, while the devout kneel on the road to allow the deity to be carried over them.

Folk rituals are thriving in the country, but contemporary Taiwan has also added its touches to the proceedings. It is not uncommon to see pole dancers busting moves or pink-haired youth dressed up as deities in the procession. Nothing looks out of place. Similarly, Taiwanese food may be known for its heirloom recipes, yet simmering beneath the oyster omelette is a quietly ambitious modern cuisine that engages seasonal local produce in new and inspired ways. The Taiwanese have a knack for taking liberties with their heritage and whizzing it, betel nut and all, into the future.

NEED TO KNOW
This four-day trail involves a combination of walking and using Taiwan's metro, bus and train network.

In the arts, Taiwan was regarded as the last bastion of Chinese civilisation until the nativist movement of the '70s and '80s saw native Taiwanese reasserting their cultural authority and rejecting traditional Chinese culture. Artists and writers mined their own histories for ideas, while manifesting Chinese culture with a Taiwanese sensibility. Sculptor Ju Ming and choreographer Lin Hwai-min, who burst onto the scene in the 1970s, are two of Asia's most revered artists.

For more examples, you need only visit the island's many museums. The National Museum of Taiwan Literature articulates how local writers came into their own; at the Kaohsiung Museum of Fine Arts, you'll find contemporary indigenous art. But some of the most interesting enactments of Taiwanese culture are found in less obvious places. On this island, tradition and modernity sashay about each other, as they do the lives of the people — with the ease of a pole dancer and the shrewdness of a sage.

① GRAFFITI IN XIMENDING

In the central Taipei shopping hub of Ximending, massive technicolour murals, often in a bright mix of pop and folk styles, leap out at pedestrians as they walk past.

Jimmy Cheng of Citymarx, one of the artists featured, says that Taiwan's home-grown graffiti writers like to borrow from their roots. 'Indigenous culture, the way of life of the Hakka migrants from China, and traditional art all come into play in the creative process,' he explains.

You'll see murals in Ximending's Taipei Cinema Park and, close by, smaller works in a range of styles bomb the lanes shooting off Emei St and Wuchang St. To get to Ximending, head to Ximen metro station.

'Nantian Temple shows scenes from hell using animatronic dioramas in period clothing and unabashedly torturous sound effects'

② SHIATZY CHEN FASHION

This Taiwanese luxury brand infuses Western clothing with Chinese details to create what is known as 'neo-Chinese chic' — an imaginative and immensely clever take on fusion aesthetics. Its flagship store is in the Zhongshan district of northern Taipei, near Zhongshan metro station.

Exotic Chinoiserie it is not; the pieces also steer clear of Orientalist dragon-and-phoenix stereotypes.

One collection themed on the Chinese classic, *Journey to the West*, includes a yellow skirt printed with dream-like renditions of the novel's characters, and held together by a lace-up corset-belt — a nod to Victorian England.

In menswear, you might spot a mandarin collar in sheepskin peeking over the shoulders of a denim windbreaker. Shiatzy Chen's fine garments have clothed the likes of

01 Taipei skyline

02 Dragon boat racing on Lake Liyu

03-04 Offerings at the Matsu temple; celebrations during the annual Matsu Pilgrimage

former president Ma Ying-jeou and Britain's Victoria Beckham. *www.shiatzychen.com; 49-1, Sec 2, Zhongshan N Rd; 10.30am-9pm Mon-Fri, to 8pm Sat & Sun*

03 JUMING MUSEUM

The works of Taiwan's preeminent sculptor Ju Ming (b 1938) are strewn all over the world, but the collection at the artist's sprawling personal museum on Taiwan's northeast coast is the most sizeable and, what's more, displayed in a beautiful garden.

Ju, who apprenticed under a temple craftsman, stunned the art scene in 1976 with dynamic wood pieces that explored the Taiwanese identity. In the celebrated Taichi series, Ju pared down the human figure to abstract

blocks in order to liberate the poetic essence of his subjects. You'll see them at the museum — monumental shadow-boxers in poses of stoic fluidity, as expressive in their form as in the marks of the artist's tools on their robes.

The museum is in Jinshan, about 38km from downtown Taipei, and can be reached by bus from Taipei Train Station; there's a free museum shuttle from the Jinshan District Office. *www.juming.org.tw; tel +886 2 2498 9940; 2, Xishihu, Jinshan; 10am-6pm May-Oct, to 5pm Nov-Apr*

04 CLOUD GATE DANCE THEATRE

Taiwan's premier modern dance troupe draws richly from folk tales, mythology and history to create spectacles

of movement that hypnotise with their technical brilliance and sublime artistry. Catching a performance at the troupe's ultra-modern headquarters in Tamsui, a northerly coastal district of New Taipei City, is a must. Heavy metal, Bach, calligraphy and roller-skating could all feature in the performances, as could meditation, martial arts and qigong in the dancers' daily routines.

In *Songs of the Wanderers*, a work inspired as much by Asian religions as by Hermann Hesse's account of Buddhism, a stream of golden rice grains shimmers down onto a monk's head, to the ethereal undulations of Georgian folk songs. Imagery — poetic, distinctly Asian, and resonant with humanity — is strong in Cloud Gate works. Choreographer Lin Hwai-min

04 © twospeeds / Shutterstock

(05)

trained under Martha Graham in New York before founding the company in 1973, and has made it one of Cloud Gate's missions to explore what it is to be Taiwanese. If there are no performances scheduled at Tamsui during your visit, the company also plays elsewhere on the island. *site.cloudgate.org.tw/eng/theater; tel +886 2 2629 8558; No 36, Ln 6, Sec 1, Zhongzheng Rd, Tamsui*

05 NANTIAN TEMPLE

In the southern foothills of Baguashan is the Nantian Temple, where it was once the custom for parents, particularly those in rural areas, to take their children to scare them into obedience. The temple has a gallery of horrors named 'The 18 Levels of Hell' after the deliciously gruesome purgatory of Chinese legends.

It shows scenes from this hell using animatronic dioramas in period clothing, copious green and red lighting, and unabashedly torturous sound effects. You'll see thieves, adulterers and their ilk fried in oil, stabbed, disembowelled and sawn in half, over and over again.

'These temples were obligatory stops on primary school outings in the '70s and '80s,' says local Trista Liao, who was taken to this temple herself as a child. 'The intense palette and shocking imagery of the style evoke Japanese artist Tadanori Yokoo. Puppet theatre backdrops had a similar style.'

The temple is in Changhua City, a two-hour high-speed rail ride from Taipei. From Hell, it's a 20-minute stroll to Nanyao Temple. *Ln 187, Sec 1, 12 Gongyuan Rd, Changhua; 8am-7pm*

06 NANYAO TEMPLE

Finish your tour at historic Nanyao Temple, a 20-minute stroll from Nantian Temple and a stop on the annual Matsu Pilgrimage. The highlight is the middle hall dedicated to the Goddess of Mercy. At a glance more like a mansion than a sanctum, this squarish structure is designed in an unusual mix of Japanese, Western and Chinese styles.

It was raised in 1917 under Japanese rule, at a time when Japan was shedding feudalism and embracing Western aesthetics. You'll notice the double eaves of many temples,

but here the lower eave flaunts a fringe of European-style balustrades. Below it, a corridor whips around the hall, bordered by Doric columns and a ceiling patterned with the chrysanthemum, a symbol of Japan. Inside the hall, the ceiling has a square three-tiered vault with simple lines and geometric petal embellishments, quite different to the sumptuous affairs of Fujian-style temples.

Cast your eyes further — large Classical-style plaques feature the 18 *arhats* (saints) in relief. The shrines are Japanese but, overall, the hall's architectural vocabulary defies definition by Chinese, Japanese and Western conventions.

43 Nanyao Rd, Changhua; 6am-8pm
BY PIERA CHEN

06 © Lamia Lin / 500 px

05 A Cloud Gate Dance Theatre performance

06 A woman carries baskets past a temple in Kinmen

WHERE TO STAY

FLIP FLOP HOSTEL
Formerly a dormitory for railway workers, clean and cosy Flip Flop offers 11 dorms and several private rooms in a historical setting. There's also a cheerful-looking reception and a wooden bar and lounge area. Be warned that there is no lift, which means a good workout for guests staying on the fifth floor.
www.flipflophostel.com; tel +886 2 2558 3553; 103 Huayin St, Taipei

ESLITE HOTEL
A quiet and tasteful place run by the bookstore chain of the same name, Eslite has 100 spacious rooms in white and olive green. Those facing the park also have good views of Taipei 101 in the distance.
www.eslitehotel.com; tel +886 2 6626 2888; 98 Yanchang Rd, Taipei

WHERE TO EAT & DRINK

RAW
Owned by chef Andre Chiang, this high-end restaurant in Taipei's Zhongshan District introduces haute cuisine to Taiwan with an eight-course menu exquisitely crafted with local produce. The setting is casual-contemporary with lots of light-toned wood, and prices are reasonable. Book two weeks in advance.
www.raw.com.tw; tel +886 2 8501 5800; Sec 3, 301 Lequn Rd, Taipei; 11.30am-2.30pm & 6-10pm Wed-Sun

FONG DA COFFEE
One of Taipei's original coffee shops and roasteries, Fong Da in the Ximending area dates from 1956 and still uses some of the original equipment. It is always busy, testament to the great brews to be had here.
Tel +886 2 2371 9577; 42 Chengdu Rd; 8am-10pm

CELEBRATIONS

MATSU PILGRIMAGE
The annual nine-day Matsu Pilgrimage sees hundreds of thousands of pilgrims and spectators escort a palanquin, graced by a statue of Matsu (Goddess of the Sea), from Taichung to Chiayi, and then back again, covering a distance of more than 350km. Dates change each year and are announced in March.

USA

VINTAGE HOLLYWOOD

Peel back the glitzy celluloid layers and Los Angeles can transport you back to its early 20th-century Golden Age, when glamour and intrigue inspired life, film and fiction.

On the sunny coast of Southern California, Los Angeles – no matter if you call it 'La La Land' or the 'City of Angels'– is a dreamscape. Here in the early 20th century, enterprising filmmakers began churning out movies to entertain the rest of the country and, soon enough, the entire world.

As much as 'The Industry' (that's what locals call the TV and movie biz) has sold celluloid images of SoCal's golden beaches, muscled lifeguards and bikini-clad volleyball players to audiences worldwide, LA has always had a seamy underbelly too.

Just think about the corruption and twisted betrayals seen in classic noir films of the late 1940s and '50s, or the hardboiled detective novels of Raymond Chandler, who began publishing after the Great Depression.

More recently, a renaissance of noir crime fiction has

NEED TO KNOW
Most of Hollywood is walkable, drive or taxi to Beverly Hills, Santa Monica and Downtown LA. Set aside two days for this trail.

been led by James Ellroy, an LA-born novelist who often writes about Hollywood's Golden Age, sometimes based on events that actually happened such as the Black Dahlia murder.

On this trail, you can travel back in time to glimpse Old Hollywood, both the glamorous lives of celebrities such as Ava Gardner and Clark Gable, and also the dark side of LA crime fiction set in the 1930s, '40s and '50s. Step inside the nightspots where movie stars and literary luminaries boozed it up with their friends, as well as places where actors showed up in diamonds and designer wear for film premieres and Academy Awards ceremonies.

Often the same spots where the stars were known to hang out in real life also appear in noir crime novels, especially Raymond Chandler's tales of private eye Philip Marlowe in shadowy 'Bay City'.

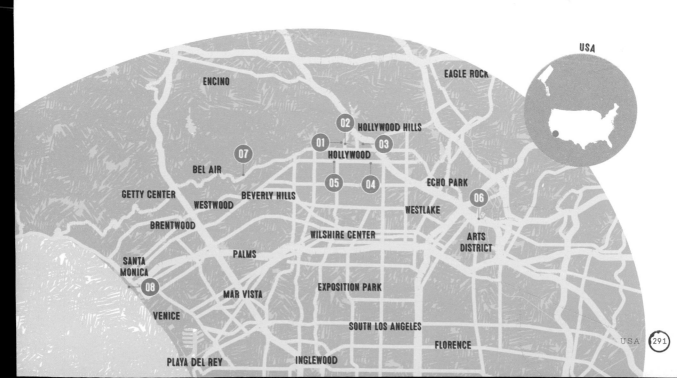

01 YØ 6e K Adams / 590px

02 © Sean Pavone / Shutterstock

01 TCL CHINESE THEATRE

On its grand opening night in 1927, this Hollywood movie palace premiered a silent epic, *The King of Kings*, directed by Cecil B DeMille. Originally co-owned by silent-film stars Douglas Fairbanks and Mary Pickford (aka 'America's Sweetheart'), the theatre has a fantastical façade imitating a Chinese palace, complete with a pagoda roof and temple bells.

Outside in the concrete forecourt, generations of celebrities have left handprints, footprints and other lasting impressions such as pin-up girl Betty Grable's legs and the hoofprints of Roy Rogers' beloved horse Trigger. The theatre still shows regular movies and hosts premieres. *www.tclchinesetheatres.com; tel +1 323 461 3331; 6925 Hollywood Blvd; daily show times vary*

02 THE HOLLYWOOD MUSEUM

Follow the Hollywood Walk of Fame, looking for your favourite artist's name on a coral pink star marked with a brass emblem signifying in which part of 'The Industry' — that is, film, TV, radio, music or theatre — they made their mark.

Past the Spanish Baroque-style El Capitan Theatre, detour to the elegant art deco Max Factor building. Here, stars such as blonde bombshell Marilyn Monroe and sassy redhead Lucille Ball had Max Factor himself do their make-up and styling before movie premieres. Today it houses the Hollywood Museum, an eclectic collection of more than 10,000 pieces of movie-making memorabilia. Gawk at set pieces, props and costumes — anything from Elvis's favourite bathrobe to Rocky's boxing gloves. *www.thehollywoodmuseum.com; tel +1 323 464 7776; 1660 N Highland Ave; 10am-5pm Wed-Sun*

03 FROLIC ROOM

Back on the Hollywood Walk of Fame, you'll pass the Egyptian Theatre, another classic movie palace by impresario Sid Grauman. Built in

'Here, stars such as Marilyn Monroe and Lucille Ball had Max Factor himself do their styling before premieres'

01 LA's iconic skyline

02 The fantastical façade of TCL Chinese Theatre, still in use today

03 Hollywood Walk of Fame

04 Outside Frolic Room, which has a star-studded history

1922, its over-the-top design reflects the worldwide craze for Egyptian decor following the discovery of King Tut's tomb.

A half-mile walk brings you to the Frolic Room, a dive bar with a staggering pedigree, standing in the shadow of the 1930s Pantages Theater. As seen in the movie *LA Confidential*, based on James Ellroy's neo-noir novel, the Frolic Room was a popular watering hole for movie stars in Hollywood's Golden Age.

Slide into a red booth after picking out some songs on the jukebox. The cocktails are stiff, which you'll appreciate after finding out that this might have been the last place the

real 'Black Dahlia', Elizabeth Short, was seen alive before being brutally murdered in 1947.
Tel +1 323 462 5890; 6245 Hollywood Blvd; 11am-2am daily

04 HOLLYWOOD FOREVER

It's a quick taxi ride down to this bizarrely touristy cemetery, the final resting place of dozens of Hollywood stars from yesteryear. Buy a map from the flower shop, then go hunting for the marble tomb of Douglas Fairbanks, Cecil B DeMille's stone sarcophagus or the crypt of silent-film heart throb Rudolph Valentino.

Pay your respects to the modest headstone of John Huston, who

directed the classic noir film *The Maltese Falcon* (1941), originally a novel by hardboiled crime-fiction writer Dashiell Hammett. Sometimes on summer nights, movies are projected onto a supersized outdoor screen here (cinespia.org) and a DJ spins electronica while couples picnic under the stars.
www.hollywoodforever.com; tel +1 323 469 1181; 6000 Santa Monica Blvd; 8am-5pm daily

05 FORMOSA CAFE

Hop in another taxi to West Hollywood's fabled Formosa Cafe, which first opened in 1925 inside a converted trolley car. It quickly

03 © Ian G Dagnall / Alamy; 04 © Steve Hamblin / Alamy

became a gathering spot for stars working at nearby movie studio lots. You may recognise the 1930s building's signature red exterior with the black-and-white awnings from *LA Confidential*. Currently this historical landmark is closed; check to see if it has reopened. Fingers crossed, you'll be able to step inside and peruse head shots of the bar's most (in)famous patrons, including gangster 'Bugsy' Siegel and movie stars such as Humphrey Bogart and Grace Kelly. *7156 Santa Monica Blvd*

06 UNION STATION

In Downtown LA, Union Station was one of the last great railway stations built in the USA. A mix of art deco and California's Spanish-influenced Mission Revival architectural style,

this landmark opened in 1939. With a cavernous and hauntingly beautiful waiting room, Union Station has starred in countless movies and TV shows. It also featured in Raymond Chandler's final novel *Playback*, in which private eye Philip Marlowe meets a mysterious woman arriving on the Super Chief from Chicago. Many Hollywood stars also took that same train route back in the day.

A 10-minute walk away, through the plazas and shopping streets of El Pueblo de Los Angeles historical monument, you'll find LA's City Hall (1928) — an impressively triple-tiered art-deco tower seen in the 1950s TV series *Dragnet* and the film *LA Confidential*. It also makes an appearance in a Chandler novel, *Trouble Is My Business*, when

Marlowe smokes a cigarette in the dark on the steps outside. *www.unionstationla.com; 800 N Alameda St; 4am-1am*

07 POLO LOUNGE

A see-and-be-seen spot where many starlets have been discovered, this restaurant is at the ritzy Beverly Hills Hotel, a 40-minute drive from Downtown LA. Snag a table on the sun-kissed outdoor patio, where fuchsia-coloured bougainvillea flowers cascade over the hotel's signature pink stucco walls. Star sightings are still practically guaranteed here and also in the hotel's Fountain Coffee Room, where Marilyn Monroe once perched at the counter. *www.dorchestercollection.com; tel +1 310 887 2777; 9641 Sunset Blvd; 7am-1.30am*

⑧ SANTA MONICA PIER

Wind west on Sunset Blvd all the way to the Pacific Ocean, where the seaside town of Santa Monica was reimagined by Raymond Chandler as 'Bay City'. It was filled with corrupt cops, two-faced women and rough-and-tumble mobsters, as seen in the 1946 movie adaptation of Chandler's novel *The Big Sleep*, starring Humphrey Bogart and siren Lauren Bacall.

You won't find offshore gambling ships or bootleggers here anymore, but you can walk out onto the pier like Marlowe moodily did. It best evokes Chandler's chilling novels on foggy, moonless nights. *santamonicapier.org; tel +1 310 458 8901; pier 24hr*
BY SARA BENSON

06 © Chris Putnam / Alamy

05 Santa
Monica Pier

06 The art deco
interior of Union
Street Station

WHERE TO STAY

HOLLYWOOD ROOSEVELT HOTEL
Gorgeously renovated, this 1926 hotel mixes old Hollywood glamour with contemporary design. Sleep in a mod poolside cabana like Marilyn Monroe did, or book a sumptuously furnished studio inside the historic tower. *www.thehollywoodroosevelt.com; tel +1 323 856 1970; 7000 Hollywood Blvd*

CHATEAU MARMONT
Hollywood's version of a French chateau, this elite address is where movie stars still stay today, along with celebutantes, rock 'n' roll musicians and the merely rich, but not yet famous. Lovers can retreat to a garden cottage or poolside bungalow. *www.chateaumarmont.com; tel +1 323 656 1010; 8221 Sunset Blvd*

WHERE TO EAT & DRINK

MUSSO & FRANK GRILL
Hollywood's oldest restaurant (since 1919), this clubby Italian-American chophouse has been the haunt of many movie stars, including Charlie Chaplin, as well as crime novelists and screenplay writers, Raymond Chandler among them. *www.mussoandfrank.com; tel +1 323 467 7788; 6667 Hollywood Blvd*

YAMASHIRO HOLLYWOOD
With spectacular views over LA from its perch in the Hollywood Hills, this faux Asian temple built by quirky art collectors later became a spot for Hollywood hobnobbing. Come for Cal-Asian fusion food and neon-coloured cocktails. *yamashirohollywood.com; tel +1 323 466 5125; 1999 N Sycamore Ave*

CELEBRATIONS

ACADEMY AWARDS
Every February, A-list movie stars sashay down the red carpet into the Dolby Theatre to attend this annual awards ceremony, first held at the Hollywood Roosevelt Hotel in 1929. *(www.oscars.org)*

STAR CEREMONIES
On the Hollywood Walk of Fame, join the public spectacle whenever a new star is revealed, which happens several times a year. Check the website for upcoming ceremonies. *(www.walkoffame.com)*

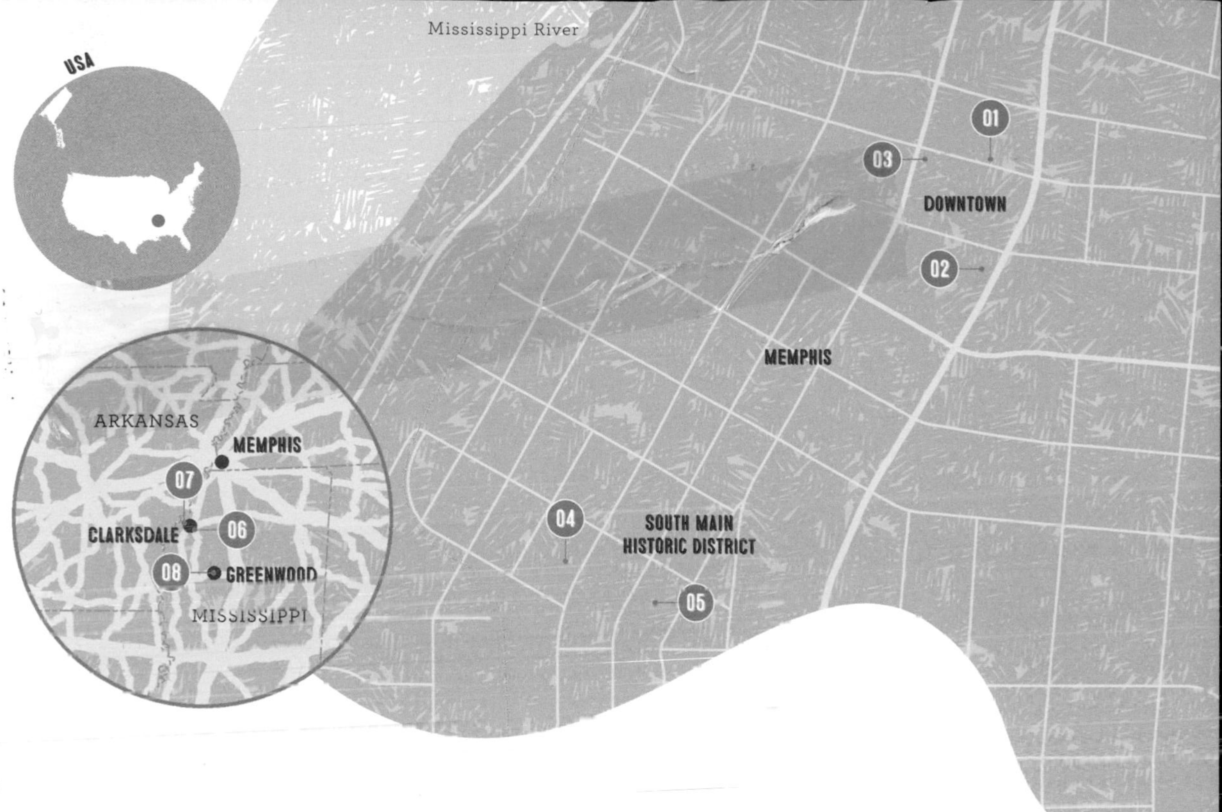

USA map labels: USA, ARKANSAS, MEMPHIS, CLARKSDALE, GREENWOOD, MISSISSIPPI, 07, 06, 08, DOWNTOWN, 01, 03, 02, MEMPHIS, 04, SOUTH MAIN HISTORIC DISTRICT, 05

USA

DEEP SOUTH BLUES TRAIL

In the early 20th century wandering bluesmen found their soul in Memphis, winning fans with rough-and-ready plantation sounds that created a pilgrimage scene still alive today.

Few things can be tracked so perfectly to the landscape as the music of the Deep South. The winding country lanes and backwater towns of the Mississippi Delta are a three-dimensional roadmap of the blues, immortalised in song, steeped in legend and nostalgically lost in time.

Listen carefully as you weave your way between the weatherboard chapels and vanished plantations and you just might hear a blast of harmonica or the rattle of a timeworn Gibson guitar floating on the breeze.

The cities of the delta have come a long way since the heyday of the blues, when legends such as BB King and Muddy Waters played nightly to full houses, and share-cropping and servitude finally gave way to desegregation and liberation. But drift out along the country roads of the South, and you'll enter a landscape straight from the songs of Tom Patton and Robert Johnson — lonely crossroads, dirt tracks to nowhere, peeling wooden cabins and leaning road signs pointing to vanished townships.

NEED TO KNOW
Spend a day on foot in Memphis, then hit the highway in a car to explore the sleepy hinterland of the blues.

For fans of the blues, a trip to the delta is not just a vacation but a pilgrimage. The Mississippi Delta is like a map of the stars for the blues; every twist in the road is a chord change, every street corner is a song lyric. Back roads snake like guitar cables between the country towns where the blues was first performed and recorded, and the lonely cabins and plantations that gave the music its passion and soul.

This musical tour is our pick from hundreds of landmark locations in the story of the blues and, ultimately, of rock and roll. For more ideas, point your wheels towards the Blues Trail (www.msbluestrail.org), whose organisers have installed nearly 200 blue signs at key blues sites around the American South.

> 'The blues drew on a fevered climate of segregation and injustice; BB King was born into servitude in Mississippi'

01 BEALE STREET

There's only one place to start a tour of the blues lands: Memphis, Tennessee. It was here that itinerant blues musicians started to congregate in the 1900s, creating one of the first 'scenes' in modern music. Given musical clout by local band leader WC Handy, the rough-and-ready plantation sounds of the wandering bluesmen found a wider audience in the cafes, parks and theatres that throng Beale St in downtown Memphis.

One musician more than any other put Beale St on the map: Riley B King, later BB King (1925-2015). The Beale Street Blues Boy — as he was known, later shortened to Blues Boy King and then BB King — rolled in from Indianola after WWII and took up residence at the Palace Theatre at 380 Beale St, and anywhere else that would let him play.

His signature vibrato and lyrical phrasing lives on in the style of pretty much every blues guitarist. Before leaving, drop into Handy Park to tip your hat to the eponymous band leader statue, then stroll south along South BB King Boulevard.
www.bealestreet.com

02 GIBSON GUITAR WORKSHOP

At the time of the Memphis blues explosion, the guitars used by the world's top blues musicians were still being made in Kalamazoo, Michigan. The first guitars only rolled off the factory floor in Memphis in 2000, but this is now the birthplace of all of Gibson's hollow-body guitars, including BB King's signature model, Lucille, named after the iconic Gibson ES-335 that King rescued from a burning theatre in Twist, Arkansas in 1949.

Fret-nuts still gather daily for guided factory tours to witness the creation of the next generation of Gibsons —

01 Beale St in Memphis: blues heartland

02 Clarksdale's Devils Crossroads

03 A Beale St blues bar, bedecked with guitars

04 The most likely resting place of blues legend Robert Johnson

05 Muddy Waters house at the Delta Blues Museum

all inspired by the prototype electric guitar that pioneer luthier and guitarist Lester Polsfuss (aka Les Paul) created by wedging a wooden block inside an arch-top in 1940. *www.gibson.com; 145 Lieutenant George W Lee Ave; 10am-6pm Mon-Sat, noon-4pm Sun*

03 BB KING'S BLUES CLUB

As darkness falls, set your sights back on Beale St, where the first sound checks will be spilling out into the night air. Although its founder died in 2015, BB King's Blues Club is still a major showcase for up-and-coming blues talent. King himself continued to play more than 200 shows a year well into his 80s, and appeared regularly at this classic Beale St club. *www.bbkings.com/memphis; tel +1 901-524-5464; 143 Beale St; show times vary*

04 BLUES HALL OF FAME

Start day two by following South Main St into south Memphis. Everyone from white-haired virtuoso Johnny Winter to the 'Three Kings' — Albert, Freddie and BB — gets hero status at the Blues Foundation's official Hall of Fame. As well as browsing the blues memorabilia (Muddy Waters' satin jacket, Koko Taylor's gold boots), you might get lucky and see the induction of a new blues legend. Brit-rocker John Mayall made the list in 2016. *blues.org/hall-of-fame; 421 South Main St; 10am-5pm Mon-Sat, 1-5pm Sun*

05 NATIONAL CIVIL RIGHTS MUSEUM

It would be remiss to visit Memphis without pausing to consider the social conditions that gave rise to the blues. A block away from the Blues Hall of Fame at 450 Mulberry St, the National Civil Rights Museum occupies the

former Lorraine Motel, where Martin Luther King Jr fell to a sniper's bullet in 1968. The blues drew on a fevered climate of segregation and injustice; consider for a moment that BB King was born into servitude on a cotton plantation near Itta Bena, Mississippi. *www.civilrightsmuseum.org, 450 Mulberry St; 9am-5pm Wed-Mon*

06 DEVIL'S CROSSROADS

If you've got a soul to sell, Clarksdale, Mississippi might well be the place to sell it. A short drive south from Memphis along Hwy 61 and Hwy 49, this sleepy southern town was reputedly the setting for one of the founding legends of the blues.

As the tale goes, a down-on-his-luck musician named Robert Johnson (1911–1938) had a mysterious midnight meeting with a smartly dressed man at a deserted crossroads, and traded his immortal soul for virtuosity on the guitar. Whole theses have been written about the symbolism of the devil and the crossroads, citing everything from Beninese animism to white tropes about the blues as 'devil's music'.

What is certain is that the myth has mass appeal — at least four towns claim to be the location of the crossroads, and Clarksdale has staked its claim with three guitars mounted on a pole at the junction of Hwy 61 and Hwy 49. *Cnr North State St & Desoto Ave, Clarksdale*

07 DELTA BLUES MUSEUM

While in town, you can detour to several more points of pilgrimage on the Blues Trail. Prioritise Muddy Waters' cabin, which originally stood on Stovall Rd in north Clarksdale.

This modest home now endures the centuries inside the Delta Blues Museum on Blues Alley — complete except for the timbers that were made into guitars by ZZ Top's Billy Gibbons. Whistle a chorus of 'Mannish Boy' then point your wheels south along Hwy 49 towards Greenwood. *www.deltabluesmuseum.org; 1 Blues Alley, Clarksdale; 9am-5pm Mon-Sat, from 10am Nov-Feb*

08 ROBERT JOHNSON'S GRAVE

Despite his massive influence, Robert Johnson recorded his entire catalogue in just two recording sessions in 1936 and 1937. Little is know about his life, and still less about his death.

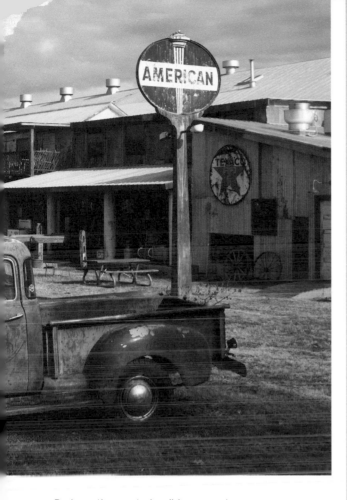

Perhaps the most plausible account, put forward by fellow bluesman Sonny Boy Williamson, is that the notorious drinker and womaniser was killed by a bottle of poisoned whisky, offered up by a jealous husband.

After his death, Johnson was buried near Greenwood, Mississippi — also the hometown of 1940s and '50s New Orleans blues musician Guitar Slim — but as a vagrant with few close kin, the site of his grave was never officially recorded.

The most likely location, according to interviews with people alive at the time, is under the trees at Little Zion Missionary Baptist Church, marked by a small stone memorial draped with offerings.
Money Rd, Greenwood
BY JOE BINDLOSS

07 © Tim Graham / Getty Images

06 Memphis's BB King Blues Club

07 An old Clarksdale cotton plantation, now a retro B&B

WHERE TO STAY
PEABODY HOTEL
This huge neon-topped edifice in the heart of downtown has been the top choice for Memphis movers and shakers since it opened in 1925. Come for stylish rooms, Italian Renaissance decor, and a nightly parade of ducks marching through the lobby.
www.peabodymemphis. com; tel + 1 901 529 4000; 149 Union Ave, Memphis

RIVERSIDE HOTEL
It might look simple from the outside, but the brick-fronted Riverside was good enough for Sonny Boy Williamson II, Ike Turner, and Betty Smith, who passed away here back when the hotel was a hospital in 1937.
Tel +1 662 624 9163; 615 Sunflower Ave, Clarksdale

WHERE TO EAT & DRINK
GUS'S WORLD FAMOUS FRIED CHICKEN
The tacky decor at this rough-and-ready chicken shed doesn't put off the punters, who flock here to tuck in to the house speciality. This is chicken fried the southern way — spicy, fluffy and served on a bed of white bread.
www.gusfriedchicken. com; tel +1 901 527 4877; 310 Front St, Memphis

WILD BILL'S
While mainstreamers are partying on Beale St, folk who like their blues down and dirty congregate at this spit and sawdust bar every Friday and Saturday for the real, soulful deal.
Tel +1 901 207 3975; 1580 Vollintine Ave, Memphis

CELEBRATIONS
BEALE STREET MUSIC FESTIVAL
This three-day Memphis celebration of guitar music on the first weekend in May covers all genres – past line-ups have included everyone from Stevie Ray Vaughan and James Brown to Public Enemy and Ed Sheeran.
(www.memphisinmay.org)

INTERNATIONAL BLUES CHALLENGE
The annual Blues Challenge in Memphis is the closest thing to a real-life *Crossroads* the movie. Every January/February over 200 bands and soloists come together to compete.
(www.blues.org/internat ional-blues-challenge)

USA
DYLAN & THE VILLAGE

On the run from Middle America, Bob Dylan blew into New York City in 1961, finding fame and fortune amid the folk scene of Greenwich Village, where his Beatnik legacy lives on.

Long before the Nobel prize and the sobriquet 'greatest living poet', before the civil rights anthems and the Electric Dylan controversy, Robert Zimmerman — later Bob Dylan — was a footloose, freewheeling teenager, drifting around America in search of an audience. It was in the folk clubs of New York's Greenwich Village that the young Bob Dylan first found an appreciative ear, and set off on the path to becoming a living legend.

America's greatest singer-songwriter was born in the anonymous setting of Duluth, Minnesota, a sleepy port city on Lake Superior, whose population peaked at 108,000 in 1960 and declined steadily every year thereafter. Being geographically stuck in the back end of beyond, it was inevitable that Dylan drifted towards the brightest light on the east coast — 1960s New York, the centre of the biggest folk scene of the modern age.

NEED TO KNOW
Use foot-power, buses and the subway for this two-day traipse around Dylan's old stomping grounds.

Dylan's first port of call in NYC was the Greystone Park Psychiatric Hospital, where he stopped in on an ailing Woody Guthrie, before touting his wares at the hip folk clubs littered around Greenwich Village. He hooked up with girlfriend Suze Rotolo — who graced the iconic cover of *The Freewheelin' Bob Dylan* — and discovered political activism and the civil rights movement, immortalising the city in a string of ballads, from *Talkin' New York* to *Positively 4th Street*.

New York has come a long way since the footloose winter of 1961, but Dylan landmarks are still scattered around the streets of Greenwich Village, including clubs where the American bard first strummed a chord. Spend a weekend freewheeling around New York from 4th Street to the Chelsea Hotel and tap into the unpredictable, rebellious spirit of music's prickliest minstrel.

01 © Tupungato / shutterst ck

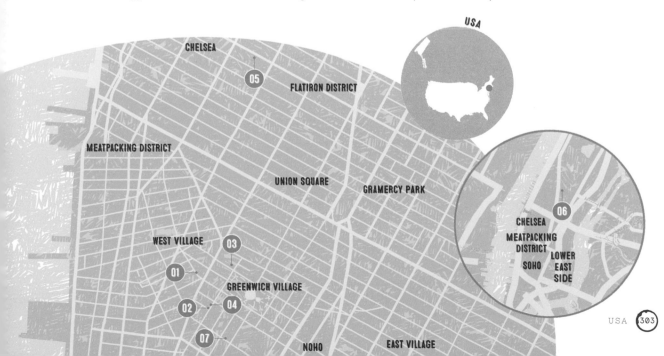

USA

CHELSEA
05
FLATIRON DISTRICT
MEATPACKING DISTRICT
UNION SQUARE
GRAMERCY PARK
CHELSEA
06
MEATPACKING DISTRICT
LOWER EAST SIDE
SOHO
WEST VILLAGE
03
01
GREENWICH VILLAGE
02   04
07
NOHO
EAST VILLAGE

01 161 WEST 4TH STREET

Put yourself in Bob Dylan's shoes. You've just dropped out of college, the songs of Woody Guthrie are flowing through your veins, and you're fleeing small-town America in the winter of 1961. You don't have much more to your name than a guitar, a harmonica and a dream. Where are you going to go?

For Dylan, the answer was simple. Greenwich Village in 1961 was a fiery hotbed of activism, music and ideas. The young musician soared to success off the back of performances in the coffee shops on MacDougal St and moved into an apartment at 161 West 4th St with new girlfriend Suze Rotolo, still flush with adrenaline from recording his first album, *Bob Dylan*.

'The Sunday meets became so popular they soon attracted the ire of the authorities, culminating in the Beatnik Riot of 1961'

There's no plaque to mark the apartment, so look for the doorway squeezed between adult shops just before the corner of 4th and 6th. One block northwest on Jones Street, you can pause for a photo op at the exact spot where Dylan and Rotolo were snapped for the iconic cover of Dylan's follow-up LP, *The Freewheelin' Bob Dylan*.
161 West 4th St, Greenwich Village

02 CAFFE REGGIO

Now that the spirit of Dylan is coursing in your veins, take a freewheeling stroll southeast along 4th St, then turn south onto MacDougal St. You are now in the heart of Dylan country. 'Blowin' in the Wind' was written at No 105, at what used to be The Commons coffee shop, and Dylan blew some of his first harmonica solos at Caffe Reggio at No 119.

01 Washington Square Park — an old Beat generation hang-out

02 On the streets of Greenwich Village

03 Rainbow flags on Christopher St

04 Cafe Wha?, where Dylan used to play, is still going strong

Caffe Reggio's legacy goes beyond Dylan. This was reputedly the spot where the first cappuccino ever served in America was brewed, and the cafe has been pepping up the Village since 1927. You might recognise the place from cinematic cameos in *The Godfather II*, cult classic *Shaft*, and Dave van Ronk-homage *Inside Llewyn Davis*. *www.caffereggio.com; tel +1 212 475 9557; 119 MacDougal St; 8am-3am, to 4.30am Fri & Sat*

03 WASHINGTON SQUARE HOTEL

Suitably refreshed, it's time to unwind. Amble back up MacDougal St to Washington Square Park, the lungs of Greenwich Village. This green bower was where the Beat generation came to unwind on Sundays, trading poems, songs and philosophical ideas over beers and narcotics. The Sunday meets became so popular they soon attracted the ire of the authorities, culminating in the Beatnik Riot of 1961.

Tucked away at the northeast corner on Waverly Place, the Washington Square Hotel has been a landmark since Dylan's time. It was here in room 305 that he holed up with Joan Baez in 1964, during the affair which ended his relationship with Suze Rotolo.

Baez later immortalised the place as the 'crummy hotel' on Washington Square (we're duty bound to say it's nicer today) in her 1974 hit music track called *Diamonds and Rust*. *www.washingtonsquarehotel.com; tel +1 212 777 9515; 103 Waverly Place*

04 CAFE WHA?

As night comes around, it's time to dig into — and dig — the nightlife that has been the beating heart of Greenwich Village since Dylan's day. Back on MacDougal St at Cafe Wha?, you can sip a beer beside the same stage where Dylan played on his very first night in New York City.

These days, the soundtrack at this bustling bar has moved on from folk music to funk, blues and soul, but that still fits the legacy; 'Greenwich Village's Swingingest Coffee House' has hosted everyone

from Springsteen to Hendrix. *www.cafewha.com; tel +1 212 254 3706; 115 MacDougal St; performances 6pm or 8pm nightly*

05 HOTEL CHELSEA

Start day two by heading north on the subway to West 23rd St to view another Dylan landmark. The Hotel Chelsea at number 222 has hosted more epic moments in popular culture than Woodstock.

This was the spot where Jack Kerouac wrote his classic Beat novel *On the Road*, where Leonard Cohen got it on with Janis Joplin, and where, tragically, Dylan Thomas drank himself to death and Sid Vicious murdered Nancy Spungen.

Bob Dylan, meanwhile, wrote *Sad Eyed Lady of the Lowlands*, a tribute to his then wife Sara, while a long-time guest in room 211. Later, he name-checked the hotel in his haunting ballad 'Sara' as the marriage foundered.

Alas, after hosting the cream of New York's creative talent for half a century, the Chelsea Hotel has fallen on hard times – the last resident artists were served eviction notices in 2016. The property is now being renovated, and is due to reopen some time in 2017. *Chelsea Hotel, 222 West 23rd St*

06 CARNEGIE HALL

For the next slice of Dylan, take a bus north on 8th Ave past a string of Broadway theatres. Hop off between West 57th and West 58th and wander two blocks east to admire the grand frontage of Carnegie Hall. It was here in 1961 that Dylan played his first concert outside of the Greenwich coffee house scene, and where he recorded his first live LP – the simply titled *Live at Carnegie Hall 1963*.

The interior is even more impressive. On a Carnegie Hall tour (book in advance via the website or box office) you can view the stalls where a rather surprised non-Greenwich Village audience first encountered the gravelly rumble of Dylan's unique take on American folk music. *www.carnegiehall.org; tel +1 212 903 9765; 57th St & 7th Ave; tours on fixed dates at 11.30am, 12.30pm or 2pm*

06

07 THE BITTER END

An appropriate finish to a Dylan-ographic perambulation. Ride the subway back to West 4th St, then drift down to Bleecker St. At No 147, the Bitter End is Greenwich's oldest club, still going strong five decades after opening the year Dylan blew into town.

Even better, it still hosts open jam sessions for aspiring musicians on Mondays and every second Sunday. The young singer was a regular at the Bitter End, and it was at a similar hootenanny on MacDougal St that Dylan got his first big break. *www.bitterend.com; tel +1 212 673 7030; 147 Bleecker St; performances from 7pm*
BY JOE BINDLOSS

05 Carnegie Hall, where Dylan recorded his first live LP

06 Beat history lives in the walls of Hotel Chelsea

WHERE TO STAY
WASHINGTON SQUARE HOTEL
The hotel where Dylan and Baez frolicked is still going strong. The building went up in 1902 but the hotel had its heyday in the Beat years, when poets and pop stars gravitated towards the cheap rooms overlooking the park. *www.washingtonsquare hotel.com; tel +1 212 777 9515; 103 Waverly Pl*

LARCHMONT HOTEL
Bargain rates are the draw at the Larchmont, which has modest, pocket-sized rooms. You also get a great location, just minutes north of Washington Square Park. *www.larchmonthotel.com; tel +1 212 989 9333; 27 West 11th St*

WHERE TO EAT & DRINK
BLUE HILL
This might be the city that never sleeps, but everything slows right down at Blue Hill. Ingredients for its innovative slow-food menu are sourced from upstate farms or the owner's family homestead. *www.bluehillfarm.com/dine/new-york; +1 212 539 1776; 75 Washington Pl*

WHITE HORSE TAVERN
This West Village watering hole was a regular haunt for two Dylans (Bob and Dylan Thomas), plus a who's who of New York literary talent. Prop yourself against the same bar that once supported Normal Mailer, Hunter S Thompson and Jack Kerouac. *Tel +1 212 989 3956; 567 Hudson St*

CELEBRATIONS
GREENWICH VILLAGE FILM FESTIVAL
This agreeably local indie film festival is an exuberant celebration of short-form and documentary cinema, with a special prize for the best depiction of Greenwich Village in film. *(www.greenwichvillage filmfestival.com)*

GOVERNOR'S BALL MUSIC FESTIVAL
Head to Randall's Island in June for three high-octane days of music from every genre. The bard's influence is certainly tangible in much of the music on stage. *(www.governorsball musicfestival.com)*

USA

LITERARY LANDSCAPES OF CAPE COD

There's something about the Cape's natural splendour, quiet towns and placid waters that has inspired generations of America's literary greats, many of whom came and never left.

Cape Cod (or just 'the Cape', as locals call it) has long been a popular destination for tourists, primarily for its wealth of pristine beaches and accompanying seafood joints. What fewer people realise is how many writers have lived on or travelled to this curious peninsula and its islands, and how many works of literature these lands have spawned.

Part of that inspiration has come just from the Cape's pure beauty: here there is a quaint, quiet radiance that shines in all four seasons. Trellises exploding with Cape rose blooms. A stretch of beach washed footprintless by the incoming tide. A herring gull hanging motionless in an updraft. A doe looking across the fog and stillness of a hidden kettle pond. Some of the world's most iconic, memorable literature has been inspired by the Cape's landscape and its denizens. Herman Melville, Henry David Thoreau, Peter Benchley, Norman Mailer and

NEED TO KNOW
Rental car is the ideal mode of transport on the Cape, which makes an easy two-day trail; four days with the islands.

more all came here and left (or didn't!) with the Cape deeply imprinted in their minds and their muses. While the landscape that brought Thoreau and naturalist/writer Henry Beston contemplative solitude has changed substantially from the rolling pasturelands of their time, the area — now pine and scrub oak forests — still holds wonder at nearly every turn.

Modern writers such as Norman Mailer, Paul Theroux and Edward Gorey found inspiration, tranquility and solace here just as their fellow writers did decades or centuries before. Peter Benchley's bestseller *Jaws* and the cult-classic movie it became was inspired by Martha's Vineyard, and filmed there.

The Cape is just over an hour's drive from Boston's Logan International Airport. To make more of this trail, add extra days for ferry rides across to popular islands Martha's Vineyard and Nantucket — the latter being Herman Melville's inspiration for *Moby Dick*.

① SANDWICH BOARDWALK

Start in Sandwich, the summer home of travel writer and novelist Paul Theroux (b 1941), whose works include the gripping novel *The Mosquito Coast*, made into a movie starring Harrison Ford. Theroux kayaks frequently around Cape waters, and here in Sandwich you can take in the beauty of its estuaries without even needing your own canoe.

While the winding brackish tributaries and spartina grass thickets aren't quite the jungles of Central America depicted in *The Mosquito Coast*, it isn't hard to imagine Theroux feeling like an explorer around every turn. The boardwalk extends for about 270 metres over the estuary before ending at Town Neck Beach. *www.sandwichmass.org; tel +1 508 888 4361; 6am-10pm*

② BARNSTABLE

Although born in Indiana, literary heavyweight Kurt Vonnegut (1922-2007) spent two very formative decades of his life not far away from Sandwich, in Barnstable village. Best known for his breakout anti-war novel *Slaugherhouse 5*, Vonnegut was never one to mince words. He often antagonised establishment elites with writing that mocked the waste and futility of war, or the short-sightedness of humans as a species.

His short story collection *Welcome to the Monkey House* opens with a homage to his Cape home. 'Where I Live', originally titled 'You've Never Been to Barnstable', discusses the narrow-mindedness of Cape Codders and their aversion to change with the author's trademark wit and sarcasm.

While his house is not open to the public, you'll pass by it as you head to Sturgis Library. Within walking distance of Vonnegut's home, this is America's oldest library building and includes an important collection of his works. *www.sturgislibrary.org; tel +1 508 362 6636; 3090 Main Street; 10am-6pm Mon & Wed, to 5pm Thu-Fri, to 4pm Sat, 1-8pm*

'These placid waters and quiet towns provided perfect inspiration for Benchley to tap into innate human fears'

01 Lighthouse on Nantucket Island

02 The Cape is beloved for its long sandy beaches

03 Quaint buildings line Commercial St in Provincetown

04 A humpback whale breaches near Provincetown

03 © Loop Images Ltd / Alamy; 04 © Bryce Flynn / Getty Images

03 EDWARD GOREY HOUSE

Decades before Goth fashion became a cliché, Edward Gorey (1925-2000) — cat-loving, bald and bearded — was out and about on the Cape wearing black, fur coats, silver jewellery, and writing and illustrating bizarre books so macabre that they were — and remain — in a class entirely their own.

Some, like the *Gashleycrumb Tinies*, have become cult classics, popular with both children and adults. Many viewers of the PBS network's *Mystery!* TV series know the pen-and-ink illustrations of the opener for that iconic show. Gorey died in 2000, but his house in Yarmouth Port was turned into this museum and it remains as he

was: curious, surprising and macabre. *www.edwardgoreyhouse.org; tel +1 508 362 3909; 8 Strawberry Lane; 11am-4pm Thu-Sat, noon-4pm Sun*

04 MARTHA'S VINEYARD

To go from macabre to downright terrifying, take a one-hour ferry to the idyllic island of Martha's Vineyard that set the scene for Peter Benchley's 1974 lurking horror tale, *Jaws*.

Katama (aka South) Beach is where a skinny-dipping college student is devoured by a gargantuan-sized predator. These placid waters and quiet tourist towns provided the perfect inspiration for Benchley to tap into innate human fears of the

unknown. There has not been a fatal shark attack on the Cape and its Islands since 1931, but there are great white sharks in the area.

Writer Paul Theroux has been known to kayak solo from Hyannis to Martha's Vineyard just to drop in for lunch with an islander friend — sharks be damned. Stand on Katama Beach and you might just hear the unforgettable theme come back to you: *Dun-nun. Dun-nun. Dunundunun...*

05 NANTUCKET WHALING MUSEUM

If time and budget allow, take another one-hour ferry and visit the Nantucket Whaling Museum, where

you'll see the maritime heritage that inspired Herman Melville (1819-1891) when he wrote his seminal work and 19th-century classic *Moby Dick*.

The museum holds a whale boat, oil lamps, scrimshaw and even a suspended whale skeleton, which make this museum a memorable stop. The town's cobblestone streets, brick-and-shingle buildings and the Athenaeum library all remain much as they did in Melville's day. *www.nha.org; tel +1 508 228 1894; 15 Broad Street; hours vary*

06 NAUSET LIGHT BEACH

Philosopher Henry David Thoreau (1817-1862) was another literary heavyweight that spent formative time on the Cape. For one of his most well-known books, *Walden*, he

spent a year living in isolation in a tiny cabin in the woods; in his travel memoir *Cape Cod*, he takes life-changing treks through the pastures, farmland, communities and desolate wave-washed shores that now make up the Cape Cod National Seashore. Both works question the significance of the self in the grandness of nature; others sparked important discussions about the value of government and its role that still continue.

Today, the Cape Cod National Seashore is a vast park that has protected much of the Lower Cape from the ravishes of development, leaving what is lovingly described as 'the elbow' of Orleans all the way north to Provincetown relatively pristine. Nauset Light Beach, with its picturesque lighthouse (first erected

during Thoreau's lifetime, in 1838) and steep eroded scarp, is a perfect place to experience the grandeur of these beaches. You only have to walk a few minutes away from the parking lot to experience the same lonely solitude that imprinted so deeply on one of America's most important writers. *www.nps.gov/caco/planyourvisit/ nauset-light-beach.htm; tel +1 508 255 3421*

07 PROVINCETOWN

No visit to the Cape is complete without a trip to 'P-town': part artist community, part Portuguese fisher-village, part LGBT mecca and part dune-swept barrens,

Provincetown has always captivated writers' imaginations and hearts. Mary Oliver, masterful poet and

teacher, lives here. Novelist Norman Mailer, a resident for much of his life, set his murder novel *Tough Guys Don't Dance* here (Mailer himself is buried in Provincetown Cemetery). But to understand the profundity of Melville's greatest work is to go whale hunting yourself: with a camera in place of a harpoon.

Whale watching offers incredible chances to see the ocean and these fascinating creatures up close. The Race Point Lighthouse will just be vanishing behind you when you arrive at Stellwagen Bank; you'll hear the captain slow the boat for an approach. Get the camera ready. Thar she blows! *www.whalewatch.com; tel +1 508 240 3636; 307 Commercial Street #1, May–Sep*
BY RAYMOND BARTLETT

05 Old North Wharf, Nantucket Island

06 Sandwich Boardwalk

WHERE TO STAY

LAND'S END INN
This Provincetown place offers fantastic views of the harbour and estuary within striking distance of the shops and craziness of Commercial Street. It has spick-and-span rooms and a funky parlour full of flair. *www.landsendinn.com; tel +1 508 487 0706; 22 Commercial St*

WHITE ELEPHANT
This hotel is so large you practically get lost in it. The price tag is similarly grand but the amenities are incredible: wall-sized TVs, wine waiting for you, enormous bedrooms, and a luxurious dining-kitchen-living room that will make you feel like you're living in a magazine. *www.whiteelephanthotel. com; tel +1 508 228 2500; 50 Easton St, Nantucket*

WHERE TO EAT & DRINK

NAPI'S
This Portuguese restaurant has been a Provincetown mainstay for decades. Stop in for its local specialities, fresh fish, calamari and, of course, boiled Maine lobster with steamer clams, corn on the cob, plenty of butter and even a plastic bib so you don't get lobster juice all over your clothes. *www.napisptown.com; tel +1 508 487 1145; 7 Freeman St*

JACK'S OUTBACK II
Jack's is where Edward Gorey often came for breakfast. Jack (as unique a character as Gorey) passed away years ago, but you might sit where Gorey did — eating, sketching and staring off into the land only he could see. *Tel +1 508 362 6690; 161 Main St, Yarmouth*

CELEBRATIONS

CAPE COD WRITERS' CENTER CONFERENCE
This event draws writers, agents and readers from around the globe. Workshop your current manuscript, chat with agents, or listen to writers read from current work. *(capecodwriters center.org)*

BLESSING OF THE FLEET
This Provincetown Festival event brings traffic to a standstill. It's an amazing spectacle, as thousands of onlookers watch the boats come in to be anointed. *(provincetownportuguese festival.com)*

06 © Hemis / Alamy

USA

POLITICO WASHINGTON ON THE SMALL SCREEN

Take a trip through the political landscape around Washington, DC, as seen on screen in TV dramas such as House of Cards *and their gripping renditions of America's corridors of power.*

Political intrigue and scandal — not to mention seismic events with global repercussions — are all part of the great Washington experience. The US capital is famed for its marble-filled halls of power and its monolithic monuments, which seem to tout American exceptionalism in all its brazen glory. Its grand avenues, speeding motorcades and gargantuan office buildings with cryptic signage form an irresistible backdrop for those interested in exploring a city shaped by the highs and lows of American power.

Washington has played a starring role in political thrillers and disaster films, though in more recent years it has been centre stage for one ruthless, Machiavellian character who connives his way into the highest post in the land. The gifted orator in question is Francis ('Frank') J Underwood (played by Kevin Spacey) and his Lady Macbeth-like wife (Robin Wright), both of whom embody the darkest side of political ambition in the epic series *House of Cards*.

NEED TO KNOW
Spend one to two days in DC and a day each in Annapolis and Baltimore; travel DC by metro, but hire a car for the rest.

On their rise through power, the US Capitol, the White House, the National Gallery and even the metro with its cinematic coffered ceilings are key set pieces to this addictive drama with its heavy underpinnings of Shakespearean treachery. For a rosier portrait of the American presidency — but with equally brilliant writing — *The West Wing* (which aired from 1999 to 2006, but continues to win over audiences today) portrays Washington in all its brainy, big-hearted complexity.

Owing to the difficulty of filming in the capital, much of *House of Cards* was shot at nearby sites in Maryland, including the state's scenic capital of Annapolis. Baltimore, an easy drive from Washington, also warrants a visit, with its brick row houses, picturesque waterfront and old-school dining and drinking scene. It's also the setting for key sites from both *House of Cards* and award-winning series *The Wire*. Together, these three cities form a neat loop for this politico TV fan trail.

USA

'Walking through the marble corridors, it is easy to picture Underwood making blackmail threats in the shadows'

01 THE CAPITOL BUILDING

Nothing says Washington quite like the iconic 285ft cast-iron dome of the US Capitol, which looms large physically and figuratively over the city's landscape. The opening credits for *House of Cards* seem to be an exercise in filming as many different dramatic angles of this imposing building as possible. And while no scenes were shot inside the building, the Capitol plays a starring role in the series as Underwood schemes his way through the halls of Congress and into the presidency.

Plenty of dramatic real-life events have also played out in and around these halls — not least, the torching of the building when it was still under construction by the British in 1814. In the 1970s, the marble steps earned a degree of notoriety after Congressman John Jenrette revealed he and his wife used to slip out of late-night congressional sessions for sexual escapades in the open air (the comedy troupe Capitol Steps took its name from these moonlight trysts).

For better or worse, visitors will be treated to a much less sordid experience on guided hour-long tours that take in the statue-laden hall and several ornate chambers. *www.visitthecapitol.gov; tel +1 202 226 8000; 1st St NE & E Capitol St; 8.30am-4.30pm Mon-Sat*

02 NATIONAL PORTRAIT GALLERY

Washington has a spread of museums housing world-class collections, including the National Gallery of Art and the Hirshhorn Museum, all within an easy stroll of one another on National Mall. But for followers of the *House of Cards*, it's the National Portrait Gallery that matters most.

In an example of art imitating life imitating art, a 6ft by 6ft portrait of

01 Washington's
Capitol Building

02 Jefferson
Memorial

03 Annapolis
street scene, with
Maryland State
House in the
background

04 Oriole Park
at Camden Yards,
Baltimore

05 Lincoln
Memorial at sunrise

President Francis J Underwood (or, rather, Kevin Spacey) painted by British artist Jonathan Yeo, was unveiled in the National Portrait Gallery in the programme's fourth season.

Curiously enough, the painting did indeed hang in the gallery for much of 2016, in the same room as portraits of President Lyndon Johnson (who declared his own painted likeness the ugliest thing he'd ever seen) and a rather romanticised Nixon by famed American artist Norman Rockwell. Even if you can no longer study Underwood's painting in person, it's still worth seeing the collection of all American heads of state (and many other luminaries), including Gilbert Stuart's celebrated portrait of George Washington.

The gallery is about 1.4 miles northwest of the Capitol, right by Gallery Place Chinatown metro station. *npg.si.edu; tel +1 202 633 8300; 8th & F Streets NW; 11.30am-7pm*

03 KENNEDY CENTER

Overlooking the Potomac River, the glittering Kennedy Center is one of the world's great performing arts venues. More than 2000 performances are staged here each year among its multiple venues, which include a concert hall, opera house, theatre and cinema. There are also free daily performances (at 6pm) in the Grand Foyer, as well as tours on offer (also gratis). The centre, with its hand-blown Orrefors crystal chandelier and regal red carpet, looks quite elegant on film, and makes a fine backdrop for one dramatic episode of *The West Wing* ('Galileo', from the second season). President Clinton even allowed use of his presidential box for the filming.

Although *House of Cards* hasn't filmed in the centre (the Underwoods prefer attending performances at the

fictitious Washington Opera House, which is actually Baltimore's Lyric Opera House), music from *House of Cards'* Emmy-award winning score made its world premier performance on stage here in 2016.

The centre is a little over two miles west of the portrait gallery. Bus 80 from H and 9th Sts will get you close. *www.kennedy-center.org; tel +1 202 467 4600; 2700 F St NW; 10am-9pm Mon-Sat, from noon Sun*

04 MARYLAND STATE HOUSE

If you really want to see the interior of the US Capitol as depicted in *House of Cards*, head 32 miles east of DC to Annapolis, Maryland. The Maryland State house does a fine job as stand-in — which is fitting, since it played just that role back in the late 18th century.

Construction, which began in 1772, was interrupted by a little skirmish known as the Revolutionary War, and work wasn't completed until 1797. For nearly a year following the war, the Continental Congress of the newly independent nation met here.

Walking through its marble corridors, one can almost imagine George Washington tendering his resignation as commander-in-chief of the Continental Army and wig- and spectacle-wearing representatives celebrating over the Treaty of Paris, which was also ratified here. But it's perhaps even easier to picture a smooth-talking Underwood making subtle blackmail threats to legislative opponents in the shadows. *www.msa.maryland.gov; tel +1 410 260 6445; 91 State Circle; 9am-5pm*

05 ORIOLE PARK AT CAMDEN YARDS

There's a long tradition of presidents throwing out the ceremonial first pitch of the national baseball season dating all the way back to 1909. Camden Yards, the beautifully designed retro park in downtown Baltimore, has hosted its share of ceremonial pitches both in real life and on screen.

Kevin Spacey threw the game's first pitch both as a celebrity in 2014 and as diabolical vice-president Underwood in season two of *House of Cards*. Other fictitious presidents played by Sheen (*The West Wing*), Kevin Kline (*Dave*) and Chris Rock (*Head of State*) have also taken the mound.

The ballpark stands have been featured in *The Wire* in several scenes, notably in season three when

detectives Jimmy McNulty and Bunk Moreland take their sons to a game. Don't pass up the opportunity to see a game live, and consider a stadium tour.

Camden Yards is a 32-mile drive north of Annapolis near Baltimore's pretty Inner Harbor. *baltimore.orioles.mlb.com; tel +1 410 547 6234; 333 Camden St; tours 10am & noon Mon-Sat, noon & 2pm Sun Mar-Nov*

06 WERNER'S

For iconic old-school diners, Charm City (aka Baltimore) has few rivals. Topping the charts is downtown Werner's, a midcentury classic with wood-panelled walls, formica-topped tables and chrome-trimmed fixtures. Not surprisingly, it feels like just the right place for discussing politics far from the ears and eyes of political insiders. Frank Underwood's henchmen held subterfuge meetings here, as did Thomas Carcetti, Baltimore's mayor on *The Wire*. Werner's was also a favourite meeting spot for real-life Maryland Governor William Donald Schaefer.

It's the perfect spot for traditional diner fare, including pancakes and bottomless cups of coffee. *www.facebook.com/Werners Baltimore, tel +1 443 842 7430; 231 E Redwood St, 8am-3pm Mon-Fri*
BY REGIS ST LOUIS

06 Inside Maryland State House

07 George Peabody Library, Baltimore

08 Washington Monument, cherry blossom season

09 The exterior of Washington's John F Kennedy Memorial Center of the Performing Arts

WHERE TO STAY
THE WILLARD INTERCONTINENTAL
One of Washington DC's most celebrated hotels, The Willard was where President Grant coined the term 'lobbyist' for the political wranglers trolling the lobby. It has hallways strung with chandeliers, a plush bar and opulent rooms. *www.washington. Intercontinental.com; tel +1 202 628 9100; 1401 Pennsylvania Ave NW*

GEORGETOWN INN
This classy guesthouse has an easy-going elegance, with rooms set amid restored 18th-century townhouses near the heart of historic Georgetown. *www.georgetowninn.com; tel +1 866 344 8750; 1310 Wisconsin Ave NW*

WHERE TO EAT & DRINK
COMET PING PONG
No, you won't find a child-trafficking ring operated by Hillary Clinton here (not even Underwood would peddle such nonsense — look up 'pizzagate' and 'fake news'). Instead, you'll find delicious thin-crust pizzas, a festive crowd and plenty of family-friendly amusement, including ping pong. *www.cometpingpong. com; tel +1 202 364 0404; 5037 Connecticut Ave NW*

BREWER'S ART
Inside an atmospheric 20th-century Baltimore mansion, Brewer's Art serves excellent Belgian-style microbrews and seasonal dishes. This is where Mario was seduced by Devonne in *The Wire*. *www.thebrewersart.com, +1 410 547 6925, 1106 North Charles St*

CELEBRATIONS
NATIONAL CHERRY BLOSSOM FESTIVAL
The best-loved festival in Washington DC celebrates spring's arrival with boat rides, evening walks by lantern light, concerts and a parade. From late March to mid-April. *(www.nationalcherry blossomfestival.org)*

PASSPORT DC
Each May, some 70 embassies and 40 other DC institutions throw open their doors for a global cultural fest. Expect music, dancing, crafts, fashion and great world food. *(www.culturaltourismdc.org)*

CULTURE TRAILS

Published in October 2017 by Lonely Planet Global Limited
CRN 554153
www.lonelyplanet.com
ISBN 978 1 7865 7968 3
© Lonely Planet 2017
Printed in Malaysia
10 9 8 7 6 5 4 3 2 1

Managing Director Piers Pickard
Associate Publisher Robin Barton
Commissioning Editor Lorna Parkes
Art Direction Daniel Di Paolo
Editor Rebecca Tromans
Cartographers Wayne Murphy, Gabe Lindquist
Print Production Larissa Frost, Nigel Longuet

Thanks to Jessica Cole, Barbara di Castro

Authors Brett Atkinson (North Island, New Zealand), Alexis Averbuck (Greece), Raymond Bartlett (Cape Cod, USA), Robin Barton (Victoria, Australia), Sara Benson (Los Angeles, USA), Joe Bindloss (Mumbai, India; Deep South & New York, USA), Jai Breitnauer (Oamaru, New Zealand), John Brunton (Belgium; Hungary; Indonesia; Venice, Italy; Lebanon), Piera Chen (Hong Kong, China; Taiwan), Kerry Christiani (Austria; Finland; Morocco; Portugal) James Clasper (Denmark), Bridget Gleeson (Brazil), Anthony Ham (Northern Territory, Australia; Ethiopia), Carolyn B Heller (Canada; Chile), Anita Isalska (Bulgaria; Romania), Anna Kaminski (Jamaica; Catalonia, Spain), Daniel McCrohan (Rajasthan, India; Beijing, China), Rebecca Milner (Tokyo, Japan), Karyn Noble (London, England), Etain O'Carroll (Oxford, England; Ireland), Lorna Parkes (Scotland), Brandon Presser (Iceland), Charles Rawlings-Way (Adelaide & Tasmania, Australia), Brendan Sainsbury (Cuba; Seville, Spain), Phillip Tang (Naoshima, Japan; Mexico), Regis St Louis (Washington DC, USA), Clifton Wilkinson (Madrid, Spain), Nicola Williams (Florence, Italy; France)

STAY IN TOUCH lonelyplanet.com/contact

AUSTRALIA The Malt Store, Level 3, 551 Swanston St, Carlton, Victoria 3053 T: 03 8379 8000

USA 124 Linden St, Oakland, CA 94607 T: 510 250 6400

IRELAND Unit E, Digital Court, The Digital Hub, Rainsford St, Dublin 8

UK 240 Blackfriars Rd, London SE1 8NW T: 020 3771 5100

Paper in this book is certified against the Forest Stewardship Council™ standards. FSC™ promotes environmentally responsible, socially beneficial and economically viable management of the world's forests.